Always in the Picture

An Inseparable Pair: the late Arthur Lavington on his Mark VIII KTT at the top of May Hill during the fourth lap of the 1961 Junior TT.

Always in the Picture

R. W. Burgess and J. R. Clew

ISBN 0 85429 266 7

First published, under the same title, by Goose and Son in 1971
This revised and enlarged edition published May 1980
Reprinted 1981 and 1988

A FOULIS Motorcycling Book

Published by:
Haynes Publishing Group
Sparkford, Yeovil, Somerset BA22 7JJ, England

Distributed in USA by:
Haynes Publications Inc.
861 Lawrence Drive, Newbury Park, California 91320, USA

Contents

Acknowledgements

The authors gratefully thank their many friends for their generous help in the preparation of this book.

They are particularly indebted to Mr B. J. Goodman for his unqualified permission to reproduce any material that is subject to Veloce copyright, to Mr and Mrs G. Denley for their invaluable assistance and comments on the manuscript, to Mr H. W. Louis and Mr J. Orchard of *The Motor Cycle* for their help with research and for their permission to use photographs and extracts from *The Motor Cycle* and *Motor Cycling*, and to Mr Ivan Rhodes and Mr 'Titch' Allen, who were kind enough to make a critical review of the complete manuscript and suggest amendments. Also their thanks to Dr Joseph Bayley for his advice about Brooklands photographs of Velocette exponents.

They also thank those good friends who have unhesitatingly given permission for the reproduction of their photographs and Mrs Jo Edwardes, Mrs Jenny Pateman, and Mrs Margaret Day who have shared the arduous task of typing the manuscript.

IN MEMORIAM BOB BURGESS

Whilst this book was being reprinted, I received the sad news that my co-author and friend of many years standing, Bob Burgess, had died in his Isle of Man home after only a short illness.

Velocette enthusiasts throughout the world will, I am sure, join with me in paying humble respects to Bob. He, more than any other person, did most to keep the Velocette name to the fore, especially after the Company went into voluntary liquidation. There can be few who have not benefited from his kindly and helpful advice at some time or other, either through correspondence or by reading one of the many short articles he wrote about Hall Green topics.

Whilst it is unlikely that Bob will ever be forgotten when Velocettes are mentioned, I can think of no better way of perpetuating his memory than the reprinting of this book. I can say with all honesty that without his help, *Always in the Picture* may never have materialised at all, for it was truly part of him. I am proud to have been so closely associated with Bob in this respect, for the world will be all the poorer without him.

JEFF CLEW
Queen Camel,
July 1973

Preface

As I am of the third generation of the Velocette story, it is with pleasure
that I contribute the foreword to this book. Two enthusiasts, Jeff Clew
and Bob Burgess, quite voluntarily and without financial backing, undertook this very onerous task and have spent considerable time and painstaking research in order to ensure that all information given herein is
as accurate as possible. Vintage owners, past and present, and Velocette
enthusiasts all over the world, will appreciate the technical details and,
to most, the information given should prove extremely useful.

I am sure that Velocette enthusiasts and many others will enjoy reading
about the origin of the firm and the many struggles that have taken place,
but most particularly, they will enjoy the Racing Period, when the 'Boys
of the Times' from all over the world came to race on the Isle of Man and
other circuits. Those were the days and it is about them that this story is
chiefly written.

For all concerned I trust this book will be a success and a tribute to all
those who played their part.

B.H.Goodman

Introduction by Alec Bennett

When I was asked if I would write an Introduction to this book I did not know whether I had been invited because I have had the pleasure for so long in having been one of Veloce's Main Agents, or whether the fact that I piloted to victory the first Velocette to win an Isle of Man TT race prompted the Authors to approach me. In either case I suppose the thought was understandable. Although it is now over forty years since my faith in the late Percy Goodman's new overhead-camshaft design led me to assure him that I could win the Junior TT.

But whatever the reason I am only too pleased to comply with the request, if only because of the whole-hearted admiration and respect in which I have always held the designer of an engine that established a milestone in motor-cycle history. To appreciate fully the greatness of the achievement of the designer and his loyal band of helpers, it is necessary to remember that the 1926 series of TT races were the first in which alcohol fuel was prohibited. Furthermore, the distance of each race was increased by an additional lap of the severe mountain course to make a total of seven per race, 264 miles.

Even with these handicaps my Velocette enabled me to complete the course at an average speed of 0·22 mph less than the average speed of the 1925 Senior winner and finish more than ten minutes ahead of the second man!

I am glad that an enthusiastic Velocette-owner has joined forces with a former member of that happy band of Veloce employees to produce this story of so much that lies behind the production of this popular make. They are well qualified to tell this interesting story of a truly family concern, especially since they have been given so much invaluable help in connection with the early days of the Company by one of Percy's sisters and her husband, George Denley.

1
The Formative Years

The earliest mention of the trade-name 'Veloce' in association with a two-wheeled vehicle occurs much earlier than one would expect. It relates to a velocipede, or 'bone-shaker' as it was more commonly known, made during the late 1860s. Although the vehicle concerned had no connection with the present company of Veloce Limited some of the facts are none the less worth recording in passing. There is a strange parallel in the sense that this vehicle represented a significant technical advance in design.

The velocipede was manufactured by the Veloce Company of 16 Northumberland Street, Strand, London W.C.2, that ran a large show-room-cum-gymnasium at Brewers Lane, beneath Charing Cross railway station. Their design, known as the 'Veloce' and covered by Royal Letters Patent, had some surprisingly novel features which included metal wheels constructed from gunmetal and steel, a radical departure from the more customary wooden articles. The wheelbase had been kept short to prevent trapping the legs between the wheels and there was an ingenious pad and lever brake mechanism which operated on the periphery of the rear wheel through a linking mechanism of the wire and pulley variety. Six different models were marketed, including a special racing version. The latter model

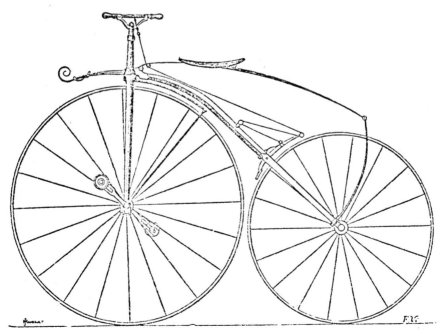

The Velocé.

John Goodman (1857–1929).
The founder of the business
known as Veloce Limited.

was the most expensive in the range for its specification included a polished steel frame, morocco leather saddle, gunmetal governor and brake, and a 'patent differential' front wheel of 40 in. diameter. It sold at £20 exactly.

Unhappily, there is no record of the success of this venture or the ultimate fate of the company and it is not until just after the turn of the century that the first mention of a motor cycle occurs.

The founder of the present Company was Johannes Gütgemann, whose father was a merchant in Oberwinter on the Rhine. The family had often been burgomasters of the district but Johannes's mother had ambitions for him to become an Evangelical minister. He had already served the first year of his training and had spent three months of his compulsory military service when his father died quite suddenly. The resulting change in the family fortunes would have curtailed the furtherance of his career and rather than face the prospects of army service and living in barracks, he made the bold decision to leave for England and settle in Birmingham, where his father had connections with nail-makers. The year was 1876 and he was nineteen years old.

In due course Johannes met Elizabeth Ore, who lived at the Windmill House, Smethwick. Her father was an artist who specialized in papier-mâché work and later became associated with the police force when the papiermâché trade went out of fashion. He was a descendant of the Ore family who originally lived in the Shropshire village of Tong. It is from the Ore family that the first signs of a mechanical interest can be noted.

Thomas Ore was an eighteenth-century watch- and clockmaker of some repute, a Wolverhampton craftsman in whom Matthew Boulton took some interest. One of his specialities was musical clocks and an excellent example of his work is in the hands of the Cadbury family. Boulton thought highly of his work, and there is mention of him employing Thomas Ore to work on his spinning-machines.

Despite some family opposition as the result of Johannes's ancestry, which was soon overcome, he married Elizabeth in 1884 and settled in Birmingham. It was here that his first venture into business occurred when he met a man named Barrett who had inherited a pill-manufacturing

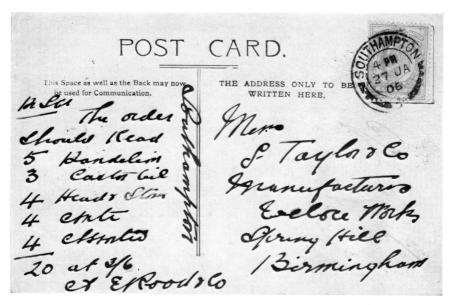

An order for pills dated 27 January 1906. Although addressed to Isaac Taylor and Co., Veloce Works is included in the directive.

business under the name of Isaac Taylor and Company. Johannes bought the business and it was the capital from this that subsidized his venture into cycle manufacture, which he began in the early 1890s, in a small workshop off Great Hampton Street.

While looking for larger premises Johannes met William Gue, a cycle-maker. At this time Johannes had adopted the name of John Taylor, following his acquisition of Isaac Taylor and Company. The two formed Taylor, Gue and Company, cycle-manufacturers and dealers, with premises at Hampton Works, Peel Street, Birmingham. The cycles they made were sold under the trade-name 'Hampton'.

During December 1896 the business became a limited company and in 1900 there was a further change of name to Taylor Gue Limited. By now their activities had expanded and they built rickshaws fitted with a basket-work body made by J. J. Plater and Son, of Bradford Street. They also became associated with a Mr Howell in a project to construct a forecar, and this was John's first connection with motor-cycle manufacture.

A rare photograph of one of the Veloce rickshaws, taken in Birmingham. The basketwork body was made by J. J. Plater and Son.

At this time the motor-cycle industry was still in its infancy and most of the machines made in this country employed either imported engines or those made under licence to continental designers. A typical machine was the Ormonde, a popular model from 1901 to 1904 to which the Kelecom engine was fitted. Of Belgian origin, this engine had the customary automatic inlet-valve and battery-operated trembler-coil ignition of the era. The Ormonde had the doubtful distinction of having the engine mounted in the old and somewhat cramped De Dion position, between the saddle-tube and the rear wheel. The manufacturers of the Ormonde employed Taylor Gue Limited to make their frames, an activity that supplemented their other activities. It should be recalled that the bicycle boom was still in full swing at that period and there was a growing export market.

Early in 1904 the Kelecom and Ormonde interests merged at the former's Wells Street West address in London. Design changes that followed indicated a more conventional engine position, and the opportunity was taken to redesign the engine. The new engine had both valves mechanically operated, and 'square' bore and stroke dimensions of 80 × 80 mm. To cope with an expected increase in power an H-section connecting-rod was specified. But this joint venture failed before the new design had materialized. By the end of the year Taylor Gue purchased the entire assets and goodwill of Kelecom Motors Limited and took over the Wells Street premises. They were thus able to enter the trade as manufacturers of a complete motor cycle.

In 1905 John Taylor decided to market his products under the trade-name 'Veloce', although it is not clear why he selected this particular name. It seems feasible that he intended it to convey the impression of rapidity, for the word 'velocity' stems from the same Latin root. Whatever the

14

One of the early Taylor, Gue advertisements published during 1905. This was one of the first occasions that the trade-name 'Veloce' was used in its own right.

reason, the new design of engine was displayed at Wells Street under the trade-name, to be followed by a complete Veloce motor cycle. An early advertisement shows this to be a 2 hp model which sold at twenty-five guineas. There is also a footnote offering a few 1904 Ormonde models as available at reduced prices, obviously an attempt to clear the old stock.

In March 1905 the 2 hp Veloce made its début at the Stanley Show, held in the Agricultural Hall, Islington, a building that still exists today. Advertising copy made great play of the lightness in weight of the machine, a mere 65 lb, which was claimed to obviate the dreaded side-slip. But success was not destined to follow. Taylor Gue had lost money as the result of the collapse of the Ormonde/Kelecom merger and they too succumbed in due course. On 19 October 1905 they went into voluntary liquidation.

Fortunately, John had maintained his faith in the future of the bicycle as a cheap, convenient means of transport for the proletariat. In June 1905, with the financial backing of Edward Williams, a prominent chainwheel manufacturer, he formed Veloce Limited after acquiring premises at Gisholt Passage, Spring Hill, Birmingham. The initial objectives of the new company were the manufacture of cycles and their components, together with the provision of a nickel-plating service for chainwheels and cranks. The original subscribers were: John Taylor, cycle-maker; Arthur Williams, machinist; Thomas Henry Tolley, commercial clerk; Edward Williams, machinist; Arthur Leslie Crockford, solicitor; Arthur Ward, gentleman; Arthur John Hookway, solicitor's clerk. The company had a capital of £1,000 in the form of 1,000 shares of £1 each, a not inconsiderable sum of money in those days.

The family pill business was eventually transferred to two maiden ladies during 1906. At one stage, John was approached by a person who had perfected a formula for the manufacture of custard-powder, but he decided not to take up this offer. If he had, the whole future of the Company may have been quite different, for the offer was eventually taken up by Birds!

Neither of John's two sons took part in the early activities of Veloce Limited. Percy, the eldest son, was apprenticed to a pattern-maker and had developed a keen interest in mechanical engineering. As the result of an acquaintanceship with an Indian Parsee named Lal Kaka, a customer for bicycles, he decided to accompany the latter on his return to India. This proved to be a very interesting period of his life, for the motor car was only just being introduced into India. He handled the importation of Wolseley cars and when the army became interested he had the distinction of dealing with Kitchener, who was then in command. He also took part in a drive from Bombay to Delhi to help publicize the cars, no mean feat when the condition of the Indian roads at that period is taken into account. Meanwhile, his younger brother Eugene was serving what was to prove a very useful apprenticeship in the Tool Room of the New Hudson Works in Birmingham.

Percy returned to England quite suddenly during July 1907 with the ambition to build his own car. John saw a great future for the motor car and gave him every encouragement. As a result he was joined by Eugene, and New Veloce Motors was formed, to operate from the same Spring Hill Works as Veloce Limited. Percy was responsible for the design and Eugene supervised the construction. The car was finally completed during September 1908. The 20 hp engine was supplied by Johnson, Hurley and Martin of Coventry and other parts were made by F. E. Baker and the Kirkstall Forge Company. It is interesting to record that the body was made by the firm of Thomas Startin of Aston, who are still in business there today. John Marston, the manufacturer of the radiator, and F. E. Baker were later to achieve much prominence on their own account in the motor-cycle world.

A photograph of the Veloce motor car manufactured by New Veloce Motors.

16

Manuel Canto, the Spanish Agent for Veloce Limited, leaves the Works for an overland journey home. John Goodman and George Denley can be seen to his immediate left, and behind the sidecar, Harold Willis and Percy Goodman. The date was 4 July 1927.

Even now success was evasive. Although the prototype was successfully used and demonstrated, orders failed to materialize and the project was abandoned. The car was finally driven to the scrap-heap by George Denley in 1919.

New Veloce hurriedly diversified into motor-car repairs and general engineering. During the roller-skating boom of 1908–9 they even made large numbers of roller-skates.[1] Later still, it is alleged that the Company undertook the grinding of crankshafts for the Levis two-stroke. But the business gradually ran down until it was finally completely absorbed by Veloce Limited in August 1916.

In the meantime, Veloce Limited had built up a healthy business with the manufacture and export of bicycles, to say nothing of their plating service, and additional premises had been acquired at Fleet Street, Birmingham. There was evidence of demand for a cheaper cycle than their standard model and so a number of subsidiary companies were formed that each marketed their own brand of cycle under trade-names such as 'Warrior' and 'Herald' in direct competition to the 'Veloce'. Needless to say the last still remained the quality product.

Despite his earlier setback, John still had faith in the motor cycle and in 1908 he decided to start work on a new motor cycle in the premises at Fleet Street. Percy and Eugene agreed to produce the engines at Spring Hill, which would then be married up with the frame assembly at John's

[1] British Patent 15,377 by P. J. Taylor. Application made during 1909 but subsequently abandoned.

The Veloce Works, York Road, Hall Green in the year 1928. These were the premises previously occupied by Messrs Humphries and Dawes, manufacturers of OK motor cycles.

Machine Shop, No. 2 Bay, in the Veloce Works during 1928. Note the model U cylinder-barrels and the flywheels for the OHC models.

premises in Fleet Street. It was apparent to Percy that an entirely new model that represented a quite radical departure from the currently accepted design practice might stand a good chance of success. He again sat down at his drawing-board and towards the end of 1909 had evolved a design[1] that created quite a sensation when the first announcement was made.

The engine/gearbox unit was built on the unit-construction principle, the engine having a bore and stroke of 68 mm × 76 mm to give a capacity of 276 cc and a 2½ hp rating. Oil was carried in the integral sump whence it was distributed by a non-adjustable mechanical-vane type oil-pump. The valve arrangement was of the inlet-over-exhaust variety, the very first models having an automatic inlet-valve. This was subsequently replaced by one of mechanical operation in order to improve performance. The two-speed gear was also located within the engine casting whence it drove the rear wheel by pulley and belt via two metal cone clutches, one per gear. A curious feature of the engine was that it ran 'backwards', so that the gear train was located in front of the engine to reverse the rotation for the drive. Much of the smoothness of the engine was attributed to the large outside flywheel on the offside of the machine. An overhung crank arrangement was employed, the beginning of a Veloce design trend which was to persist for the next eighteen years.

The engine was provided with the simple, but nevertheless effective, oil-feed indicator protruding from the crankcase consisting of a length of rod that was caused to pulsate by the flow of oil from the pump. A visitor to one of the early Motor Cycle Shows at which the Veloce was exhibited was apparently rather critical of the scheme and must have said as much to John. Eugene once related how his father had patiently explained that when riding at night, if the pulsations of the rod could not be seen, the rider could easily reassure himself that the pump was working by resting a finger-tip on the indicator-rod. John became very impatient at last with such niggling criticism. He turned to the critic and suggested that they might modify the rod to keep the rider happy about the lubrication by setting it to prod his bottom!

Sales were disappointing. Perhaps the design was too advanced for the public is always reluctant to accept change. In order to rectify matters and, hopefully, to give the new model time to become more widely accepted, a second very different model was designed along more conventional lines. At a casual glance it bore a very close resemblance to the contemporary 500 cc Triumph, a machine already renowned for its unfailing reliability. But the differences included the fitting of Druid forks and an Xl-All saddle, with such standard proprietary components of the day as a Bosch magneto and a B and B carburetter. The engine had the customary side-by-side valve arrangement and bore and stroke measurements of 85 mm × 88 mm which gave a cubic capacity of 499 cc. Drive was direct to the rear wheel by the familiar V-belt. The machine was originally marketed as the VMC (Veloce Motor Company) and it sold at forty guineas.

[1] British Patent 24,499 by P. J. Taylor (21 October 1910).

The engine fitting section in 1928. A group of model U crankcases can be seen in the left foreground, while model K OHC engines can be seen in various states of assembly on the right.

The finished component stores. It required careful budgeting to keep many of these items closely in step with the current level of production.

During 1911 John made successful application to the Home Office for his naturalization. The papers were signed by none less than Winston Churchill, as yet to achieve greater fame. But it was not until 1917 that he changed his surname to Goodman by deed poll.

A current method of obtaining good publicity was to seek out a notoriously steep hill and give a demonstration of the machine's climbing ability before the assembled Press and members of the public. Veloce Limited were no exception to the rule for during the early part of 1912 the $2\frac{1}{2}$ hp model made a convincing climb of Gough Street, Birmingham which had a gradient of 1 in $7\frac{1}{2}$. A repeat performance with a passenger proved even more convincing, especially since both tests were made from a standing start. This was no mean achievement for such a small-capacity engine of that era.

It is worth noting that at this period Veloce Limited did not normally exhibit machines on a stand bearing their own name, a trend which has rendered many a search through early indices quite perplexing. It was their practice to acquire space through their London agents, the Wilton Cycle and Motor Company of 110 Wilton Road, London, S.W. This latter company also held agencies for Clyno and Matchless machines which they exhibited alongside the Veloce models and sidecars of their own design and manufacture.

The year 1912 also saw the beginnings of the cycle-car movement, a cult which was to expand so rapidly during the year that it would shortly support its own trade magazine. With an eye on fresh markets, Veloce Limited announced their intention of manufacturing a twin-cylinder engine especially for cycle-car use, but regrettably this was a project which never materialized. No doubt the distant rumblings of the impending war helped prevent its realization.

Motor-cycling had now become accepted as a respectable pastime for ladies and a $2\frac{1}{2}$ hp ladies' model was exhibited for the first time at the 1912 Olympia Show, complete with open frame and dress-guards. Muriel Lord, a well-known motor-cyclist who wrote a regular column for *Motor Cycling* commented very favourably on this model in an early 1913 test report. She found the engine easy to start and throughout the entire test period of several weeks she had recourse to adjust the driving-belt only once. The little machine climbed Edge Hill and Sunrising without difficulty and also Saintbury, all notorious gradients, which would quickly show up the shortcomings of any machine. Vintage enthusiasts who have taken part in the Vintage Motor Cycle Club's annual Banbury Run will appreciate the severity of these tests, especially since the roads were narrower and waterbound in those days.

It is probable that the introduction of the ladies' model underlined the need for a footstarter, for by the end of 1913 the standard and the ladies' models were so equipped. The ladies' model sold at fifty guineas just two guineas more than the standard model.

Despite the success of the $2\frac{1}{2}$ hp models, the 1914 Catalogue still listed the old 499 cc model in company with a more recent version, which had a three-speed Sturmey Archer hub gear. Admittedly, some modifications to the original design had been made in accord with the fashion of the day, the most obvious being the reshaping of the rear end of the top frame-tube to give a lower riding position. These models sold at forty and forty-eight guineas respectively. There was also a sidecar outfit based on the same design, which could be purchased for sixty guineas. The sidecar was of the coach-built type, with seating for one passenger. The Company was obviously very proud of its success, for the Catalogue contained a number of illustrations showing the various machining operations in the factory. Also included in the Catalogue were reprints of test reports from the Press and numerous testimonials from satisfied private owners. Although no mention is made of the fact, it is interesting to note that the bore size of the $2\frac{1}{2}$ hp engine had been increased by 2 mm to 70 mm, giving a cubic capacity of 293 cc.

The onset of the First World War soon curtailed the activities of this expanding industry and the production of civilian machines finally ceased for the duration in 1916 by order of the Ministry of Munitions. Like most other manufacturers, Veloce Limited was quickly occupied with essential engineering work for the military authorities and it is significant that part of this work was for Rolls-Royce Limited.

It is sad to reflect that only one of the $2\frac{1}{2}$ hp models appears to have survived, a standard model of 1913. Fortunately it is a runner and in the good care of an enthusiast who is well aware of its value. The Hall Green Works have most parts of an earlier 499 cc model, again apparently the only survivor. It is hoped this too will be completely restored some day for use on the road.

2
Development of the two-stroke

In the year 1913, two quite significant events occurred in the history of the Company. For some time there had been a growing interest in the potential of the lightweight motor cycle or 'motorcyclette' as it was then known, as a cheap and economic form of transport. By the end of the year there was a very representative range of these machines on view at the Olympia Show, including the first two-stroke model to originate from the Spring Hill Works of Veloce Limited.

The Company had obviously decided that there were prospects of a hitherto untapped market, no doubt inspired by John Goodman's dream of an 'Everyman's' machine for the working classes. Percy Goodman evolved the design and the model was marketed as the 'Velocette', presumably in an attempt to identify this model quite separately from its larger brothers. Yet another precedent had been created, albeit unknowingly, for this was the trade-name destined to outlive the original.

The newcomer had an engine of 206 cc capacity (bore and stroke 60·5 mm × 73 mm) which was housed in a neat loop frame. The crankshaft arrangement was of the overhung type and there was a large outside flywheel mounted on the nearside. The cylinder was of the desaxé type with the cylinder and head cast integral. A patent lubrication system drew oil from a separate crankcase compartment and delivered it to various parts of the engine by exhaust pressure. The oil supply could be regulated by a simple control valve, and it was claimed that a single filling of oil would suffice for approximately 200 miles. Forks were of the unbraced lightweight Druid pattern and an Amac or Senspray carburetter looked after the mixture while there was a choice of Bosch or UH magneto for ignition.

By 1914 three variations of the original basic model were available. The cheapest, which sold at twenty-five guineas, had direct belt drive to the rear wheel and was virtually the equivalent of the 1913 model. It weighed only 112 lb and it had 6 in. ground clearance. For an additional five guineas a two-speed version with simple dog clutches was available, with all-chain transmission. The trio was completed by a ladies' model with open frame and dress-guards. This too had all-chain drive and a two-speed gear; it sold at thirty-two guineas. All three models were fitted with a neat cast-aluminium expansion chamber and a short extension pipe, which gave the engine a very subdued exhaust-note without any marked loss in performance. There was also a handlebar-controlled compression release, which vented the combustion chamber into the exhaust-port via an internal passageway cast in the cylinder. Gear control was by Bowden

This 1913 Velocette two-stroke was presented to Mrs E. Denley by W. T. Tiffen, the Carlisle trials rider and agent. It is now in the Birmingham Science Museum.

A ladies' model two-stroke of about 1922 vintage. The aluminium cowl round the cylinder-head acts as a dress-guard.

wire from the handlebar and footboards could be supplied as optional extras on payment of 12s. 6d. Twenty-four inch wheels were fitted as standard, but 26 in. wheels were available to special order.

In 1915 the engine unit underwent some design changes, the most noticeable being a new crankcase casting identified by a projecting centre-boss on the offside. Revised bore and stroke measurements of 62 mm × 73 mm raised the cubic capacity to 220 cc. This model, in company with a similarly engined ladies' model continued unchanged until 1916, when the war necessitated the termination of civilian motor-cycle manufacture.

With the war over, the production of motor cycles was resumed early in 1919. The only models listed were two-strokes, and two variations were available, known as the 'D1' and the 'DL1'. These models were virtually the gentlemen's and ladies' versions of 1915 models, unchanged apart from the refinement of an internal expanding rear hub-brake. They sold at £48 and £50 respectively.

Later in the year two models were announced, the D2 and the DL2. Signs of further development were very evident, for they both had distinguishing features such as a new double-front down-tube frame, an improved design of steering-head[1] with more positive means of adjustment, and a new type of engine[2] with a larger monobloc crankcase casting, the rear portion of which provided a mounting-platform for the gear-driven magneto. Access to the overhung crankshaft assembly could be gained through a large screwed circular opening on the offside of the machine, normally closed by a circular cover which was sealed off from the crankcase by a removable inner casting which itself formed the crankcase outer wall. Thus it was now possible to remove the piston, connecting-rod, and crankshaft from the engine without having to take the crankcase out of the frame. The big-end bearing took the form of a plain phosphor-bronze bush that was retained laterally by a tapered left-hand thread screw, which also blanked off the crankpin at its extremity.

The rotating and reciprocating oil-pump[3] was mounted from the top of the crankcase and it fed direct to the crankshaft main bush from the oil supply contained in an enlarged sump compartment. Oil passed through the hollow mainshaft to the big-end bearing, whence it was thrown by centrifugal force to lubricate the other engine internals. The rate of flow could be governed by an adjuster which either increased or decreased the stroke of the pump-plunger. It is interesting to note that throughout the whole period that this type of pump was in use, not a single case of failure was ever reported to the manufacturers.

Veloce Limited now found that the cast-aluminium silencer had proved unsatisfactory in long-term service, no doubt due to embrittlement that resulted from the continual expansion and contraction. The new design had the barrel and lugs made of steel, and featured a much longer flattened tail-pipe. The gearbox was still of the clutchless variety, but it had a selector of the rack and pinion type.[4] Gear control was by a polished metal knob on the offside of the petrol-tank, not unlike a bath-tap in appearance, which was connected to the selector mechanism by a stout metal rod. The rear sprocket incorporated a spring shock-absorber, which helped ease the 'snatch' on the dog clutches during gear changes.

The more sophisticated appearance of the model D2 resulted from the shapely tapered wedge tank of $1\frac{3}{4}$ gal capacity, which was suspended from the top frame-tube. Both models were fitted with lightweight Brampton

[1] British Patent 137,186 by P. J. Goodman (20 March 1919).
[2] British Patent 133,588 by P. J. Goodman (7 January 1919).
[3] British Patent 135,694 by P. J. Goodman (23 January 1919).
[4] British Patent 137,688 by P. J. Goodman (27 March 1919).

forks, which replaced the earlier Druid forks and gave a more comfortable ride. The D2 and DL2 models sold at £52 10s. and £55 respectively; both weighed about 155 lb.

The early 1919 Catalogue gave preliminary data about the D2 and DL2 models, and also mentioned the prospects of a spring frame, flywheel clutch, and three-speed gearbox. But with the exception of the last, these announcements proved premature. Pressure of work precluded the deployment of time on such ambitious development projects as rear suspension which, as will appear, did not materialize for many years.

It was now apparent to John Goodman that a move to larger premises would be necessary if the present continuing rate of production was to be maintained. In June the capital of the Company was increased to £10,000 by the creation of 9,000 new shares of £1 each and two of the main subscribers were a Mr R. E. Riley and the Member of Parliament for Deritend, a gentleman by the name of Smedley-Crooke. On 20 October a mortgage was secured for the purchase of freehold land in Victoria Road, Aston, including a cottage known as Victoria Cottage and works known as Victoria Works. The registered office of the Company was transferred to this address during February 1920.

At the 1919 Olympia Show only two models were exhibited, both of the D2 type. One was the standard production model which was to continue unchanged for 1920 and the other was the actual works machine that had won a Gold Medal in the 1919 ACU Six Days' Trial. To prove this was no fluke win, Veloce Limited entered three machines in the 1920 event and secured three Gold Medals and third place in the Manufacturers' Team Prize.

In retrospect, the two-stroke engine of fifty years ago may seem a somewhat crude device, especially when compared with today's advanced designs. Even so, the little Velocette was well in advance of its contemporaries. Good basic design, helped no doubt by the desaxé cylinder arrangement and the separate lubrication system, gave a unique combination of good performance and excellent petrol economy. The standard model D2 would reach about 50 mph in full road trim and it was not exceptional to record anything up to 200 mpg petrol consumption and 2,000 mpg of oil. A petrol-consumption test held in Tasmania was won by a Velocette, which recorded the incredible over-all figure of 229·5 mpg, a

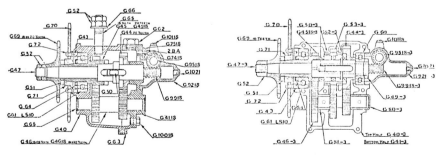

Gearbox. *Left* Model D2 (1920–1). *Right* Model D3 (1920–1).

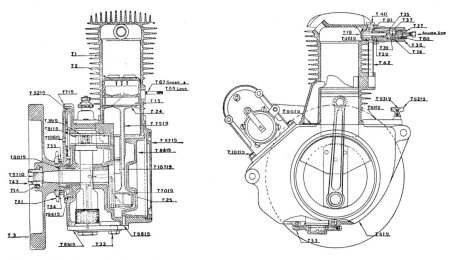

The model D two-stroke engine.

test which was immediately repeated to dispel any doubts about the possibility of a freak performance. Although the weather had deteriorated, the second test returned an over-all figure of 217·3 mpg – proof enough. It is worth taking into account the facts that the rider, a Mr T. Searell, was in his sixtieth year and that his machine was the only Velocette entered for the competition.

A new model, the D3, appeared in 1921 that had a three-speed gearbox based on the earlier two-speed design, but was still clutchless. The D3 was also fitted with a new internal expanding front hub-brake, made by H. C. Webb but designed by Percy Goodman.[1]

Before internal expanding front brakes were available on motor cycles, horse-shoe types were fitted. These were essentially an enlarged version of the normal sort of brakes used on pedal cycles. The brake-blocks rubbing on the front rim were almost ineffective as a means of retarding the machine's progress and became positively dangerous if the rim was even slightly buckled. The shoes were sometimes known to work loose, jam in the spokes, and riders were thrown off. Most riders preferred to remove the shoes, in the interests of personal safety, and run the risk of prosecution if the shortage of the brake-blocks be noticed.

Percy Goodman designed and patented an arrangement whereby the contracting spring that kept the shoes 'closed' was in the form of a split spring ring surrounding the shoes in a recess underneath the friction-liners. In such a small-diameter brake there was no space in which to fit orthodox coil springs.

With unpleasant memories of the old 'rim-scratchers' still very vividly in mind, few motor-cyclists would have used a front brake even if they had had one, and presumably it would have been a waste of effort and money to have fitted a larger and more effective front brake at that time. The little Webb brake was largely useless as a 'stopper' even when in good order and as wet and dirt very soon wore out the linings and drum it was

[1] British Patent 169,067 by P. J. Goodman (24 July 1920).

really a 'bobby-dodger'! The royalties from the use of the patent undoubtedly came in useful however!

Extras in the form of aluminium leg-shields were available on payment of an extra 30*s*. They could also be supplied for the D2 and DL2 models, which had continued unchanged in specification.

By 1922 the Company realized the limitations of their two- and three-speed gearboxes through the lack of a clutch, probably as a result of the knowledge they had gained from the Isle of Man TT entries. The gearboxes were redesigned and both versions now incorporated a single-plate cork-insert clutch which retained the original narrow chain-line. A gate-change control was fitted for the first time. The clutch-operating mechanism was somewhat unorthodox in the sense that a face-cam mechanism behind the clutch body was employed to separate the plates. Operation was from a thrust-cup and ball thrust-race carried in a pressed-steel lever with an enlarged end to encircle the thrust-race. This part was nicknamed the 'frying-pan' which it resembled in outline. It worked in a recess in the gearbox face adjacent to the sleeve-gear ball-race. The circular part round the thrust-cup was pressed to form three raised portions that rested in depressions machined in the hardened ball-race retaining ring. Movement of the lever caused the raised parts to ride up the 'ramps' or face cams in the hardened ring and move the thrust-cup and ball thrust-race outwards.

The thrust-cup operated the now familiar three thrust-pins in the back-plate of the clutch. To get the operation to function correctly, the retaining ring has to be set during initial assembly so that the 'frying-pan' lever lay in the right relation to the gearbox. Operation of the clutch-lever drew the upper end of the 'frying-pan' lever forward to free the clutch and as this part of the mechanism was exposed the method of adjustment (by means of the spring carrier in the front clutch-plate) was not quite so baffling to those unfamiliar with this somewhat unorthodox method of clutch operation.

The three-speed gearboxes were available with standard or close ratios. Since the middle gear of the former was of the same ratio as the first gear of the two-speed version, close ratios were favoured by the more discerning rider who liked to maintain good speed on hills and appreciated rapid acceleration.

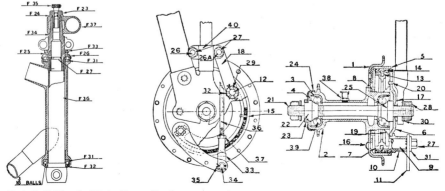

Left Ball Head. *Right* Front Brake.

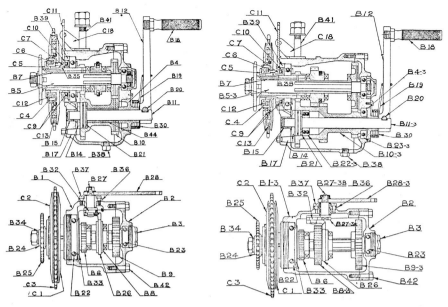

Velocette two- and three-speed gearboxes clutch and KS.

A kickstarter[1] which was now fitted to both the two- and three-speed gearboxes worked through the layshaft by means of a spring-loaded single roller which was forced into engagement with internal serrations in the layshaft by an inclined plane on the kickstarter-shaft. It was a reasonably effective means of starting, but it had the curious feature of occasionally permitting the kickstarter to revolve of its own accord when bottom gear was engaged. Fortunately, this occurred only after a considerable amount of wear had taken place on the layshaft bearings or if the tension of the main return spring had relaxed somewhat, but it seldom occurred on types fitted with ball-bearing layshafts.

Those interested in design features may like to know that the roller-type kickstart mechanism was retained on the model K four-stroke of 1925 but was found somewhat unsatisfactory with the increased loading of the larger engine. The design was modified to include three rollers carried on a suitably altered shaft. The internal serrations on the layshaft were discontinued at the same time. This modification did not prove satisfactory, and very shortly the arrangement was changed again to employ two rollers operating on a suitable shaft and engaging with an internally serrated layshaft. This remained the standard practice until the three-speed gearboxes became obsolete and all models had four-speed gearboxes with an entirely different mechanism.

Other 1922 modifications included the fitting of a proprietary Carb-Jector silencer which contained a patented spiral baffle assembly, and the standardization of the rectangular exhaust-port, a feature previously found only in the sports engines. The front forks now had buffer and rebound springs embodied in the top links, and were known as the Brampton Biflex type. The freedom of horizontal movement that this arrangement allowed

[1] British Patent 124,339 by P. J. Goodman (15 June 1918).

29

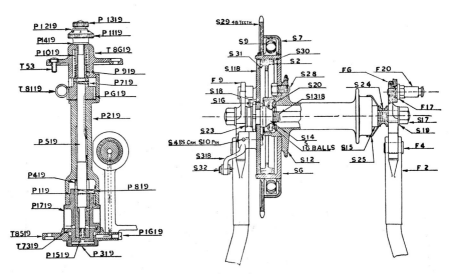

Left Oil-pump. *Right* Rear brake and spring drive.

brought about considerable changes in wheelbase and did not improve navigation over rough roads! Five models were listed, the E2, EL2, and E3 models and the S2 and S3 sports models. These latter machines had engines with revised bore and stroke measurements of 63 mm × 80 mm, giving a cubic capacity of 249 cc. They also used a special lightweight racing Brampton fork, which dispensed with the horizontal springs. All models with the suffix 'L' were designed for ladies' use and featured the characteristic open-frame layout. The numerals related directly to the number of gears.

About this time electrical lighting sets were making their first serious bid to challenge the superiority of acetylene as equipment. An ML Maglita with variable ignition control could be fitted for an extra £10, this instrument representing one of the first wide-scale attempts to combine a magneto and DC generator in one compact unit. Although the Maglita was driven at engine speed the charging rate of the generator was still somewhat low. It was a temperamental instrument even at its very best, for electrics were still in their infancy as far as two-wheelers were concerned.

In 1923 further engine design changes were made, and all the range now had the revised bore and stroke measurements of 63 mm × 80 mm to standardize the cubic capacity at 249 cc. The cylinder, still of the desaxé type, was much thicker in the walls, had deeper cooling-fins, and there were two separate exhaust-ports. This change had been dictated by ever-increasing speeds, for the earlier sports models had had a tendency to overheat when held at prolonged high speed. These latter engines had a large single exhaust-port which had been bridged to prevent the piston-rings from becoming trapped. Subsequent investigations showed that the bridge overheated, for it was at the centre of the hot exhaust gas stream. By providing a two-port layout the required port area could be obtained without the necessity for a bridge and the cylinder wall between the ports could be finned externally and kept sufficiently cool. Other smaller modifi-

30

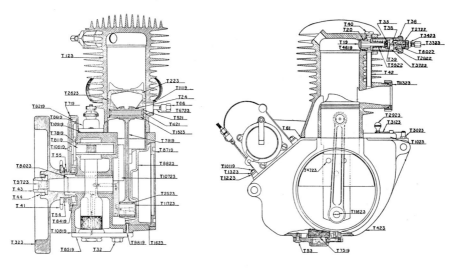

Engine of H, HC, G, and GC models (1923–6). EL, single port.

cations included the use of a new pattern piston and an increase in diameter of the crankshaft from $\frac{3}{4}$ in. to $\frac{7}{8}$ in.

Two touring models were listed, the G2 and the G3, which sold at £62 and £65 respectively. There were also two sports models, the GS2 and GS3 which were available at the same prices, a G3 combination with a single-seat sidecar at £85, and the ladies' models EL2 and EL3 (£63 and £66). Close or wide ratio gearboxes were optional.

As the top tube of any conventional cycle, or motor-cycle, frame contributes very considerably to the strength of the frame its absence from the open-type frames employed upon ladies' models, makes these less robust than the normal types. Eugene Goodman, always a rather dashing rider, used to recall an occasion upon which he was riding a ladies' model, probably his wife's Velocette, and drove over a sharp humpbacked bridge far too exuberantly. The machine took off and jumped quite a long way before landing very heavily. The open frame folded up and ended up with its wheelbase greatly lengthened!

Veloce Limited now guaranteed 120–130 mpg of petrol consumption with even greater oil economy, proof of their faith in the new designs. Gearboxes, clutches, and brakes were unaltered, but the top tube of the frame was lowered to give an improved riding position. The sports models had a toe-operated rear brake instead of the heel-operated type fitted to the standard models. Later in the year an additional model with 26 in. wheels was added to the range, the GC or 'Colonial' model, designed for use where the going was tough.

Overseas conditions were popularly supposed to include service over roads that would have been thought atrocious in the United Kingdom, and presumably those who rode or drove in those places to which vehicles were exported would require very much increased ground clearance. Many motor-car makers produced cars with modified axles, etc., to provide this and it was customary to describe such designs as 'Colonial' models. Veloce

The 'Light Two-Fifty' model A of 1924, one of the few Veloce models to have belt drive. The unusual tank motif is very distinctive.

One of the rare model HSS racing two-strokes. The rider is Charlie Goody, of the Vintage MCC.

were not remiss in offering motor cycles suitable for overseas or other exceptional conditions. Hence the modified versions of standard models were fitted with larger diameter wheels.

The G models proved very successful and they were continued in 1924 with only minor modifications. But with signs of demand for a cheaper model – again in keeping with John Goodman's concept of an 'Everyman's' machine, Veloce Limited decided to market two versions of what was known as the 'Light Two-Fifty'. To achieve some reduction in weight, the frame reverted to the single-loop arrangement used earlier, and lightweight Brampton forks of a type without the horizontal springs were substituted. The engine was of simplified design, having a central, single exhaust-port and a lubrication system dependent on crankcase compression – basically the system used successfully in the 1913–14 models. Apart from the savings effected by such radical changes in the specification of the cycle parts, the elimination of an oil-pump itself represented a significant saving, for the mechanical pump was a costly component to manufacture. A simple split-clamp fitting was adopted for the front crankcase mounting, leaving the rearmost portion to be supported by the two rear engine-plates, bolted to a lug on the frame. The magneto was chain driven, from a small sprocket behind the flywheel. Some further economy was effected by employing plain bushes to supersede ball-races to support the layshafts of the gearboxes.

The model A had a two-speed gearbox and chain-cum-belt transmission, the first time Veloce Limited had used a belt since 1915. There was also a heel-operated brake which pressed a block on to the belt rim, although a front brake of the internal expanding type was retained in the interests of safety. Obviously this model had its limitations, for it sold at only £38, a very competitive price well below that of the G models.

The second model, the model B, had all-chain drive and a three-speed close ratio gearbox. Internal expanding brakes were fitted to both wheels and aluminium footboards replaced the more customary foot-rests. At £45 this machine clearly represented the better buy, especially in terms of all-round performance. A distinguishing feature of both 'Light Two-Fifty' models was the special tank motif, which comprised the name 'Velocette' contained within an oval outline formed by the continuation of the tail of the final letter 'E'.

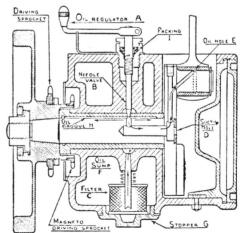

Plan of crankcase showing lubrication system used on models A, AC, and B.

The model numbers were changed to H in 1925 although the machines, with few alterations, were virtually the same as the corresponding 1923–4 G models. One fixed aluminium end-cap was used in the gudgeon-pin in place of the earlier fixing. The end-cap was pinned to the gudgeon-pin, so that, as it was larger in diameter than the pin to which it was fixed, it prevented the gudgeon-pin from working along towards the inlet-port. The depth of the recess in which it lay in the piston kept it clear of the cylinder-wall. Not only was it easier to fit than the two steel caps and threaded stud that it superseded but it eliminated the trouble that had occasionally occurred if the previous arrangement had worked loose.

The crankcase, gearbox shell, clutch, rear hub, and frame were also slightly modified. There were four models in the H series, the H2, H3, HS2, and HS3. The ladies' models EL2 and EL3 continued unchanged, as did the 'Light Two-Fifty' model B.

As may be expected, the belt-drive model A had not proved successful, hardly surprising in view of its somewhat primitive specification. It was replaced by the model AC, a two-speed all-chain version with internal expanding brakes on both wheels. Despite these refinements, the price was still slightly reduced, mainly due to production economies.

Manufacture of two-strokes terminated at the end of 1926, albeit only temporarily. The new OHC model K was in production and all the factory resources were concentrated on this revolutionary model. As may be expected, the two-strokes manufactured during the year were virtually unchanged, although the catalogue included an illustration of a new addition, known as the model HC3. This was a special, heavy-duty touring model which sold at £46 and replaced the earlier GC 'Colonial' model. The model AC now had a three-speed gearbox as standard but it still sold for £38, representing even better value for money. Minor improvements to the range as a whole were confined to the gearbox which had gear pinions with wider teeth and larger dogs.

A very limited number of super sports H models (HSS) raced with fair success, mostly in Spain. These were fitted with large-diameter cast-aluminium exhaust-pipes fitted to screwed adapters screwed on to the external threads of the exhaust-stubs of the cylinders. These pipes extended to a point just ahead of the gearbox where they entered two steel extensions running right to the rear. The ends of these pipes carried adapters and smaller diameter outlet-pipes. The high level of exhaust noise precluded the machines being used under normal road conditions.

Despite the success of the model K four-stroke, it was to the surprise of many that a new two-stroke was exhibited at the 1927 Olympia Show. Known as the 'model U', the design was brought up to date by larger and better brakes, and made more attractive looking by the fitting of a saddle-tank. The engine was of the two-port variety, using an H-type cylinder, but it had a roller-bearing big end – a design feature to be continued in later models. Capacity was still 249 cc, the old bore and stroke measurements of 63 mm × 80 mm being retained. The Brampton fork had at last been discarded in favour of a lightweight Webb design, which improved the handling. No steering-damper was fitted, nor side friction-dampers. The wheels each had new 6 in. diameter brakes, the front having a water-deflector formed integral with the steel brake-plate. In accord with the fashion of the day $1\frac{1}{4}$ in. twin exhaust-pipes were specified, each of which terminated in a black-painted barrel-type silencer. The normal, three-speed gearbox with the frying-pan clutch operation was retained, driving through a twenty-two-tooth gearbox sprocket. An extra front engine mounting-clip was fitted to the bottom of the crankcase, presumably in an attempt to reduce the vibration which was occasionally experienced in the earlier models.

The model U (for utility) sold at £36 and it weighed 193 lb. It quickly established a reputation for reliability under all manner of conditions thus proving a worthy successor to the two-stroke range.

In 1929 the USS or super sports version of the model was produced, 'Utility Super Sports', surely a contradiction in terms! Although the same frame and gearbox were used, the engine differed in many respects, having a new, more generously finned cylinder-barrel and a detachable cast-iron cylinder-head with a forward-facing sparking-plug. Internally all ports were polished and contoured to aid gas flow and a large-bore Type 6 Amal carburetter bolted directly to the inlet-port. Two large-diameter ($1\frac{3}{4}$ in.) exhausts were attached to adapters screwed into the cylinder by means of finned ring-nuts as used on the OHC engine. These pipes led the exhaust into two barrel-type plated silencers with integral fishtails. As a concession to higher speeds, the Webb forks incorporated side friction-dampers and a steering-damper. The appearance of the machine was

A close-up of the engine of the 1929 model USS two-stroke. Note the large-bore carburetter bolted direct to the inlet-port.

A near-original 1929 model 32 Velocette two-stroke photographed at the Sunbeam MCC's 1953 Newlands Corner Rally.

further enhanced by a more shapely petrol-tank holding just under 2 gal of fuel. The USS sold at £42 and weighed 205 lb. The improved performance of the engine permitted a twenty-tooth final-drive sprocket to be fitted as standard as opposed to the twenty-two-tooth sprocket of the model U.

As may be expected, the model USS was quickly accepted by the sporting fraternity and it was not uncommon to see these models successfully competing in grass-track events, even to the extent of winning Centre Championships. On the road there was little to choose between the model U or the USS, although the latter was undoubtedly faster. But unless the carburation was near correct, the USS was more prone to seize and would do so with lightning rapidity, the only advance warning being a slight harshness in the exhaust-note followed by the characteristic two-stroke rattle. Fortunately, little harm was caused if the clutch was promptly lifted; in most cases the engine would free sufficiently to permit the machine to be carefully driven away again within a minute or two. Petrol consumption averaged about 75 mpg on both models in normal give and take conditions, but the oil consumption was a little on the high side due to a tendency to over-oil at low speeds. The model USS was much noisier, due no doubt to the resonance of the hollow 'Oxford Bag' silencers. Road-holding and brakes conformed to the usual exemplary Velocette standards, although the model U was more skittish at high speeds due to the absence of friction-dampers on the forks.

Mention of the 1929 two-strokes would not be complete without including a third model announced towards the end of 1929. This was a variant of the model U known as the model 32, presumably because it sold at £32. It could be readily distinguished from the model U by virtue of its blue-coloured petrol-tank, the first departure from the traditional black and gold finish. Otherwise the general specification was very close to that of the model U. Needless to say the break with tradition in the choice of petrol-tank colour was regretted by many of the more conservative Veloce enthusiasts.

The year 1929 marked the end of an era, for the U series models were the last to employ the overhung crank layout, a distinctive Veloce design feature since the inception of their two-strokes. Presumably the hoped-for sales targets had not materialized, particularly in view of the success of the now well-established K series four-strokes. Certainly, few of the saddle-tank two-stroke models have survived the passage of time, for there are only two models known to be in full running order – a model 32 and a model USS, both of 1929 vintage.

An entirely new design of two-stroke was exhibited at the 1929 Olympia Show, where it caused quite a sensation. The model GTP had arrived, a step much nearer the 'Everyman's' machine envisaged by John Goodman so long ago and now close to the heart of his sons, Percy and Eugene. It is significant that this new model sold for £38, fully equipped.

The GTP used a quite different frame from the earlier models in the sense that it was not a 'cradle' type and the engine formed an integral part of it from front down-tube to seat-tube. Webb forks (Type 300 B and D) complete with a steering-damper and side friction-dampers were fitted and both wheels had 6 in. diameter brakes with the now familiar water-deflector as on the U models. The engine itself was completely new, although the cylinder-head, barrel, piston, and connecting-rod were virtually identical with those used in the USS series models. But there the similarity ended. The crankpin was now of the conventional double-ended type and was a press fit into two balance-weights. The left-hand shaft carried the large outside flywheel and primary-drive sprocket and the right-hand shaft drove the oil-pump by worm-gear and carried the contact-breaker cam at its extremity. The whole assembly was mounted in a small,

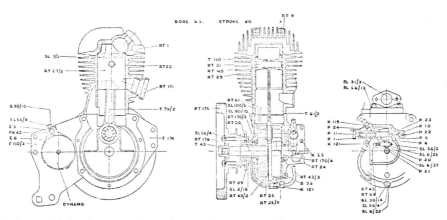

The model GTP two-stroke engine and its reciprocating oil-pump.

The late Freddie Hicks astride his very successful record-breaking model. Note the minimum ground clearance, the small-capacity petrol-tank, and the use of a lever-operated throttle. This photograph was taken during March 1929, outside the Vickers hangar at Brooklands.

The sidecar outfit used by the late Freddie Hicks to secure the 200 mile 350 cc sidecar record at Brooklands on 5 May 1929. Earlier in the year he had taken the three-hour 350 cc sidecar record at an average speed of 70·97 mph at the same venue. As can be seen, a special large-capacity petrol-tank was fitted for the occasion.

very rigid crankcase, with two large-diameter phosphor-bronze bushes as the main bearings. It was now necessary to remove the engine and separate the crankcase halves to gain access to the crankshaft assembly.

The gearbox had been slightly modified by the addition of a notched gear-selector quadrant carried internally. This worked in conjunction with a spring-loaded plunger, thus making gear selection more positive, and less reliant on the gearchange gate. Another change in specification concerned the clutch-operating mechanism. The 'frying-pan' clutch assembly was abandoned in favour of the now-familiar design which operates through an internal bell-crank and a hinged 'trapdoor' which abuts against the three thrust-pins. In these respects the GTP gearbox followed the model K design.

Perhaps the most sensational departure from current practice was the adoption of coil ignition, previously associated with cars only. The coil was mounted vertically within a special compartment which occupied part of the petrol compartment of the tank[1] (another portion of the tank contained the separate oil content whence the oil fed to the reciprocating oil-pump in the offside crankcase half by gravity) so that a short high-tension lead connected directly with the plug. Current was supplied by a 6 volt, 13 amp-hour battery mounted on the offside of the frame which was kept charged by a dynamo, belt driven from a pulley integral with the flywheel. During daylight hours the charge could be regulated by changing the position of the headlamp-switch. In the 'Off' position, a half-charge resistance was brought into the circuit which reduced the charging rate quite considerably. This resistance was automatically cut out when the switch was in the 'Charge' position, or when any of the lights were in use. To dispel any doubts about the efficacy of the system it was claimed the machine could be started with a flat battery if the switch was moved to the 'Charge' position and one ran with the machine in bottom gear. But the manufacturers neglected to mention one would have to run up to about 15 mph before the dynamo would cut in and give a sufficiently good charge! There was much still to be learnt about motor-cycle electrics even if this was one of the first attempts to devise an emergency-start procedure.

The GTP continued unchanged into 1931, but in 1932 two further modifications were incorporated in the design. The cast-iron cylinder-head was replaced with one of light alloy, mainly as an aid to weight reduction and the cheap tax concession. More important, the lubrication system was improved by directly linking the oil-pump adjuster with the carburetter throttle-valve. This altered the supply of oil from the oil-pump in accord with the throttle-opening, although the feed was never cut off entirely. It successfully overcame the objection to petroil lubrication (which Veloce Limited had always eschewed) with which an engine can become starved of oil or even seize on a long descent when the throttle is closed. The principle of metering the oil into the engine in direct proportion to

[1] The original patent, British Patent 338,704 by Eugene Goodman (27 November 1930), also had provision for a tank top panel containing an ammeter and lighting switch. The wiring was to be carried within a conduit formed integrally with the tank.

Road Testers leaving the Works on a batch of model U two-strokes.

Assembling Section One for the two-stroke models.

the throttle-opening was achieved by the addition of a control-rod from the carburetter to a modified adjuster on the oil-pump. While this refinement was described as a special feature in the catalogue of the period, nothing like the 'song and dance' about it was made as the quite unfounded claim that some Japanese firms thought up recently when they introduced a similar system – some thirty-odd years after the Hall Green engineers had used it! Twin upswept exhaust-pipes were also available for the first time, to give a more sporting illusion to those who used their machine for other than daily transportation.

40

In 1934 some changes were made to the cylinder and piston presumably to improve low-speed running, increase the power output, and reduce the risk of piston seizures. Experiments were entrusted to Alan Edwards formerly an employee of Butterfields Limited, the makers of the well-known Levis two-stroke motor cycles. Edwards had a lot of experience of engines similar to the Velocettes for some years, having been a consistent Gold Medallist in numerous reliability trials. He had also ridden in the Isle of Man TT on Levis machines. Possibly with the so-called 'six-port' Levis engine in mind, Edwards prevailed upon the Veloce designer to modify the GTP transfer-port arrangement to one that resembled the Levis design.

The transfer-passage in the cylinder that had originally run down from the twin ports in the rear wall of the cylinder to the cylinder-base was altered to run back and re-enter the cylinder-wall just below the twin outlets by means of a rectangular port. The piston was modified to delete the cut-away in the back of the skirt, which thus became continuous, and a rectangular opening was cut about an inch up from the bottom of the skirt. Gas was thus transferred from the crankcase via the opening in the piston rear wall to the passage in the cylinder and through the twin ports above. The idea underlying the design was apparently to improve the piston-skirt, and to aid its cooling by the passage of the mixture up the inside of it, which it was expected would cool the underside of the crown.

Happily, the modifications did not complicate the supply of spares to any marked extent and did not affect the reboring of worn cylinders and the supply of oversize pistons. Used together the two components were fully interchangeable with the first type. Later in the year the four-speed gearbox was fitted, a move which necessitated a somewhat lighter flywheel with a detachable centre. An oil-bath primary chaincase and a special valance on the chainstay of the rear mudguard to protect the top and bottom runs of the rear chain from mud completed the process of modernization.

Apart from the fitting of a much deeper and more stylish petrol-tank in the immediate pre-war years, the GTP continued virtually unchanged until 1940 when the Second World War again necessitated the cessation of civilian motor-cycle manufacture. A small batch of GTP models, all destined for export, were built to the pre-war specification in 1945–6, when motor-cycle production was again fully resumed. But these models differed in one respect – they all had magneto ignition, the magneto being mounted on a platform over the rear engine-plates. A chain sprocket fitted in place of the ignition cam and the contact-breaker cover was replaced by a neat polished chaincase which carried no acknowledgement to the manufacturer. For some strange reason, none of these models appears to have survived, even though there are many examples of the standard coil-ignition model still in daily use. To all intents, 1940 can be regarded as the last year of manufacture of the GTP.

A 1939 road test of the GTP conducted by *Motor Cycling* describes the machine in glowing terms and makes particular mention of the smooth

The ultimate of a long line – the 1939 version of the GTP two-stroke.

The very first Velocette model LE, a hand-built prototype produced during 1944–5. Note the twin headlamps mounted on the leg-shields and also the original design of the rear-wheel bevel cover. The position of the filler and level plugs would have been inaccurately located if the cover was refitted incorrectly.

running and high standard of road-holding. Starting was easy in all circumstances and the machine would cruise quite happily in the 40–45 mph range at half-throttle. Maximum speed was 57 mph and the petrol consumption averaged 78 mpg in town and 86 mpg in the country. Oil consumption was 1,210 mpg and both brakes would bring the machine to a halt in 34 ft from 30 mph. The model tested (1939) weighed 248 lb fully equipped but without fuel. It sold at £44.

It was not until 1960 that the name of Veloce Limited was again associated with a two-stroke design. Although the model LE was by then well established it was not a cheap machine to buy. As a motor cycle it failed to appeal to such a large potential market as had been opened up by the conventional types of scooters. It was felt that a really good design of scooter, backed by the high reputation enjoyed by all Veloce products could take advantage of the new two-wheeled transport.

The basic conception of the design is alleged to have occurred as far back as 1955 when the Works Director, Peter Goodman, was using an experimentally cut-down LE as a hack. One of the objections to any form of motor cycle, in the eyes of many buyers, is the type of frame that requires a leg to be raised to negotiate the tank when mounting or dismounting. The experimental LE employed a specially built 'open' frame constructed from standard LE components but cut away midway along to provide the 'opening' to make access and dismounting easier. As might have been expected the modification greatly reduced the strength of the structure, and the idea was dropped.

Later on a special frame of 'open' type was built, into which an LE power and transmission unit was fitted. This was based on suggestions from Tony Reynolds and Bertie Goodman, the latter having just taken over the Company's sales organization. This interesting machine was extensively road tested, and at one stage was fitted with entirely changed front-wheel mounting. Initially, it had used a cut-down and suitably modified LE front fork, but as many scooters on the market employ single-side mountings for their front wheels, which simplifies front-wheel assembly and removal, a special front-wheel suspension scheme was devised. This consisted of a single member below the steering-column that carried a stub axle at its lower end upon which the front hub, brake, and bearings were carried.

The assembly included suitable springing. The bulk of the weight was thus supported on one side only and was offset to the steering-column. The verdict of every member of the Works personnel who rode the finished article was that the very noticeable 'pull' to one side when in motion was quite unacceptable. Bearing in mind that many scooters get away with single-side front-wheel mountings some experiments were carried out using weights fixed in strategic places to endeavour to 'balance' the steering. None of them was successful in achieving a standard of 'navigation' that even remotely approached the criterion required of a Velocette.

Having decided to enter the scooter market, however, a new design was started from scratch and the project was placed in the hands of the Chief Designer, Charles Udall, who had been responsible for the LE some years before. In order to avoid some of the less satisfactory characteristics of other scooters being perpetuated in the new machine, as much as possible was learned of the steering qualities and general behaviour of some of the better-known makes, including at least one German design.

Noting that many scooters were very often called upon to carry pillion-passengers, and luggage when touring, not to mention being cluttered up

The Viceroy Scooter, a new approach to scooter design with a forward-mounted engine. This was the first Velocette model to use petroil lubrication.

with accessories of all sorts – some of these being useless weight in the form of dummy radio aerials and such-like – Veloce decided that more engine power was essential, and they disliked the bad weight distribution that resulted from carrying the power and transmission unit so far back and mostly over the rear wheel. They further considered that the wheel size should be bigger to obtain greater safety; in point of fact there was little of the usually accepted scooter design that found favour with them.

In the interests of simplicity, and economy in production, a two-stroke engine was chosen to propel the Velocette scooter, and to reduce vibration as much as possible it was made a horizontally opposed twin. It was air cooled. This engine was carried well forward suspended from the main, and very large-diameter tube of an entirely new frame. Behind the fly-wheel a tubular propeller-shaft drove a short shaft contained in a cast-aluminium housing that formed part of a transmission unit carrying the rear wheel and crown-wheel. From the short shaft a pre-stretched duplex roller-chain drove a large sprocket on a multi-plate clutch and four-speed foot-controlled gearbox. The gearbox terminated in a bevel pinion that meshed with a crown-wheel. The crown-wheel shaft carried the rear hub fitted to it on a tapered extension.

The transmission unit including reduction drive, clutch, gearbox, and final bevel drive was pivoted to the frame upon Silentbloc bushes; the whole controlled by a single oil-damped spring suspension unit.

The front end was supported upon a modified type of LE front fork. Wheels, larger in diameter than those customarily used on scooters, were bolted to their respective hubs, and being of welded pressed-steel construction could accommodate tubeless tyres.

Students of motor-cycle and scooter design may wish for further details of the engine and the following information is included accordingly.

Induction was controlled by twin reed-valves seating in a siamesed induction-tract that branched after leaving the engine side of the Amal

Monobloc carburetter which was fitted with a remotely operated butter-fly-choke and a combined air-cleaner and silencer to muffle intake roar. The cylinders took the form of light cast-alloy barrels shrunk on to steel liners that each had one exhaust-port and two transfer-ports. The die-cast cylinder-heads were machined to provide 'squish' by conforming to the domed crowns of the pistons that carried two compression-rings and had double-ported skirts for gas transfer. 'Torrington' needle-roller bearings were used in the connecting-rod small ends and the big ends ran on double rows of caged rollers. The crankshaft was built up from two mainshafts, each with its integral bob-weight, a central disc, and two hardened and ground taper-shanked crankpins. For the first time in the Company's history one of their engines was lubricated by petroil!

A Lucas 12 volt, 60 watt alternator was fitted to the forward mainshaft and enclosed in a neat domed cover fixed to the crankcase. The accumulators, two 6 volt banks making up the battery, were accommodated below the rider's seat together with the tool-kit. The 12 volt system was selected so that a car-type electric starter could be included in the specification. Charging was through a full-wave rectifier.

Engine capacity was 250 cc (54 mm × 54 mm) which gave the machine an adequate cruising speed of 55–60 mph. The exceptionally good road-holding, probably due to the inbred experience of the designers, and the use of 12 in. diameter wheels, was demonstrated by hands-off steering down to 20 mph.

The price of the model that was named the 'Viceroy' when announced, was £198 inclusive of Purchase Tax. Various extras including wheel trims, spare wheel and carrier, and a windscreen, were listed. Standard finish was bright red with white piping (with blue as an alternative) and off-white wheels. The seat was upholstered in grey 'Vynide' and the dry weight of the machine was 302 lb. The need for maintenance was reduced to an absolute minimum – not even a grease-nipple was in evidence.

The Viceroy was yet another attempt by Veloce to produce a modern concept of the late John Goodman's vision of a true 'Everyman's' machine.

Unfortunately, the Viceroy never enjoyed the success that was intended and expected. Possibly it reached the market too late, but it is more probable that it fell between two stools, and perhaps was neither the scooter-man's idea of a scooter, nor the motor-cyclist's idea of a motor cycle. The average scooter-buyer is oblivious to technical innovation and prefers the 'devil he knows' in the form of an imported foreign model to the technically very much better design that he doesn't know. To the dyed in the wool Velocette enthusiast, accustomed to more conventional sporting machines, it would not appeal either.

Few were surprised when the Viceroy was quietly dropped from the Company's range only a few years after it was first listed, and it is strange to relate that its efficient engine survives only in the somewhat unusual role of a power unit for hovercraft. In this guise the power output is alleged to be 16 bhp at 5,000 rpm. The specification includes an electromagnetic starter. The engine normally runs within the range 4,500–5,000 rpm.

3
The model K and its successors

In 1923 the Veloce Board made a decision that was to have a far-reaching effect on the prestige of the Company within the next decade. They decided to manufacture a four-stroke model again despite such lengthy experience with lightweight two-stroke designs.

The underlying reasons were not difficult to understand. The two-strokes had established an enviable reputation in the hands of a large number of customers and they had performed well in competitive events, even to the extent of holding several speed records at Brooklands and elsewhere. But there was clearly a need to produce a higher powered model, and as a single cylinder of 250 cc capacity was considered to be the largest size that could economically be made efficient in single-cylinder two-stroke form, the two-stroke principle was discarded. About 1923–4 the current trend was towards overhead valves, especially since engines of this type were not only getting faster than two-strokes, but what was of greater importance, were becoming more reliable.

Veloce Limited had experimented with a 250 cc engine by including a poppet-type inlet-valve in the crankcase of a two-stroke engine in an endeavour to obtain more power. But although the machine fitted with this engine was undoubtedly very fast it was not reliable, being subject to frequent piston seizures and the difficulty of getting the valve motion accurately to follow the 'engine-speed' cam. In consequence, the project was ultimately abandoned. In the light of the frequent use nowadays of disc inlet-valves in racing two-strokes it may be wondered why a poppet-valve was chosen instead of a form of valve that it would not have been difficult to use on the Velocette. The answer would seem to be a reluctance to risk objection on the ground of infringement by another motor-cycle manufacturer in Birmingham. It seems that a certain firm had, at one time, threatened action against Veloce for employing the overhung crankshaft which they claimed was one of their own ideas!

Another design of engine that they tried utilized a separate pumping cylinder behind the working one, in a manner somewhat reminiscent of the Griffon Bichrone, manufactured just after the turn of the century. This too was a failure and it is alleged the engine would not even run properly on the test-bench, or to use a phrase often heard in the motor and motor-cycle trades, 'Wouldn't pull the skin off a rice-pudding!' It became increasingly obvious that to attempt to boost two-stroke power by adding valves and other mechanical 'complications' was going to be less profitable than using valves in an up-to-date four-stroke design.

An added incentive for the new design was the need for a high-class

The first Velocette OHC engine designed by the late P. J. Goodman and built during 1924. In this form the engine did not go into production but was modified and produced in 1925.

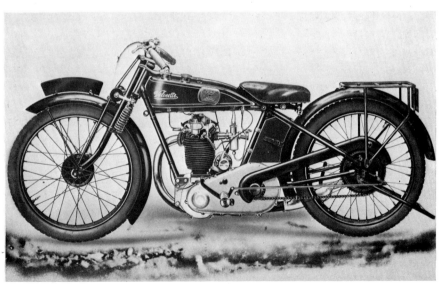

A nearside view of the prototype model K of which only three were built during 1924–5. The absence of a separate oil-tank denotes the total loss lubrication system. The oil-pump can be seen to the left of the cam-box.

production model which would adequately uphold the Company's reputation for performance and quality and even enhance it. There was also need for a higher degree of exhaust silencing than could be achieved without too much sacrifice of power. And so an overhead camshaft was selected as being the most efficient, and one that allowed the maximum enclosure of working parts and their thorough and constant lubrication. This would contrast favourably with the currently accepted standards of open-valve gear and push-rods, usually only scantily lubricated by the occasional application of a grease-gun.

Percy Goodman produced drawings towards the end of 1923, although some considerable time elapsed before the prototype was seen. The design had an overhead-camshaft engine of 348 cc (74 mm × 81 mm) as expected, with bevel-camshaft drive via a vertical shaft. Veloce tradition was followed by setting the primary chain-line inside that of the rear chain, giving a narrow but very rigid crankcase assembly. The gearbox was virtually a modified version of that used for the H series two-strokes, the internals being identical except for a ball-bearing layshaft. A single-plate, cork-lined clutch was employed, but this was to prove inadequate for the much greater power of the larger capacity engine, as explained later.

The 1924 prototype differed in many respects from the type that eventually went into production. The lubrication system was of the total-loss variety, oil being fed from a compartment within the petrol-tank to the cams and rocker-skids by a small rotating-reciprocating plunger-pump. This pump, driven off the left-hand extremity of the camshaft, was a modified smaller version of the pump used on the two-strokes. The stroke of the plunger could be adjusted to vary the amount of oil delivered to the engine. Unlike the vertical drive that was eventually standardized, the first design employed splined ends on the vertical shaft that mated with internally splined bevels. The cams were cut on a much larger base circle than was ultimately adopted, and the rockers carried rollers at their inner ends to bear on the cams. None of these features appeared on the production engines which began to reach the public in mid 1925.

In appearance, the prototype engine had a long, narrow look accentuated by the scantily finned cylinder-head and the parallel-sided magneto chaincase-cover that carried no maker's identification. In accord with the fashion of the day, the specification included Druid forks, 650 mm × 65 mm beaded-edge tyres on flat-base rims, and wide D-section mudguards, the rear mudguard having a tubular metal carrier above it. The petrol-tank held $1\frac{1}{3}$ gal of petrol and $\frac{3}{8}$ gal of oil were contained within the separate oil compartment.

During the intensive testing period that followed, which included entry in such diverse events as the 1925 Junior TT and the Colmore Cup Trial, it was found that the lubrication was not satisfactory. Oil refused to drain down the vertical-shaft cover as had been intended, preferring to build up round the shaft and bevels, so that the bottom end of the engine ran under-lubricated. In consequence a number of important design changes had to be made before production commenced. The most noticeable

One of the earliest K models; engine number K23. This superb example of the year 1925 has been restored by Eric Thompson of the VMCC.

A 1925–6 model KE fitted with an unusual front fork assembly.

change was to a dry-sump lubrication system, utilizing a double-gear pump housed in the offside crankcase half and driven from the mainshaft. The vertical-drive shaft and bevels were modified to use Oldham couplings in place of the splines. A 'hunting-tooth' arrangement was employed to ensure the heaviest loading did not occur consecutively on the same set of mating teeth. The design was patented under British Patent 252,822 dated 13 March 1925.

The first production machines (designated model K) were delivered mid-1925 under the trade-name 'Veloce' according to Company policy, for they could not be classified as lightweights. All had 'Veloce' transfers on the tank and the rear mudguard. But the public had very largely forgotten a name which had not appeared on a motor cycle since the First World War. In consequence the name was changed to 'Velocette' within a month or so of the first deliveries being made, no doubt due to representations from dealers who wanted to take advantage of the goodwill built up by the Velocette two-strokes produced by the firm in recent years. It was probably this change in policy that prompted the Company to register the trade-name 'Velocette' for the first time with the Trade Marks Registry on 21 January 1926.

It is perhaps not surprising that the new model suffered from a succession of 'teething' troubles and on at least one example of a quite newly delivered model K the screwed ring that retains the mainshaft shock-absorber spring worked out sufficiently to catch the inside of the dome on the cast-aluminium primary chaincase-cover which was torn open, allowing the ring, and spring to fly out on to the road, effectively stopping the progress of the machine.

The new owner, possibly not quite so proud now of his recent purchase, telephoned the dealer who had sold it to him and was towed home. To protect the good name of Veloce the machine was taken right to the back of the dealer's premises and covered over to hide it from view until it could be taken back to the Works in Six Ways Aston the next day. A modification was made at once and the possibility of any repetitions prevented by changing the threads of ring and shock-absorber body from right- to left-hand threads.

Valve-spring breakages were so frequent that full enjoyment of an exciting new design was sadly marred, riders having to 'limp' home at much-reduced speed when it was discovered that one, or even both valves were relying upon only one spring to close them. There was never any reluctance on Veloce's part to supply replacement springs gratis and these were obtained by them from various spring specialists in an endeavour to find some that would stand up sufficiently well.

Customers' work in changing springs was made much easier when Veloce produced a small tool that could be attached to the lower tank-rail by means of which the valve-spring collars could be depressed to permit broken springs to be removed and new ones to be installed without the bother of having to remove the cam-box and cylinder-head. With this piece of equipment, easily carried in one of the tool-boxes, and some springs previously compressed and wired up at home before setting out, new springs could be fitted reasonably easily at the roadside.

After a time this trouble ceased but petrol-tank leakages were only too prevalent, and, as in the case of the valve springs, the wares of several petrol-tank makers were tried in an endeavour to overcome a very real source of annoyance to owners.

Oil leakages from the engine were another 'fly in the ointment' and were not eliminated by the substitution of a disc for a ball in the non-return valve in the drain-pipe from the cam-box to the crankcase. At least the removal of the valve for cleaning out and reseating was made easier when it was transferred from the offside crankcase to the nearside, but it must be admitted that until, in later years, the KTT came along with its little cam-box scavenge-pump, leakages from the rocker-slots were never entirely eliminated. As a matter of interest, the design of the Veloce cam-box owes something to the design of certain overhead camshaft aero engines produced by Rolls-Royce as a study of some published patent specifications of theirs makes fairly evident.

The practice of packing the vertical-shaft gland-nuts with asbestos string usually enabled owners to keep the oil inside the cover, but it is germane to the subject to mention here that at one time rubber rings were employed instead of the asbestos. They certainly sealed the joints very efficiently, but when it became necessary to unscrew the gland-nuts to dismantle an engine it was almost impossible to move them! Veloce soon reverted to asbestos string which remained in vogue for the whole production 'life' of the OHC type.

The introduction of screwed-in rocker-pin end-caps removed one source of sweating oil from the top end of the engine; this modification is dealt with elsewhere.

When the Instruction Book that had done duty for some years was revised for Harold Willis's modified KTS and KSS models, which formed the mainstay of the 1932 programme, the directions for dealing with possible oil leakages were moved to a less prominent place in the book. The person responsible for the revision pointed out to Willis that in the original edition of the book the introductory instructions for starting a new machine were *immediately* followed by a prominent sub-heading reading 'Curing oil leaks'. This, it was suggested to Willis, led to the obvious inference that oil leakages were to be expected very soon in the life of the machine, very much as a standard feature of the design! With his broad sense of humour, Willis wholeheartedly agreed that the transfer of the paragraphs concerned to a later and less prominent part of the book had much to commend it and the revision proceeded along the lines suggested.

A rather peculiar 'flat spot' was noticeable in certain wind conditions when riding the first K models, presumably because the carburetter air-trumpet was very close indeed to the front face of the oil-tank. The height of the British Thompson Houston magneto with which many K models were turned out required a long induction-pipe to set the B & B carburetter back far enough to clear the magneto. When an ML magneto was fitted a much shorter pipe was used and there was plenty of room between the trumpet and the tank and it was found that machines so equipped did not 'catch their breath' occasionally like their BTH-carrying fellows.

It has been stated already that the clutch of the 1925 K models was a single-plate one with cork friction-inserts. Looking back it is remarkable that this clutch worked as well as it did, as not only was it run only at a very little higher speed than the MAC clutch, when the latter was fitted with a nineteen-toothed engine sprocket (the K had a twenty-tooth), but unlike the MAC chainwheel, the K chainwheel had no ball-race to support it on the clutch back-plate! There is little doubt that the failure to keep the chainwheel properly concentric with the back-plate, together with the overloading due to its slow rotational speed, made it a real source of trouble.

The replacement of the cork clutch with the seven-plate Ferodo type cut out all complaints of clutch slip but, as is so often the case, the curing of one ailment brings on another, the new clutch no longer acted as a 'safety-valve' to prevent the transmission gears from being overstressed. Quite soon after the Ferodo-lined clutches came into use some instances of gears becoming stripped of their teeth came to light. These breakages led to the Brown and Sharp form of gear teeth being superseded by Stub tooth gears and another cause of bother was removed. Stub tooth gearboxes acquired the prefix X to their serial number.

To anyone not well acquainted with the early OHC models, it is easy to assume from the foregoing text that they were unreliable and were plagued with troubles. Fortunately, nothing was further from the truth; our frank exposition of the problems that did occur with the early models has been made because they are characteristic of the 'teething' troubles liable to occur with any new design. It should be remembered that oil tightness was rarely a virtue of any machine made during the vintage era, although some were better in this respect than others. Most manufacturers relied upon felt pads and other simple non-mechanical devices to impede the leakage of oil, in the absence of the highly efficient oil-seals that we know today and take for granted.

There can be little doubt that the early OHC Velocette was a very handsome machine that does not look out of place amongst many of its peers made a decade later. On the road it had a performance that can only be described as exhilarating and a smoothness that was almost unknown from a single-cylinder engine at that time. Road-holding was to a very high standard; in short, the owner of an OHC Velocette rapidly acquired status among his motor-cycling companions, for it was not long before they became aware of the machine's capabilities.

During 1925 a second model capable of 80 mph was added to the Catalogue to meet the demand expected from those who required a machine with performance approaching that of the TT models. The fashion for fast machines with bare rear mudguards had been started a little earlier by John Marston Limited, of Wolverhampton, when they marketed a sports version of their 500 cc model the 'Long-stroke' Sunbeam. Because the Velocette sports model was virtually a 'K super sports' model, it acquired the designation 'KSS' – beginning a long line of models with this Catalogue symbol which continued until the road-going OHC models were finally dropped from production in 1948.

To bring the 'K' into line with racing practice was not difficult, for Webb forks had already superseded the Druid forks with which production had started. The main changes in the cycle parts were the fitting of narrow 'C'-section mudguards, the front one having a tubular stay and the rear supported by a tubular stay and lifting handle assembly. Two platforms between the rearmost stay and the vertical stay served as mountings for the tool-boxes. Except for a larger petrol-tank and quick-action filler-cap, the KSS resembled the 1926 Junior TT winner.

The KSS engine was supplied with a special slipper-piston giving a higher compression ratio. A long open exhaust-pipe could be included in the specification if the machine was to be used for racing. It is alleged the engine produced 18–19 bhp at 5,800 rpm, an increase in power helped by the use of cams which gave a more extended timing than the profile of those fitted tō the touring model provided.

It is worth recording that some minor changes had been made to the lubrication system in an endeavour to reduce the possibility of oil leakage. In the earlier system, the drain-pipe from the cam-box cover was connected to a second branch-pipe that took the oil to a ball-valve assembly fitted into the timing side crankcase behind the magneto chaincase-cover. Oil leakage from the rocker-slots was prevalent as the inertia of the ball prevented the non-return valve from operating in a satisfactory manner. It was not long before the ball was changed to a disc and then the whole assembly was transferred to a more accessible place in the driving-side crankcase-wall, above the front end of the cast-aluminium-alloy chaincase. Oil from the gutters below the open ends of the rockers still ran through two small-diameter pipes to the chaincase; a little later the rear one of these was altered to deliver oil from the rear-gutter drain to the inlet-valve guide.

The subject of oil leakage from the cam-boxes has been dealt with in the comments on the 'teething' troubles to which the model K was liable. While the diversion of oil to some place where it might do some good by lubricating the inlet-valve stem and guide as described above, the little pipe leaked some of the oil on to the fins adjacent to the inlet guide flange. But on the whole the modification was welcomed.

During 1925 the standard model K sold at £65 and the model KSS at £75. A sports sidecar with frosted-aluminium panels was available for £18 when either model was specified with sidecar gearing. Both models and the sidecar continued unchanged for the 1926 season.

At this period the Velocette two-strokes were making a great reputation for themselves as very reliable lightweights, having an exceptional performance for their capacity, yet even the most ardent Velocette enthusiast would not claim the marque was very popular. There were comparatively few examples to be seen on the roads of Great Britain, so it was not surprising that the new OHC models aroused little interest outside the immediate circle of those who were already Velocette-owners. But later in the year, after Alec Bennett won the 1926 Junior TT with a lead of approximately ten minutes over the runner-up, the situation changed with surprising rapidity. Riders who usually looked down on two-strokes and had no interest in buying one (except perhaps a Scott!) began to see possibilities in the OHC models as a means of winning races or of obtaining a very fast road model with which to 'dust-up' other motor cycles on the road.

Following Bennett's win, that famous contributor to *The Motor Cycle* who wrote under the *nom de plume* 'Ixion' prophesied that the new OHC Velocette would attract a following of enthusiastic riders and that it would be responsible for the formation of a 'clan' similar to that of those whose ideal machine is the Scott. How accurate was his forecast has been clearly demonstrated over the years that have passed since it was written.

Among other things that troubled Veloce Limited, and also of course purchasers of earlier examples of the model K, fuel leakages have been mentioned. Like the tanks of most contemporary machines, of the early 1920s, those of Velocettes were made of 'tin-plate' with soldered joints; in a word a 'tinsmith's job'. The normal method of attachment to the frame was by short bolts screwed into threaded sockets soldered into the floor of the tanks. To prevent chafing, reinforced rubber packings some $\frac{3}{16}$ in. thick were interposed between the tank and the flat lugs which supported it.

Naturally, with such mountings, the tanks suffered ill effects from vibration from which no single-cylinder engine can ever be entirely free. Seams developed cracks in the solder and it was not until tanks of welded-steel construction superseded the soldered ones, and more flexible forms of tank attachment were standardized that reasonable freedom from leakages was attained.

The flat tanks of the 1926 TT machines had been supported upon four deep rubber buffers that rested in heavy malleable lugs on the lower tank-tube that were provided with matching sockets in their upper and lower faces. Long-shouldered bolts passed through the lugs from below and each had another rubber buffer that fitted the underside of the lug between the bolt-head and its plain washer. The bolts were therefore flexibly held from any contact with the frame-lugs and their threaded sockets in the tank-floor were free from stresses.

The HRD machine to which Harold Willis ran second in the 1927 Junior TT had, like Howard Davies's Senior TT mount of 1925, been fitted with a saddle-tank. This type of tank was now becoming the accepted equipment for high-class sports-type motor cycles and Veloce had fitted them to their 1927 racers, as well as standardizing them for the production machines. These tanks were fixed in the manner of the 1926 racer for which the frame was modified to include the cupped lugs and permit the use of rubber buffers and the shouldered bolts previously described.

As saddle-tanks cannot have flat bottoms but require to be constructed to straddle the tank-tubes of the frame, it was now possible to put a 'set' in the lower tank-rail of the frame to give extra clearance with which to make the removal, and replacement, of the cam-box assembly easier, and all frames to which saddle-tanks were fitted were modified accordingly.

One consequence of this modification was to make it almost impossible to use the special valve-spring compressor that had been such a boon in the early days, but as the reliability of the valve springs had improved and

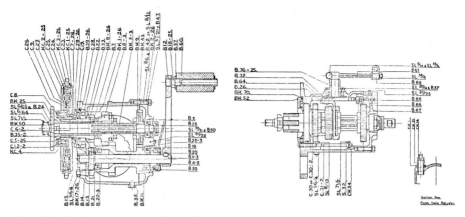

The 1927–32 three-speed gearbox (Veloce part numbers shown).

emergency changes were now seldom called for, this was not found to be of much importance.

But apart from the better tank-mounting and freedom from tank leakages the KSS, to which saddle-tanks were fitted before being standardized on the tourers, had a very much more handsome and pleasing appearance that was in keeping with its performance.

Another considerable improvement was the fitting of the new gearbox that had been used first on the TT models. The clutch-operating mechanism that had been inherited from the two-strokes was discarded and in place of the 'frying-pan' that carried the thrust-bearing, a hinged thrust-cup operated by an internal bell-crank was substituted. The 'one-sided' movement of this thrust-cup necessitated the inclusion of a spherically mounted component in the thrust-bearing to line up the clutch-plates as the clutch revolved, and as this could be fitted to clutches operated by the 'frying-pan' numerous owners of machines bought before the introduction of the new mechanism were able to improve their clutches at trifling expense.

In another respect also the new gearbox was a distinct improvement. Until then all model K gearboxes were basically but slightly modified editions of those used on the two-strokes. Admittedly, they had ball-bearing layshafts, but so had the G and some earlier models (plain bearings were used on certain less expensive models), but the retention of the gears in engagement was still dependent upon the location of the lever in the tank-side gate. As a result it was not uncommon for second-gear teeth to become prematurely worn due to running only partially engaged, sometimes due to incorrect adjustment of the gear control-rod, but also due to wear in the gate and on the lever.

In addition to the improved clutch operation, the new gearbox included a spring-loaded plunger working against an indexing segment embodied with the selector-lever. The segment was machined to provide notches into which the indexing plunger was held by its backing spring. There were four notches, one for each gear position and one for neutral. An adjustment by means of an eccentrically bored indexing plunger bush enabled the second gear to be meshed accurately with the corresponding teeth on the layshaft,

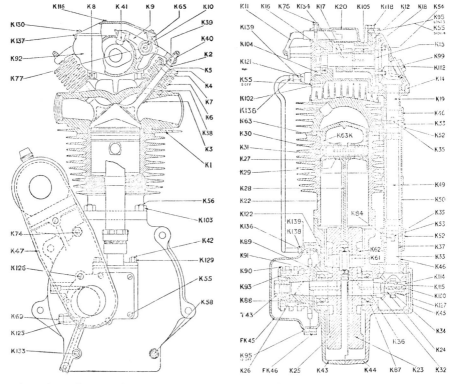

The 1926–7 OHC engine in section (Veloce part numbers shown).

and the correct engagement of the gears and driving dogs was no longer dependent upon the lever and gate. GTP gearboxes employ the same mechanisms.

For 1927 wired-edge tyres were fitted in place of the original beaded-edge variety and the flat-section rims gave place to the now universal well-base type. The standard K was continued unchanged except that as supplies of flat tanks were used up, saddle types were fitted. The model KS was in effect a KSS with a standard engine, or in other words a standard K with sports-type wheels, tyres, and mudguard equipment. (A 'sheep' in 'wolf's' clothing!)

An item of equipment supplied with the KSS was a pair of large sports-type knee-grips. These were made by the John Bull Rubber Company of Leicester and had originally been produced to a design furnished by that famous rider George Dance, a legendary figure in speed hill-climbs and road-races on Sunbeam machines. Listed at first as George Dance knee-grips, they later became known as just 'Sports' type, but at the time they were a *sine qua non* with any rider desirous of emulating the racing-men of that era. The *tout ensemble* of the KSS was indistinguishable from that of the Company's TT entries.

Even now the cam-box was not completely oil-tight, a problem which tended to become more serious as speeds gradually rose. In the current design the rocker-pins passed through phosphor-bronze bushes pressed into the side of the cam-box, where they were retained by countersunk-headed screws that passed through them and screwed into the casting on the opposite side. The cam-box was never quite clear of an external film of oil, as there was always some seepage from between the rocker-pins and the fixed bushes that supported them. In consequence the cam-box casting was yet again modified to take threaded hexagon-headed caps that carried the rocker-pins. The caps could be securely tightened against their soft copper gaskets and made oil-tight. After some instances of them working loose, they were drilled through the flats and locking wire passed through to secure them.

During 1926 the cylinder-head had been slightly altered to hold two short head steady tubes. The tubes tied the cylinder-head to the twin down-tubes of the frame and considerably improved the smooth running of the machine. The new cam-box now used only three of the cylinder-head bolts for support and the front left-hand side was bolted to an extension of the cylinder-head steady bolt lug on this side. Repositioning of the cam-box drain-pipes permitted the flow from the rearmost rocket-gutter to be fed directly to the inlet-valve. The end-cover of the nearside of the cam-box was reshaped and included provision for a new exhaust valve lifter and cable stop.

When the 1927 TT machines were seen it was noticed that much more aesthetic bevel-box covers were fitted. These were much more bulbous than the ones that they replaced and had been adopted with the object of leaving more clearance for the crown-wheel and top bevel which it was believed would confer a slight advantage by reducing oil-drag. Apparently any benefit that was obtained was thought to be unworthy of consideration as the design was not continued and never appeared on more than a very few of the machines actually used by Veloce for racing or experimental purposes. The famous spring-frame Velocette 'Spring-heeled Jack' had one of these bevel housings.

Apart from the introduction of the new cam-box in 1927, other modifications were also evident. The diameter of the steering-head races were increased to accommodate larger ball-bearings, preventing the pitting that had bedevilled the original type, reducing the need for periodic adjustment. All models were fitted with the new saddle-tank and all had the improved gearbox.

The model KSS now sold at £75 and was listed as having a guaranteed maximum speed of 80 mph when fitted with an open exhaust-pipe of the correct length. As a result of TT experience the diameter of the main oil-feed pipe from tank to crankcase was increased to bring it up to the internal diameter of that used on the Company's racers.

To enable the riders to get going at full-throttle sooner, and so save time, Percy Goodman had enlarged the oil-feed pipes for the TT races and the benefit of his foresight was passed on to his customers by making the larger bore pipe and tap standard equipment.

A tap had always been included in the feed system as a means of preventing the crankcase flooding when the engine was stationary should the ball-valve in the mainshaft fail to seat properly. Some years later, and following some engine seizures caused by forgetful riders failing to turn on the oil after turning it off when parking their machines, a plain union that only had the strainer gauze fitted to it, superseded the tap.

A special racing-type ML magneto of rectangular shape supplied the sparks and for road use a new type of silencer (described elsewhere) was fitted, often referred to as the 'water-bottle' on account of its shape. No speed guarantee was given with machines supplied with electric lighting sets.

Other models catalogued in 1928 were the K, KE, KS, and KES – all variations of the same basic design. For example, the model KS was very similar in specification to the KSS, apart from the cams, piston, and magneto. The compression ratio was lower and in consequence there was no guarantee of performance. The cheaper models, designated the KE and KES, sold for £58. Economies had been made by replacing the cast-aluminium-alloy chaincase with a sheet-metal guard and dispensing with the steering-damper, and generally the model lacked many of the refinements of the various K types that had preceded it. The shielded primary chain, which because it could not be kept as well lubricated without a case that enclosed it fully, could not be kept quiet and the noise from it, though slight, greatly reduced the pleasure of riding. Also, the life of the chain was shortened. Some saving in manufacturing cost was also made by using a lighter edition of Webb fork and the Type 275 B and D that had been standard on the other models (except the KTT) was replaced by one that had several details in which it differed from its predecessor. Webbs were not used exclusively on the KE and KES models and a few were supplied with forks made by Bramptons who had by then discarded the 'Biflex' type that had been used on the two-strokes. A standard 'round' ML magneto was fitted in place of the special racing type supplied with the KSS. Tyre sizes were 27 in. $\times$ 2·75 in. The KES differed only in respect of narrower mudguards, the absence of a rear carrier, and the use of tubular mudguard-stays.

When electric lighting was fitted to any of the models, a Lucas Magdyno was usually specified. To allow adequate clearance for the carburetter it was necessary to fit a longer induction-pipe secured by a loose ring-nut, which had a slight upward set to clear the dynamo. This modification probably accounted for the reluctance to give any guarantee relating to the machine's performance.

By 1929 it was evident that some rationalization was necessary, especially since a new TT replica model had been added to the range. This model, the ubiquitous KTT, is fully described in the chapter which covers the racing models. For an outlay of £80 one could purchase an actual TT replica capable of at least 85 mph and having the first positive-stop foot-operated gearchange.

Apart from the KTT, only three other models were listed: the KN, KNS, and KSS. The letter 'N' in the engine number prefixes indicated an improved Hoffmann thirteen-roller big end and suitably modified connecting-rod to accept the larger big-end outer ring.

The authors have no idea why the extra letter should have been used in

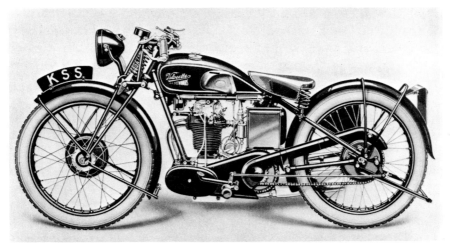

The 1930 model KSS fitted with Miller SUS lighting equipment.

An artist's drawing of the 1931 KTP coil ignition model. Note the flame trap fitted to the mouth of the carburetter.

the designations of the KN and KNS, but it was still stamped on the crankcase of the KSS until well into 1931. The thirteen-roller single-row big end was fitted to some of the early KTT engines before being superseded by a double-row cage-type bearing for a while.

There are plenty of motor-cyclists who prefer a machine that *looks* fast even if it may not be particularly so, and there was thus a market for a model that outwardly resembled the KSS. This demand was satisfied by the KNS which with its narrow mudguards, small-diameter types, and absence of rear carrier was a most attractive proposition even though it lacked the ultimate maximum of the KSS. It was less expensive to produce by virtue of having the standard 'round' ML magneto in place of the much more expensive square-type racing ML. The model had another advantage for those less wealthy and thus unable to afford the KSS as with its lower compression ratio the engine was less discriminating about fuel. The KSS insisted upon a 50/50 mixture of No. 1 Petrol and pure benzol which was

59

not obtainable from roadside pumps. The much more sedate KN was equipped with D-section mudguards and larger section tyres on 19 in. diameter wheels and was provided with a rear carrier.

With 'commuting' customers in mind, and to provide extra weather protection large rubber-covered footboards like those that had been standard equipment on the model H two-stroke were offered for the KN and for those who wished, polished aluminium leg-shields were listed. The degree of comfort with this equipment was most welcome in inclement weather, but the leg-shields amplified every little sound from the engine and transmission and reduced very greatly the rider's pleasure, and an 'open' machine seemed like a high-priced six-cylinder by contrast afterwards! Harold Willis, who used to do a lot of long-distance riding on his Velocette, had a machine fully equipped with footboards and leg-shields and called it his 'Gentleman's Road Carriage'.

In 1930 there was a curious departure from Company policy when Veloce Limited decided to pander to a very short-lived fashion for two-port cylinder-head four-stroke engines. As a result a new model, the KTP (K-Two-Port) was introduced which in common with the GTP two-stroke (introduced at the same time) employed coil ignition and of course electric lighting. The dynamo was carried in place of the magneto on the platform of the four-stroke where it was retained by special clamps. It was driven by chain from the normal spindle but at a higher speed than a magneto. This necessitated a redesigned cast-aluminium chaincase-cover which was pear-shaped in outline, to accommodate the larger diameter driving sprocket. It had the name 'Velocette' cast upon it.

The bottom end of the KTP engine was identical to that of the KSS of the same period, but the cam-box had a modified side cover to carry the contact-breaker assembly. No. 23 profile cams were fitted and the camshaft was extended to carry the ignition cam. The two-port cylinder-head was fitted with the same valves and springs as the KSS but had a machined face on the induction-port to which was fitted a flange-mounting Amal carburetter. The coil and condenser were contained within a special compartment in the underside of the petrol-tank in a manner virtually identical with that of the GTP. A ½ gal oil-tank was mounted sideways on a special platform on the offside of the machine, just above the gearbox. The other half of the platform carried the battery on the nearside of the machine where it was retained by a simple clamp.

If Veloce ever produced a 'flop' the KTP was it! Despite the very keen purchase price of £58, which included electric lights and horn (there was no Purchase Tax in those happier times!), it was far from being the success that was expected. In performance it was mediocre with a maximum that seldom bettered 65 mph and it was never a lively performer; certainly not by Veloce standards.

In addition, however, the coil ignition was rather unreliable, partly due to the fragility of the components of a system with which no manufacturer had had much experience at that time, but also due to oil that seeped through from the cam-box, fouling the contact-breaker points. Dynamo failures were not uncommon due to the armature, commutator, and other internals becoming flooded with oil that for some time could not be prevented from getting into the dynamo driving chaincase in excessive quantities. This last fault was cured by a modification to the end-face of the driving-spindle bush.

KTP-owners who over-flooded their carburetters and opened the throttle too far when endeavouring to start their engine from cold were liable to set the machine on fire. The effect of the over-opening of the throttle cut out the pilot system thus weakening the mixture, and also caused the engine to kick back. The coil-ignition system gave a spark in either direction of rotation and the resulting flame from the combustion chamber ignited the surplus petrol dripping from the over-flooded carburetter.

Later deliveries were fitted with a gauze flame-trap screwed on to the carburetter in place of the normal air-trumpet. Incidentally, the KTP was not the only machine subject to this disconcerting defect – some other makes suffered too. After a rather short and disappointing run the KTP was discreetly deleted from the range.

A few KTPs had been produced with magneto ignition to special order and many were eventually converted to single port, a modification which was quite easy if a replacement cylinder-head of the required type was purchased, together with a new exhaust-pipe. It is nevertheless interesting to note that only a few years ago the Works received a letter from a Velocette-owner in eastern Europe who was still using one of these models daily, in unmodified form.

The other OHC road model in 1930 was the KSS, which now sold at the reduced price of £62 10s. A front-wheel-driven speedometer was available as an extra, the drive being taken from a steel pinion within the front brake-drum. Full dynamo lighting was also available as an extra for £5 6s. using the Miller separate unit lighting set. The separate dynamo was carried in front of the crankcase within specially shaped front engine-plates. It was driven by a flat belt from a pulley on the engine mainshaft, the drive being fully enclosed within a pressed-steel casing. The addition of lighting equipment raised the over-all weight of the machine to just over 290 lb, an increase of approximately 25 lb. No guarantee of performance was given even if the machine was supplied without lights, a fact underlined by changing the magneto specification to the standard 'round' ML pattern.

It may be appropriate to digress at this point and outline the significance of the overhead camshaft engine prefixes. All engine numbers prior to 1932 were prefixed by one or more letters which were used to identify the type of machine and in some cases indicate modifications in design. For example, when the first 'improved' cam-box was fitted the initial letter 'C' of 'Cam-box' was added to the prefix, and the fitting of the first deeper section rockers was heralded by the use of the initial letter 'R' (for 'Rocker') in a similar manner. Some cumbersome prefixes resulted as there were successive lengthy ones such as 'KCR' and 'KCRSS'. On occasion the 'R' of these prefixes has been interpreted optimistically and quite erroneously by buyers of old machines as indicating a 'Racing' model.

Other prefixes used were the letters 'N' and 'A' which respectively indicated the use of the 'new' thirteen-roller big end and a two-port cylinder-head. It will be appreciated that the crankcase used for the 1930–1 KTP models had the prefix 'KA'. Towards the end of 1931 the letter 'N' was dropped from the prefix of the single-port OHC model engines which were then stamped 'KSS'.

No changes of any significance were made during 1931. The KTP and KSS models still had hand-operated gearchange but the latter had a more shapely petrol-tank which no longer had provision for the anchorage of the Andre steering-damper. The leather tool-boxes on both models were redesigned and the transfer on the petrol-tank now included the words '26–28–29 TT Winners' as a token of the Company's successes in the Isle of Man. For the first time all bright parts were chromium plated as standard, in place of the nickel plating used previously.

For reasons that it is not too easy to ascertain, the KSS models of the late twenties and the very early thirties could by no means have been expected with any degree of certainty to have exceeded 80 mph. Motor-cyclists were becoming 'softer' perhaps and required what had previously been 'extras' such as built-in speedometers and lighting equipment, not to mention pillion-seats and foot-rests for their passengers. The Miller separate unit lighting set required a battery and a properly designed carrier to hold it, and although at first the pillion foot-rests and speedometer were not provided or included for the normal list price, the machine had provision for them to be fitted so that they could be purchased as 'extras' and be fitted easily by a customer for himself.

The over-all weight of the KSS had thus increased since its first appearance, but for all that it is difficult to understand why, in 1931, the maximum speed of an average example off the production-line was often some 10–12 mph slower than the earlier ones. The original slipper-type two-ringed KSS piston had been superseded by a full-skirted one with two compression rings and a slotted oil-control ring below them, and provided a compression ratio of 6·75:1, the cam was the No. 24 profile that had been used previously, and even taking into account that the racing ML magneto had, presumably on account of price, been replaced by the standard 'round' type, these things hardly explained the mediocre performance to which the KSS had deteriorated over the years.

Changes made to the touring models during 1931 included the use of the KTP-type side-mounted oil-tank and wheels with pressed-steel brake-plates. In the construction of the rear wheel, the spokes were now taken to the brake-drum, permitting the sprocket to be detachable. The KTS had WM2 × 19 in. rims and 3·25 in. × 19 in. tyres back and front. Touring-type ribbed mudguards were fitted, the front one valanced. The KSS had the usual 21 in. rims and 3 in. tyres, and narrow C-section mudguards. Both KTS and KSS models had mudguards covering a much greater proportion of the wheel peripheries and to enable the rear wheels to be removed more readily the extreme rear ends of the rear guards were made detachable and the registration-plates were attached to them. The mudguard-stays were all produced from steel strip instead of steel tubes as hitherto.

For some reason never ascertained these were the subject of many letters to the Hall Green Service Department accusing Veloce of 'cheapening' the machine by fittings unworthy of quality productions. Since concurrently Messrs John Marston Limited of Wolverhampton were still fitting their Sunbeams with similar stays, and since the Sunbeam had long been cited as a real quality motor cycle the Veloce staff never understood why something that apparently was accepted as in keeping with the Sunbeam was unacceptable to Velocette owners.

After the 1932 season tubular-steel stays were standardized, but the strip type had never given any trouble! Neither machine had a rear carrier fitted. This could be purchased separately, as could pillion foot-rests and a speedometer. Provision was made for the fitting of the latter by providing lugs on the top front-fork lug; the rear chainstays had built-in lugs to accept the pillion foot-rests, which could be folded when not in use. The petrol-tanks were modified by incorporating rubber buffers in the front mounting because the earlier type used on the KTP had shown a tendency to split and leak near the front mounting and the rubber mounting was considered necessary. They were similar in shape and fittings to the KTP pattern but had no coil-boxes.

Another similarity to the late, and unlamented, KTP model was the braking equipment. To keep down production costs at a time when the motor-cycle market was highly competitive, it was necessary to effect economies in any respect that did not detract from the efficiency, safety, or performance of the finished product. Some trouble arose from a weak front brake-plate anchorage coupled with an unfortunate setting of the front cam spindle-lever that increased the pressure of the brake-liners upon the drum when any slackness developed between the somewhat weak stop on the fork-girder and the slot in the brake-plate. Otherwise the KTP brakes had been entirely satisfactory. After modification to the front cam-lever, brakes similar to those of the KTP were standardized on the new KTS and KSS models.

The front hub was identical and a pressed-steel brake-plate was used, being considerably cheaper than the familiar cast-aluminium one that had graced the majority of the K range since 1925.

The KTS front brake-plate had a water-deflector at its lower edge, but the brake cam-lever was fixed to face rearward instead of forward as on the KTP. This entailed operating the lever by cable for the full distance between the brake and the handlebar-lever and a cable-stop pillar was fixed to the brake-plate in the position required above the extremity of the cam-lever. The effect of setting and operating the lever in this way avoided the tension upon the cable being increased when the brake was applied. In addition the stop-lug on the fork-girder was reinforced.

Although some machines were supplied with the earlier malleable rear hubs to which separate brake-drums were bolted, all later models were equipped with rear hubs similar to the KTP rears. These were pressed steel with integral brake-drums to which a separate chainwheel was bolted. Because the brake diameter prevented the provision of a flange deep enough to accommodate the necessary bolt-holes to take the chainwheel bolts, the number of teeth on the chainwheel had to be increased to fifty-six, which is one more than were cut on the malleable brake-drum that was replaced. The over-all gear ratios were thus reduced fractionally but this was not found to be of any consequence. The pressed-steel rear brake-plate used with this type of hub had the advantage of incorporating a water-deflector plate that the other type lacked.

On some occasions rear brakes in the malleable drums had become ineffective in wet weather due to water entering the drum. Special rings had been available to weld on to the brake-plates of any machine that had been afflicted with a trouble that for some unknown reason occurred only in very isolated cases.

The engines and gearboxes of both models were identical. Internally, several items had been modified to give the engines a performance more in keeping with that normally to be expected from a KSS model. The basic intention was to produce an engine that would give a high-power output without using either expensive fuel such as 50/50 petrol-benzol mixture, or sparking-plugs that cost more than the usual 6s. each. In any case, it was by then difficult to obtain pure benzol and few riders were willing to try anyway, so all engines were turned out to run on No. 1 Petrol and were fitted with two compression-plates between their cylinders and crankcases. Customers were thus able, should they wish, to increase the compression ratio and use a suitably higher octane fuel after removing one or both of the plates. As no previous Velocettes had ever been fitted with compression-plates, it was necessary to warn owners that the removal of only one plate, let alone two, made it essential to fit a shallower Oldham coupling to the vertical shaft or dire results would follow.

The hemisphere of the combustion chamber was reduced, a new slipper-type piston fitted and the valve lift increased. By modifying the end-cover of the cam-box it was possible to reposition the sparking-plug so that it came much closer to the centre of the combustion chamber. In altering the valve timing, the opportunity was taken to reduce the diameter of the cam base circle to improve the lasting qualities of the cams and the rocker-skids that bear on them, a benefit derived from the reduced surface speeds. To simplify cam removal, a thread was provided to accommodate an extractor. Maintenance was simplified by designing the cams to permit the timing to be checked with the 'running' tappet clearances. This type of cam was designated K17/5.

A comparatively inexpensive make of sparking-plug was now specified as standard equipment which, in addition to having the exact character-istics that the engine required, was very short and so fitted in nicely with the new cam-box side cover. Unfortunately, this sparking-plug had a ceramic insulator against which material there was at the time an un-reasoned prejudice in riders' minds – presumably because the majority of racing and high-heat resistance-type sparking-plugs employed mica for the purpose. Many plugs were returned to the Works as 'defective' when all they needed to make them work efficiently was cleaning. Since they were not separable for the purpose, a change was made to a suitable grade of mica-insulated KLG plug a little later.

At this juncture it is opportune to include a section that deals with the various forms of silencer that have, from time to time, been fitted by the makers to those models that comprised the K range.

The 1925 models used a small cast-aluminium silencer that was devoid of a fishtail; that item of the equipment that has become such a well-known feature of Hall Green motor cycles and has been taken as the title of the magazine issued to the members of the Velocette Owners' Club. Despite the very small volume of this silencer, only a very rudimentary form of baffle-tube was fitted into the engine side of the body, at the outlet of the exhaust-pipe from the engine. This was simply a piece of tube that had its end slit and folded over to provide some restriction. It is not to be wondered at that the exhaust was by no means adequately silenced, because the folds got straightened out by the force of the exhaust gases and the baffling effect, never very effective anyway, was removed altogether. To those who were frightened of being prosecuted for riding noisy machines Veloce kindly supplied, gratis, neat little black fishtails and clips for attachment to the short outlet-pipe of their silencers.

A little later the production machines were fitted with welded-steel silencers of rectangular side elevation and rounded upper and lower sides that were of greater volume than the aluminium ones. They incorporated a baffle-tube, but were finished in black and were not as pleasing in appearance. This type was gradually improved and later included a shroud-tube outside the baffle-tube much the same as the arrangement employed in the current type of large chromium-plated fishtail-ended silencers that grace the Vipers and Venoms.

It can be said that the present silencer is a direct descendant of the ones that were produced for the KTP model. These were produced from two 'handed' steel pressings that when welded together made a quite shapely silencer of which a fishtail formed an integral part. The pressings were shaped to provide ears with which the rear ends could be held by two studs screwed into the frame fork-end lugs. As the fishtails were not drilled there was no need to produce right- and left-hand versions for the KTP.

In the course of the experiments that Harold Willis made before modifying the KSS engine, he tried out many ideas that he had about silencers, and as silencer pressings for the KTP were plentiful it was convenient to make up a silencer for the single-port model by using one KTP silencer and to conduct his experiments with it. He produced a silencer that contained a shroud-tube, into which the outlet end of the baffle-tube was fitted and located by a special cup pressing that was welded into the end of the shroud-tube. After prolonged tests on the engine test-rig and on the road, an acceptable design was arrived at that gave a reasonable degree of silence without too great a loss of power. Exact details were formulated for the location, number, and diameter of the holes that were to be made in the baffle-tube, and a similar specification was laid down for holes to be punched in the pressing for the offside of the silencer fishtail. The final design was used as standard equipment on the 1932 KTS and KSS models and remained so until the Mark II superseded the 'iron' engines for the 1936 season.

The silencer produced for the Mark II was made up from a number of pressings and the fishtail was made separately and then welded on. When the performance of the first batch of the Mark II series was so very disappointing the subsequent investigations showed that one of the causes was the very much restricted outlet from the silencer body to the fishtail. This was probably due to the press tools having been altered to increase the volume of the silencer over and above that of the KTP type from which it derived and to improve the shape. At all events the outlet was altered and this, together with other changes made to the engine, to instructions from Percy Goodman who had intervened, brought the performance of the Mark II up to the standard usually associated with KSS models. It eventually became possible to use the same type of silencer upon all models except the GTP and, of course, the LE, Valiant, and Viceroy.

Both the KSS and the KTS very soon became firm favourites among motor-cyclists as the performance was uniformly good, but of the two the KTS was always considered the faster, although in fact there was probably little difference. This belief was due to the fact that the speedometer gearing was identical on both models but the greater rolling distance of the large-diameter front wheel on the KSS produced a fractionally slower reading. Additionally, the smaller diameter rear wheel and consequently fractionally lower gear ratio of the KTS were an advantage.

A very limited number of the 1932 models were fitted with a double row of uncaged rollers in a big-end bearing of proprietary make (as used on 1930 KTT engines) before the new sixteen-roller caged type was fitted as standard. Steel flywheels replaced the earlier cast-iron ones used up to the end of 1931. Otherwise the KSS and KTS models were outwardly similar (at a quick glance) to their predecessors. The list of optional extras had been extended and it now included such items as an air-filter, crankcase-shield, high-level exhaust-pipes and sports tyres. Although both models were still supplied with hand gearchange as standard, the most popular extra was the positive-stop foot gearchange, which added only £1 15s. to the bill.

About this time there was a theory that perhaps there would be a market for a foot-control mechanism that could be produced more cheaply than the positive-stop type, and that a 'non-positive' one would be acceptable. Accordingly, one was designed and listed but never 'took on' and was very soon dropped.

While writing of the positive-stop control that Willis originated and which inspired so many copyists, and undoubtedly was responsible for making pedal-operated gearboxes universal practice, not only for racing but for ordinary road-going models, the eventual fate of the Veloce attachment should be related.

Shortly after the gearboxes were redesigned to include the mechanism within the housing, the only need to produce further parts for the original type was to supply spares for those already in use and to the makers of the Reynolds-Scott motor cycle upon which a modified Velocette foot control was used. Not wishing to manufacture the necessarily small quantities of parts that were called for, as this was not a profitable proposition, an agreement was made with Scotts whereby they bought all finished and part-finished parts, the jigs and tools for manufacture, and all raw material for parts in stock at Hall Green. A condition of the sale was that Scotts would undertake to supply spare parts for the mechanism to such Velocette-users as should require them.

By 1933 four-speed gearboxes were coming into general use, following racing practice. One had already been successfully used on the Works racers, but it had no starting mechanism and was, therefore, unsuitable for normal road use. Nevertheless, the necessity for a four-speed gearbox for the KSS and KTS models was realized and Eugene Goodman produced a special design to suit the standard production machines. Two of these gearboxes were made in due course but they were very much larger than the three-speed type that they were intended to replace. Furthermore, since they had a protruding extension of the housing to enclose a kick-starter quadrant (a radical departure from Velocette practice), they looked exceedingly bulky. Part of this effect was due to the traditional layout of the Velocette chain-line which, as the clutch lies behind the final-drive sprocket, tends to bring the gearbox over to the offside.

Apart from the unfavourable criticism of the appearance, which possibly was not very important, the whole unit was too heavy, the ratios were somewhat ill chosen, and the very high kickstarter ratio made cold starting most difficult – there were no multi-grade oils available in those days! To test the gearbox under severe conditions one of them was fitted to a KSS sidecar outfit that Frank Cope was using in open trials such as the Colmore and Victory Cup events. Although the gearbox functioned satisfactorily it was decided not to put the design[1] into production and it was left to Harold Willis to produce a second, improved design that overcame all the objections that had been made to the first arrangement. The second design was adopted for the production models and by the end of 1932 the last three-speed K-type machine was delivered.

The modified engines proved to be very satisfactory in service and possibly the only points for criticism were the somewhat heavy valve-stem wear, due in part to the increased lift and perhaps the shortness of the guides. There also appeared to be a need for a petrol-tank of increased capacity, especially since the new tank held little more than the original KTP design. What was possibly even more important from the sales point of view was that the tank *looked* small, and did little to enhance the appearance of the machine! The two complementary models had already

[1] It is interesting to note that one of these gearboxes is still in existence.

67

A standard production KTS model of 1934.

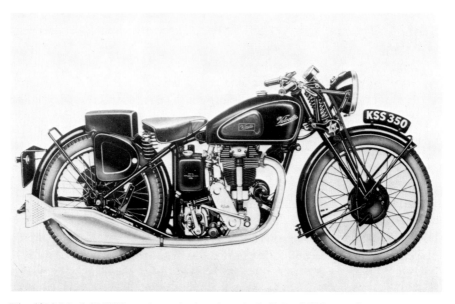

The 1938 Mark II KSS, perhaps the best loved of all the OHC models.

been brought up to date by the inclusion of the four-speed gearbox and so for the 1934 season the tank capacity was increased to about 4 gal and the mounting was much improved. Following racing practice, two tank-support lugs were added to the lower frame-tube in a manner identical to that of the Mark IV KTT frame providing a much lower mounting position. The tank was secured by four vertically fitted shouldered bolts that screwed into threaded bosses welded to the underside of the tank.

Rubber insulating buffers were interposed between the tank and the support lugs, after the fashion of the earlier K models.

Although positive-stop gear control had not been standardized before 1934, except on the KTT model, only a few buyers elected to have the standard hand control and most machines were fitted with the Veloce patent foot-control mechanism which bolted directly to the standard gearbox. And so the gearbox was further modified to include a positive-stop mechanism within the housing which made it possible to produce all the 4 gal tanks without provision for the attachment of gear-lever gates.

With the 4 gal tank and foot-controlled four-speed gearbox, the KSS and KTS models continued unchanged in specification until production finally ceased late in 1935. There was an interval during which no OHC road models were made until the so-called Mark II versions were put into production in 1936.

The incentive for a change probably originated from criticism of the exposed valves and other external parts of the valve gear. In 1933 Eugene Goodman had designed the first of the M range engines, the high cam-shaft MOV model of 250 cc capacity. Upon this engine the whole of the valve gear was enclosed, was properly lubricated, and it was proving very satisfactory in service. The same principle was also proving equally successful in the companion MAC and MSS models.

Before committing themselves too far in the matter of valve enclosure a 'mock-up' enclosure of the valves and springs had been given an extended trial on a KSS engine that powered a sidecar outfit. Any fears that may have been felt that the springs would become 'let down' by being robbed of the cooling draughts of air were fully dispelled. In the light of this exacting test and as the M types were doing so well the decision was made to redesign the K-type engine and produce two new models. To rationalize production it was decided to continue the practice of making the KSS and KTS complementary by using as many of the same parts for both as possible. As a result, the two models were to differ only in the specification of mudguards, wheel and tyre sizes, and possibly internal gear ratios.

It had been found that by relieving the bevel gears and the overhead camshaft drive-shaft and cover of oil pressure a slight improvement in power output had been gained in the cases of the KTT model and the Company's own racing engines. In consequence the lubrication system of the new KSS engine was modified during the design stage to lubricate the upper bevels and the cams and rocker-ends from jets in the upper-bevel housing and cam chamber respectively. The new engine, which Harold Willis dubbed the Mark II, differed from the previous KSS also in having the iron cylinder-barrel surmounted by a single light-alloy casting that was a combined cylinder-head, cam, and rocker-box. The rockers, outer ends of the valves, and the coil valve-springs were now fully enclosed. Rocker-clearance adjustment was effected by carrying the rockers upon spindles ground eccentric to their mountings in the housing. Rotation of a spindle thus varied the clearance between the outer end of the rocker and the tip of the valve-stem. The valve-seats, of austenitic iron in the case of the inlet and of aluminium-bronze for the exhaust, were inserted cold while the head was pre-heated, thus shrinking the head on to them and retaining them in place. A copper gasket formed the seal between the head and the cylinder-barrel. Excess oil thrown off from the cams lubricated the valve-stems and guides and after collecting in recesses below the bottom valve-spring collars, drained down through a large-diameter 'Y' shaped external oil-pipe to a union on the nearside of the crankcase.

After the Mark II went into production and examples found their way into customers' hands, the performance was found to be much below that of the KTS and KSS models that it replaced. The engines ran very 'oily' and it seemed clear that the new type of piston designed for it, that was of the full-skirted variety with a chamfered type of oil-control ring, instead of the slipper type with slotted ring that had been used for years previously, was not proving a satisfactory substitute.

A member of the staff, who had been previously employed by a motor-car firm, commented on the drawing of the piston with its chamfered ring before it had gone into production. He 'dared' to suggest that rings of that type had to be changed in the car engines after proving unsatisfactory and that they might well prove equally useless in the Mark II. He was told by the designer to mind his own business!

Faced with the problem of rectifying over-oiling and heavy oil con-sumption on customers' machines, the Service Manager sought Percy Goodman's permission to have some compression-rings altered to 'stepped' scraper-rings by turning away some of the bearing face so that they could be tried for rectifying cases of over-oiling with which the Repair Depart-ment were occupied. Some benefit was obtained and later the Service Department were authorized to buy some 'stepped' rings from Well-worthy, the piston-ring makers.

Percy Goodman, when dealing with the Mark II silencer to improve the machine's performance also modified the valve timing and reverted to a slipper-type piston and slotted oil-control ring. Fortunately, the various modifications introduced were successful in considerably improving the performance which then reached the standard required.

The bottom bevel-cover was now produced as a single casting integral with the rear of the magneto chaincase to which a cast-aluminium cover was attached by a series of screws, the whole making a much neater appearance than the 1925 conception.

Although of the same bore and stroke as its forerunner, the new engine was given a longer connecting-rod than before, produced from the same drop-forging as the MAC part. In fact it differs only from the MAC rod in that the small-end bush protrudes slightly at both ends of the small-end eye (it is flush on the MAC). The crankcase was much larger than was required to house the flywheels of a 350 cc engine and suggests the possi-bility that there may have been some intention to utilize it for a production 500 cc OHC model.

The 500 cc MSS model that had been listed first in 1935 provided a large proportion of the cycle parts of the Mark II KSS and KTS models. The same frame-forks and gearbox were used and the KTS was fitted with the same wheels, tyres, and mudguards. The KSS still had narrow sports-type mudguards and larger diameter wheels (21 in. front and 20 in. rear) but both models used the MSS front hub and brake. The rear hub of the Mark II models differed in the sense that the wheel was quickly detachable, leaving the brake, sprocket, and chain still in position.

The more technically minded may be interested to learn that the first prototype Mark II engine dispensed with a pressure of oil in the vertical-shaft cover and bevel housing, but after a brief road test the engine was considered to be far too noisy mechanically, probably due to the lack of the sound-deadening effect of the volume of oil. As a result the lubrication system was at once restored to the original arrangement in so far as pressure in the vertical-shaft cover and bevels was concerned. What can be tolerated in racing cannot always be translated in terms that will be acceptable to all buyers. Having been known for so long for maintaining a high degree of mechanical silence for all models, it would obviously have been a retrograde step to produce a new model that would have fallen so far short of the established standard.

The new models were announced just prior to the 1935 Motor Show at Olympia. They sold at £68, and now turned the scales at close to 340 lb. The standard of performance was very close to that of the earlier models, but two major advantages were soon apparent. The engine was very much quieter in the mechanical sense and there was no longer the bogy of oil leaks; an oil-tight engine resulted from the adoption of fully enclosed valve gear. Certainly the two models were even more handsome in appearance, due in no small way to the seemingly massive construction of the engine where even the cylinder-head was partially enveloped by the deep-section petrol-tank.

Both models continued virtually unchanged until all motor-cycle production ceased as the result of the Second World War. Most of the detail modifications related to the lubrication system. After a short while, the external oil-pipe feeding the cams and rockers was taken from the bevel-box cover, permitting a gauze filter to be used on the cover face, thus protecting the jet from impurities in the oil. Later still, the external pipe and jet were deleted entirely, and oil fed through grooves in the camshaft plain bush as on the 1925–35 models. Metering of the supply was achieved by not cutting the groove right across the bearing, but leaving a short section ungrooved in the centre. A flat cut on the camshaft overlapped the two grooves so that a continuous passage for the oil to travel into the cam chamber was formed at every revolution of the shaft.

The early Mark II engines had no filter between the bottom of the crankcase and the return side of the oil-pump. Following an epidemic of valve-spring breakages and the shearing of the oil-pump drive, due to pieces of spring being drawn into the pump, a gauze filter was incorporated in the bottom right-hand corner of the sump as protection. In case the connection between valve-springs and the sump is not fully understood it was found that small pieces of spring got out of the valve-spring cavities in the head and reached the sump via the large-diameter oil drain-pipes. As a temporary expedient, and until new crankcase castings could be obtained, a small filter shaped like the traditional 'witch's hat' was fitted at the bottom end of the drain-pipe. Incidentally, the reshaping of the offside crankcase half to accommodate the new suction filter has given rise to many problems with the 'special' builder, for this later type of engine is more difficult to fit into the post-war spring frame used for the M series models.

It is not intended to make this account of the overhead camshaft models a catalogue of the various troubles associated with them during the long period during which models that used this type of engine were included in the Company's manufacturing programme, but often the description of difficulties encountered and the manner in which they were surmounted is interesting to students of motor-cycle design from whose ranks we expect that some of our readers will come. And so, having written this, we will describe some of the 'teething' troubles that came to light after the Mark II was marketed and came into general use.

The enclosure of the rocker-ends, and outer parts of the valves and their guides and their consequently copious supply of oil from the cam chamber, had the disadvantage that there was now a tendency for oil to work through into the valve-ports and down the valve-guides which produced a smoky exhaust. Owing to the depression in the inlet-port, this was affected more than the exhaust.

The guides were accordingly modified to provide recesses or cups at their upper ends to accommodate leather oil-seals which were carried in pressed-steel cups retained under the inner valve-springs. This modification proved more effective than a previous expedient of shaping the top of the inlet-guides to sharp edges to scrape excess oil off the stems and increasing the working clearance of the exhaust-valve to allow exhaust gas pressure in the port to expel the oil past the guide.

The epidemic of breakages of valve-springs was attributed to fractures starting from minute surface marks on the unpolished wire from which the springs were wound. A partially successful cure instigated by Percy Goodman was found in shot-blowing all springs in stock until new supplies produced from polished wire could be obtained. The trouble was also attributed to stresses set up by the springs surging at certain engine speeds and the springs were later modified to make the inners a fairly tight working fit in the outers. The trouble was cured and the 'close-coiled' springs were standardized on all Velocette singles.

Two other changes were made in 1939. The fork-damper adjuster was replaced by an improved design which took the form of a circular knob, not unlike that usually fitted to domestic radiators. The gearchange lever was also modified, so that a greater range of adjustment could be achieved. When production finally ceased after the outbreak of the Second World War the KTS model was to disappear for all time; only the KSS was reintroduced and even then for only a short spell.

At the end of the war Veloce Limited found themselves with a range of equipment for precision engineering that was second to none, as a legacy from their Government contract work. They had been giving much thought to the evolution of new designs and had even carried out a limited amount of experimental work, as a prelude to re-entering the motor-cycle market at the cessation of hostilities. But the problem was what post-war plan should they adopt as they gradually tapered off their Government work?

There was ample evidence that there would be a steady increasing demand for new motor cycles and so a rapid reversion to full-scale production appeared to be the main consideration. Rather than delay matters by persisting with new designs they decided initially to produce most of the highly successful 1939 range, including the by now well-established KSS model. Initially, post-war production of motor cycles began with the manufacture and export of a batch of 250 GTP models, with magneto ignition. But by the time they had made their first official announcement to the Press late in 1946, every Velocette agent in Britain had at least one of the 1947 models in stock.

The 1947 KSS model differed only in very minor detail from the 1939 version. The cylinder-head was fitted with a slightly larger inlet-valve, a modification carried over from the very late 1939 models which commenced from engine number KSS 8972 onwards. The cam-plate in the gearbox was changed to give the 'down for up' and 'up for down' foot movement which corresponded with that of the majority of post-war machines. All the post-war KSS models had engine numbers which commenced at KSS 10,000. Perhaps the main difference between the 1947 and the 1939 models was the price, now £139 exclusive of the newly applied Purchase Tax.

Before the 1948 season it had been learned that Webbs had decided to discontinue the manufacture of girder forks and so it was decided to fit a new type of Oleomatic 'telescopic fork' made by Dowty Equipment Limited. Past experience with smaller units working on the same principle had shown that satisfactory springing could be obtained at the rear end of the Mark VIII KTT racing models. The Dowty fork had already been accepted by a number of other motor-cycle manufacturers as standard equipment, on machines such as the Scott, EMC, and the Panther.

The use of the telescopic fork necessitated a different shape of petrol-tank, tapered at the front to clear the fork legs when they were on full lock. A 19 in. diameter front wheel of the MAC/MSS type was also fitted, using an alloy brake-plate.

The reasons for adopting air suspension are perhaps best underlined by requoting the statement in the fork-manufacturer's literature: 'Air springs are impervious to the fatigue failures common to metal springs and give a far smoother action. Steel springs have a constant deflection per increase of unit load. Air springs, given suitable compression ratios, provide soft springing over the normal range of movement, but will absorb a considerable amount of energy for a very small movement at the extremes of the compression stroke.' The air cannot 'bottom' like a helical spring.

Externally the fork was very similar in appearance to other telescopic designs, but could be readily identified by the Kilner valves that extended from the top of each fork leg. Each leg was interconnected by an air balance pipe, in a recess below the upper fork yoke, and was filled with oil to a predetermined level. The remaining space above was charged with air, from a normal tyre-inflator.

The complete fork unit weighed about 22 lb and had a total movement of $5\frac{1}{2}$ in., equally divided between the fully extended and fully compressed positions. Static pressure with the rider seated was approximately 42 psi, a rating which rose to some 250 psi on full compression and fell to 20 psi on full recoil. The oil provided the damping medium.

In service the forks performed well and it was claimed that up to 20,000 miles could be covered before any 'topping-up' was necessary. But air is an intangible medium to keep in any confined space, especially when it is under pressure. Sooner or later leakage occurred as the synthetic-rubber seals began to wear and there was always the danger that the forks would slowly subside until they remained in the fully compressed position, for there were no conventional springs to keep them extended in an emergency.

The Dowty fork depended upon perfect cleanliness for satisfactory working, and it is likely that in cases where air was lost prematurely the fault was on the part of the person who reinflated the fork. If he was not sufficiently careful to see that his pump and connector were quite free from dust and dirt, this would immediately cause trouble if taken in with the air. However, these were not problems destined to affect the KSS in its latest guise. With the now imminent birth of the LE model, 1948 was to be the last year of manufacture of the KSS. There were many who mourned its passing, for somehow the Veloce Stand at Earls Court never looked quite the same without it. Few models can have enjoyed such a long production run; it is no coincidence that these models are now acquiring a collectors' value. It is particularly unfortunate that the ever-increasing costs of production of what was never an easy engine to make in large numbers necessitated its withdrawal from the range on grounds of basic economies. It would have been interesting to witness the birth of a spring-frame version, which may well have occurred had production continued into the 1950s.

4
The M series

By 1933 the modified overhead-camshaft models, the KSS and its complementary model the KTS, were selling well, yet there was clearly a market for a cheaper model that gave better performance than the GTP two-stroke but was not as complicated as the overhead-camshaft designs.

Although the K engine was not at all difficult to maintain there were many motor-cyclists with insufficient confidence in their abilities to undertake the job of decarbonizing an engine upon which the valve timing could be deranged by careless or inaccurate assembly during the refitting of the cylinder-head and cam-box. Furthermore, the engine was never easy to manufacture in quantity, for the two pairs of bevel gears, both of which must be most accurately meshed during the initial assembly, required the attentions of skilled fitters. With these facts in mind, consideration was given to producing a new four-stroke machine that would provide the degree of performance desired but would be more economic to manufacture because less highly skilled labour could be employed in erecting the engines to the Company's exacting standards.

A design for a 350 cc single-cylinder side-by-side valve engine was drawn out, mainly with the export market in mind. As the current fashion in motor cycles decreed that the single cylinder should be inclined forward, the design provided for the iron cylinder-barrel and its alloy cylinder-head to slope some 30 degrees from the vertical. Many existing parts were included in the make-up such as flywheels similar to the 1931 K engines and an identical Hoffmann big end carrying thirteen uncaged rollers in a single row. The lubrication system worked on the total-loss principal and depended upon a GTP-type pump interconnected with the throttle control. Valve-springs and tappets were enclosed with tubular covers.

A prototype was assembled and as the new frame that had been designed for it had not been completed the engine was mounted in a GTP frame for extended road testing. The drive was through a normal three-speed GTP gearbox.

Unfortunately, the test results were disappointing, for the performance was mediocre and the engine was not particularly quiet mechanically. It is not surprising that the engine never went into production, although it is alleged that a contributory reason may have been a change in motor-cycle taxation rates in Australia, the market for which the machine was primarily intended.

The frame that had been specially designed for the side-valve engine was completed in a short while and was seen to be a cradle type with tubes running from a lug at the bottom of the front down-tube horizontally along to lugs at the bottom of the seat-tube, and from thence upwards to pressed-steel fork-ends. The gearbox was mounted upon a cross-tube between the chainstays, behind the seat-tube, thus discontinuing the normal Velocette practice of suspending the gearbox from a specially forged bracket forming an integral part of the frame, between the seat-tube and chainstay-tubes like the K models.

Having abandoned the 350 cc side-valve engine design, Eugene Goodman set to work on an entirely new 250 cc overhead-valve engine and he produced what was to become widely known as the MOV engine.

With ease of manufacture a major consideration, the valve gear was of simple design. To reduce the weight of the reciprocating parts of the valve gear the gear-driven cams were carried high up in the crankcase and so the push-rods were kept commendably short. With the emphasis on mechanical silence the gear-train included an intermediate gear with one more tooth than the gear to which the cams were fitted. The gears consequently operated on the 'hunting-tooth' principle, a method which ensures uniform distribution of wear over all teeth. This intermediate gear was carried on a spindle that was capable of lateral adjustment to obtain very accurate meshing of the gears during assembly, thus contributing still further to silence in operation, and ease of assembly. Originally, the gears had straight-cut teeth but eventually a helical cut was employed for reasons described later. The cubic capacity of the engine was 248 cc, the almost 'square' bore and stroke measurements being 68 mm $\times$ 68·25 mm.

A prototype machine was soon available for testing, using the new frame and a new design of four-speed gearbox, the latter being a lightweight edition of the gearboxes used on the current KSS and KTS models in so far as internal parts went. It differed in appearance by having a housing with integral lugs at the bottom that were machined to fit the frame cross-tube to which it was held by steel half-clamps, studs, and nuts. Primary chain adjustment was effected by swivelling the gearbox on the cross-tube; the top of the housing carried a threaded eye-bolt adjuster that was attached to an extension of the nearside rear engine-plate. Like the first four-speed K models, the MOV was supplied with hand-change gear control, although the external positive-stop foot control could be purchased as an optional extra for attachment to it. Later the gearboxes of both the K and M types were modified. The positive stop was embodied in the selector mechanism and enclosed in the housings.

The upper parts of the first engine relied for lubrication entirely upon that stand-by so often referred to as 'oil mist' in catalogues and lists, but it soon became apparent that the rockers, which ran direct between the rocker-box and the top cover required more oil than was optimistically expected to be blown up the tubular push-rod cover from the crankcase. Fortunately, it was a simple matter to remedy this defect by running an external oil-feed pipe to the rocker-bearings from the top of the timing cover to which there was already a feed-line for the crankshaft oil-jet. Initially, the pipe was branched at the upper ends to reach the top cover above the bearings, at which point oil unions were fitted. Later, the rocker-

The assembly line for the early M series. One or two GTP models can also be detected.

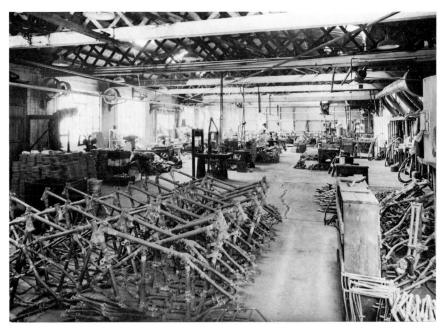

A view of the frame-building section showing a batch of MSS frames prior to cleaning up and enamelling.

box and cover were altered to make machining easier and improve appearance and the oil-pipe was simplified and connected to the cover by a banjo union and hollow bolt. At the same time it was possible to avoid a 'set' in one of the overhead rocker-arms and thus make the grinding of the bearing portion much easier.

When the new 248 cc model was first announced in 1933 it was seen to be a most attractive-looking machine, with performance and handling well in keeping with Velocette standards. Like most Velocettes, the new model was not entirely new throughout but incorporated some parts from previous models. In this case the brakes were identical to those of the GTP, but the hubs were of improved design inasmuch as taper roller-bearings were employed in place of cups, cones, and steel balls. The front fork, as usual, was made for Veloce Limited by Webbs of Birmingham and closely resembled that of the GTP apart from modifications to suit the new and larger steering-head cones and cups that the new frame carried.

The MOV sold at £47 10s. and weighed 275 lb fully equipped. Any model off the assembly-line, after being run-in, was capable of a genuine 60 mph and often more, so the sales increased rapidly. Although a maximum speed of 60 mph or so from a 250 cc engine would not be considered good today, in 1933 it was regarded as highly satisfactory and was better than that of many contemporary models of the same or even greater capacity apart from special racing machines, of course. Possibly the liveliness of the model was enhanced by the very free-working and quick-opening twist-grip control that Veloce produced for it. The mechanism did not employ return springs but the carburetter throttle-valve worked on the push-pull principle. The air-valve was operated as usual by Bowden cable and lever.

Shortly after the MOV was listed, and had obviously been well received by the motor-cycling fraternity, a complementary model that used many of the same components was announced. This was a 349 cc model produced by lengthening the stroke of the 248 cc engine to 96 mm. It was thus possible to use the same piston, valves, and cylinder-head casting as the smaller capacity engine; and so very few parts were not interchangeable between the two models.

At first the two models had the same primary-drive reduction and the higher over-all gear ratio required for the more powerful machine was achieved by substituting a twenty-two-tooth sprocket for the nineteen-tooth final-drive gearbox sprocket. But the higher powered model was prone to clutch slip and a change was made as described later.

With the additional power obtained for the larger engine, which provided more favourable power to weight ratio, the new MAC model found favour with those wanting good performance without having to pay the higher price charged for the overhead-camshaft K models. The MAC was priced at £49 10s., leaving a differential of £10. Furthermore, there was a weight advantage of almost 20 lb, in favour of the MAC. It is not surprising that some owners of the overhead-camshaft models resented such serious competition from a much cheaper machine from the same stable!

The model symbol 'MOV' means in effect 'Type M, overhead valve', a term which could equally well have applied to the 349 cc model, and so it was necessary to call the latter something different. The type letter 'M' had to be retained, but quite why the letters 'AC' were appended must remain

78

a matter for conjecture. At all events the 349 cc push-rod OHV model became the 'MAC' by which tag it has been known since, except for the use of 'MAF' to designate a 349 cc model produced for the Ministry of Supply during the Second World War.

The first batch of the two M-type engines proved troublesome to keep clean, due to oil leakages from the rocker-box cover and tappet-cover joints. In the original design the rocker-box cover had no bridge across the centre, and the centre one of the three bolts securing the rocker-box assembly to the head was shorter than the other two so that it did not pass through the upper half. The top cover was inadequately held in contact with the bottom half as a result. The provision of a bridge on later castings enabled a longer centre-bolt to be used to hold down both top cover and rocker-box and a considerable improvement was made in oil-tightness.

As it was found that the valve-stems and guides required more oil, the discs that originally were fitted to the rockers behind the rocker thrust-springs were pierced to allow oil to blow through from the push-rod tube. By carefully proportioning the diameter of these holes the flow could be controlled. The joints between the outside of the valve-spring covers and the valve-guides and those between them and the rocker-box and tappet-covers were always troublesome to make properly oil-tight and it was not until the WD model was being made during the Second World War that the valve-guide to spring-cover joint was greatly improved.

From time to time additions were made to improve the lubrication of the engine, such as a take-off from a passage in the timing cover to provide a direct feed to the cam-wheel bush. Later still, a further refinement was a feed to the rear wall of the cylinder-barrel, with the idea that piston slap would be eliminated or at least reduced. But it was found not to be worth the extra complication of the drillings and the hollow bolt (always susceptible to damage by ham-fisted owners) and was eventually discarded.

Some troubles with cracked crankcases developed on MAC models that were eventually traced to the use of unsuitable material; it stopped when the material specification was changed and at the same time the opportunity was taken to improve the crankcase design. It had been thought at one time that the trouble had been caused by the tension of the cylinder-head steady so high up the engine, and some machines were fitted with a steady from the front down-tube to the top of the crankcase. Eventually, the steady was restored to the original position.

The only component that continued to give trouble was the clutch, which was of the single-plate cork-lined type similar to that of the MOV. It was run at the same engine speed by virtue of being driven by an identically sized engine sprocket (nineteen teeth). Reluctant to substitute the multi-plate K clutch, probably on account of the increased production costs, Percy Goodman characteristically overcame the trouble by the simple expedient of replacing the nineteen-tooth engine sprocket on MAC models with one having twenty-two teeth to increase the speed of the clutch. To retain the same over-all gear ratios, the twenty-two-tooth gearbox sprocket was changed to one of nineteen teeth and all was well! Despite continuing successful results with the single-plate clutches, especially those lined with Neoprene inserts during 1939, the multi-plate K-type clutch was adopted for all the military models and was retained for post-war production.

In the opinion of many people whose judgement can be trusted, the introduction of the MOV and MAC models brought about a period of increased prosperity for the firm. In contrast to the previous mainstay, the OHC models, the M models were a much better proposition from the production aspect. Their timing gear with the adjustable intermediate timing-gear spindle lent itself to much quicker assembly than two pairs of vertical-shaft bevel gears and did not require such a high degree of skill on the part of the engine-bench staff. The profit margin was consequently much better, particularly in the case of the 350 cc model. Because of the popularity of the MAC, sales were for a long time in a very encouraging state, well outstripping those of the other types in the range.

Probably because of the success of the MAC (often known affectionately as 'The Mac'), it was decided to extend the range with a 500 cc M type and for the 1935 season another model was introduced that incorporated many of the engine components of the MOV and MAC models.

The new engine employed the same length of stroke as the MAC but with a larger diameter cylinder, producing an engine size of 81 mm × 96 mm and a capacity of 495 cc. With an identical rocker-box and similar outline timing cover, the design bore a marked resemblance to its smaller stable companions and it was mainly in the frame and gearbox layout that the difference was apparent.

A very robust cradle frame carried the engine and four-speed gearbox, mounted close together as a unit held between the rear engine-plates, that extended to encircle the gearbox, in these respects anticipating the construction later employed on the Mark II OHC models.

The 248 cc MOV model, first introduced in 1933. The example illustrated is a 1937 model. A pillion-seat and speedometer had yet to be supplied as standard equipment.

Franz Binder on a 1938 MSS model alongside the late Ted Mellors and a 500 cc racer. The cover of the 1938 catalogue (*shown below*) was based on a photograph in this series.

VELOCETTE

For learner and expert

The same internal parts as the corresponding parts of the top-mounted K gearboxes were used but the housing was drilled horizontally to take bolts that nipped it firmly between the rear engine-plates. Primary chain adjustment was effected by swivelling the housing about the single bottom fixing-bolt, the movement being controlled by a threaded eye-bolt adjuster that fitted over one of the upper fixing-bolts. The adjuster carried one adjusting-nut and a lock-nut against a yoke fixed to the right-hand engine-plate, just above the housing. With sidecar-owners in mind the heaviest Webb fork was fitted and the brakes were of 7 in. diameter with 1 in. wide linings. Size WM3-19 rims were used front and rear with 19 in. × 3·25 in. and 19 in. × 4·00 in. tyres respectively. The MSS sold at £63; it weighed 335 lb fully equipped.

With such a specification the model could hardly be classified as a 'super-sports' type and yet it was catalogued as the MSS. The use of the type letter 'M' is understandable, but with the precedents set by the previous super-sports types such as the KSS and USS models, it is difficult to imagine why the letters SS were appended. When, years later, one of the Directors had a 500 cc M-type machine built for his own use that was, in effect, an MSS with Mark II KSS wheels and mudguards, etc., it became known as the 'MTS'. It cannot be disputed that this would have been a much more suitable symbol to have used for the production model but for the fact that the pattern had already been set.

In 1936 an automatic ignition advance and retard unit was designed in collaboration with the British Thompson Houston Company which became standard equipment, so that no M machines were thereafter sent out with manual control (until the later Venoms and Vipers were announced). Until then, most motor-cyclists employed some form of manual control for the ignition, whether it was of the magneto or coil type. While those who had been riding for some time were able to use the control to the best advantage, many newcomers to the pastime had very little idea of how to use it properly. They soon learned, often by painful experience, not to leave the control too far advanced when starting, but there were doubtless many cases of engines being run with the ignition retarded, to their detriment. Greater ignorance probably existed among the ranks of car-drivers for most car engines had been equipped for years with coil-ignition sets that embodied a centrifugal advance and retard mechanism which relieved the driver of any manual control.

The automatic unit is designed so that as it advances or retards, the magneto armature is in the position of maximum flux when the contact-breaker points separate. Thus the intensity of the spark is not reduced when starting, a not inconsiderable advantage on an engine that has to be started by the physical effort of the rider. A rider of limited experience is thus able to get better results from his machine than he would be likely to obtain with a manually controlled machine, the ignition control of which he does not fully understand.

Unfortunately, the new 15-degree helical timing gears that replaced the original straight-cut ones did not give the high standard of silence required and expected and a change was made in the helix angle to 11 degrees which still left something to be desired. Finally, a 16-degree helix angle was decided upon and is still the standard for all the M range. The changes caused less difficulty than was expected in the supply of spares as details of the engine numbers at which changes were made were printed in the Spares Lists covering the models concerned. Timing gears were always replaceable in sets so that the oldest machines could, if desired, be brought up to date as far as the timing gears were concerned.

A further improvement that was made some time after the Second World War but which had no influence upon interchangeability indicates the ever-present desire at Hall Green to make the product better, often in ways that are not readily appreciated by the customers.

Very slight, but nevertheless important, changes were made in the helix angle of the timing gears, and the adjustable intermediate timing wheel was produced in a material that can best be described as tough and hard wearing rather than hard, and this was intentionally fitted initially very closely in mesh with the mating gears. The effect was to give rise to a slight, but not objectional or unacceptable whine, when a new engine was first started. In a very short time the teeth of the intermediate gear bedded in to the harder teeth of the camwheel and the crankshaft gear and ultimately the standard of silence was much better than had been obtainable prior to the modification.

The useful life of the bottom rockers was much extended by facing the tips with stellite and by directing jets of oil on to the working surfaces of the cams. This arrangement superseded the previous method of feeding oil through radial drillings in the cams and the bush from the hollow cam-spindle.

Oil leakage from the early engines has been mentioned previously and in this connection it is important to understand the effect of crankcase ventilation by means of a 'breather'. The first batches of 250 cc and 350 cc engines 'breathed' through a timed port in the crankcase behind the magneto gear. The opening and closing of the 'port', a drilling facing rearward, was arranged by recesses cut in the periphery of the magneto-gear centre-boss. To keep oil inside an engine it helps to maintain a slight negative pressure in it. The Works Technician thought that this was not being achieved in the M engine and that perhaps a slight pressure was building up instead.

It was therefore decided to dispense with the timed breather and substitute a disc-valve similar to that used for the oil-return pipe of the contemporary K engines. Accordingly, the crankcase was drilled at the rear just below the cylinder-base flange and threaded $\frac{1}{8}$ in. BSP to take the disc-valve body. A length of reinforced rubber hose was connected to the outlet of the disc-valve and led to the rear chain. When the MSS was in production a similar arrangement was used, but for some obscure reason the disc-valve was fitted by means of a right-angle adapter to the top of the timing cover, not nearly so neat an arrangement as that on the two smaller models.

On the MAC in particular the working of the disc made a curious noise when the engine was ticking over that was often mistaken for the noise that might have originated from slackness in a bearing. It was necessary to reassure anxious owners that all was well by holding a finger over the open end of the breather-hole, whereupon the noise would stop. Some time later all three models had the disc-valves deleted and the crankcase relieved of pressure by means of radial drillings into the hollow driving-side mainshafts through the shock-absorbers. More or less concurrent with this change, the three-lobe sprockets and shock-absorber clutches superseded the original five-lobe type, contributing to smooth running at low speeds.

Before the introduction of the automatic ignition timing unit the steel centre to which the magneto gear was bolted was machined to provide the relieved parts to open the crankcase breather-hole to atmosphere. This part was not required with the timing unit as this embodied a parallel portion that fitted the opening in the crankcase into which the magneto is spigoted and so to prevent oil leaking out; it was machined with a 'reverse' thread to carry back oil to the inside. So efficient is this arrangement in oil retention that the thread was discarded some years later because the plastic oil-seals on magneto armatures, which apparently like a little oil upon them, were running too dry and were deteriorating in consequence.

It will be seen that a steady progressive policy of improvement went on in the usual Veloce manner. Alterations were never made just for the sake of alteration, but such changes and modifications that were made eliminated sources of potential trouble, improved performance in all its aspects, and gave longer life or perhaps simplified production. In cases where changes were made, the supply of spares was studied so that as far as possible the design was such as to enable later types' improved parts to be fitted to the earlier models with the minimum expense to the owner.

With the various improvements mentioned, the three M models were continued until the outbreak of war in 1939. Thereafter, only the MAC remained in production, for the forces; later supplies being designated model 'MAF'. It was not until after the war that the MOV and MSS models reappeared, and then only for a brief spell. ·

As an example of a valuable alteration that was made during the war and which caused no difficulty in the supply of spare parts the rear-brake anchorage of the MAC can be quoted.

The rear brake-plate of the pre-war MAC, and the WD/MAC used sometimes to give trouble should the anchor-bolt that held the plate to the rear-fork end of the frame not be tightened securely.

When preparing the prototype of what was later to become the MAF it was decided that this must be improved and the small bolt was discarded and superseded by a torque arm from the bottom of the brake-plate to the prop-stand lug. In this way the nearside seat stay-tube was relieved of all brake reaction stresses and the load applied to the chainstay in such a manner that no bending stresses were applied.

In the event of a new rear brake-plate being required for an earlier machine the later brake-plate is supplied together with the torque arm and the two requisite bolts and nuts. The rear brake is thus greatly improved at a minimal expense.

After the war, when it was possible once more to finish Velocettes in their traditional black and gold livery, the range of MOV, MAC, and MSS models were again available. The civilian version of the MAC was not deprived of the K-type clutch that wartime service had given to it, and certain other features of the MAF were retained, including the improved cradle-type frame that embodied a substantial undershield, the folding kickstarter, and the improved gear-lever. The substitution of an alternative gearbox cam-plate on the other models which gave a 'down for up and up for down' gear-pedal movement in common with that on most other British machines, did not apply to the MAC. The linkage of the improved gear-lever inherited from the wartime MAF effected the necessary change.

To ascertain the reason for the change of gearchange movement it is necessary to go right back to the days of almost universal tank-side lever and gate control.

The Velocettes of the period all employed a lever working in a gate in which first gear was engaged with the lever at the top of the gate. The first move downwards to bring the lever to mid position in the gate engaged second (middle) gear of the three-speed gearbox. Third gear (top) was engaged when the lever was at the bottom.

When Harold Willis designed the positive-stop gear control it was made to bolt on to the normal Velocette three-speed gearbox and connected to the outside striking lever from which the usual control-rod from the hand-lever was removed. Thus the foot control merely replaced the original lever and gate.

Most other makers, when designing their own foot gear-control mechanisms made things to work so that an upward movement of the pedal selected a lower gear. There was no rule at all but it so happened that Veloce kept on with the arrangement with which they started and as the majority of their competitors differed became just about the only make with an 'up for up' gear change.

In 1948, all models were fitted with the Dowty Oleomatic telescopic front fork, which is more fully described in the chapter describing the K models. A new headlamp glass of domed pattern gave improved lighting and imparted a more pleasant look to all three models. But alas, 1948 was to be the last year of the MOV model and also the MSS in its existing form. Only the MAC was continued when the new lightweight LE model was launched.

Great things were expected of the LE, the little water-cooled machine that was such a distinct breakaway from all previous Velocette practice, and it was hoped that it would eventually constitute the sole output from the Hall Green Works. As things turned out due to popular demand the MAC had to be continued and when demand for the LE failed to reach the large quantities expected, some detailed modifications were made to it to make the design more attractive.

In 1952 the engine was greatly improved by eliminating the separate two-piece rocker-box and carrying the upper portions of the overhead-valve gear in a quite new light-alloy cylinder-head and rocker-box combined. By completely enclosing the valve-springs and rockers, the chance of oil leakage from the top part of the engine was reduced considerably. Furthermore, the new design of composite cylinder-head and rocker-box was much easier, and consequently more economical, to produce. The cylinder-barrel was also light-alloy jacketed and the timing cover was redesigned to have a more convex profile which no longer carried the manufacturer's name and trademark. But despite these changes, it was impossible to avoid the conclusion that the MAC was out of date and not a serious competitor to the newer spring-frame models now being marketed by the Company's contemporaries.

Charles Udall was given the task of modernizing the model to bring it more in line with current practice, if not actually to break new ground. Telescopic forks had already been included in the specification and the Dowty Oleomatic type with which the singles had at first been equipped in 1948 had given place to a fork of Veloce's own design, first introduced during 1951. The engine was apparently considered to require no further changes so attention was concentrated on the frame and the general appearance of the machine.

Having had much experience with the KTT models, not to mention the 'one-off' supercharged racer of 1939, rear suspension by swinging fork was a natural choice for the new MAC. In order to find room for the pivot bearings and their housing lug, the frame that had served the MOV and MAC models since their introduction had to be discarded in favour of one that owed something to the KTT for its inspiration.

A one-piece fabricated swinging-fork assembly was found to be impracticable and there had to be two separate tubular arms that were clamped to a large-diameter spindle working in bushes located in a lug brazed to the frame seat-tube. The gearbox housing was completely redesigned and its fixing into the frame brought into line with the method used in the KTT, the Mark II KSS models, and the MSS, by carrying it sandwiched between the rear engine-plates. Initially, the gearbox used the lighter MOV/MAC gears in a narrower shell, but during mid 1954 the new, wider shell with the heavier MSS/KSS gears was standardized on all M models.

Use was made of the patent taken out before the war in the name of P. E. Irving and Veloce Limited, by carrying the upper anchorages of the rear suspension units in arcuate slots in brackets attached to the frame below the seat, which made the rear suspension fully adjustable for load. The units were specially supplied by Woodhead-Monroe Limited. This patent had also been successfully employed in the adjustable rear suspension of the LE model.

A more shapely fuel-tank, and redesigned oil-tank, the latter flanked by an efficient wire-wool air-cleaner, changed the appearance of the machine considerably and brought it right up to date with contemporary practice.

For a long time the large fishtail silencers of Velocettes had been criticized in some quarters and the fitting of a cylindrical pattern had been advocated so that a slightly modified version of the silencer used on both WD/MAC and MAF models was used on civilian machines (polished and chromium plated of course!), but there was some difficulty in accommodating it with the spring-frame design MAC and a new silencer in line with pre-war Velocette designs was produced. This, with its integral fishtail, has almost become an accepted Velocette feature and owing to its generous volume and internal design provides a high degree of exhaust silencing with a minimum power loss.

The early 1953 models were available for export only despite being first exhibited at the 1952 Earls Court Show.

For the first time in Velocette history a standard production model was listed with a dual-seat; not exactly like Harold Willis's 'Loch Ness Monster' of the racing days but one with a raised rear portion to accommodate a pillion-passenger at a slightly higher level than the driver.

Although this two-level seat has not proved universally popular there is no doubt that many lady passengers preferred it to the more usual one-level pattern. Most ladies are much shorter than their male companions, and so when seated behind the driver can see little but a small area of the back of the rider's neck. It is possible that the greater sales of single-level dual-seats is due to the ladies' preferences being overruled by the males because the one-level seat is what the racing men use!

As may be expected, the spring-frame MAC was somewhat heavier than its rigid-frame counterpart – 354 lb against 330 lb. But even so the machine was very lively and would top 70 mph with ease. The handling characteristics were superb and there are many who even today consider this model to have been one of the best ever produced by the Company. It was still a good buy at £197 8s., a price somewhat 'inflated' by Purchase Tax of approximately £32.

Just under a year later a new version of the MSS was announced that had much in common with the spring-frame MAC but nevertheless incorporated many features new to the standard range of Velocettes. The KTT engine was drawn upon for certain features such as hairpin-type valve-springs and their mountings and racing experience was evident in the combustion head and port design of the large light-alloy cylinder-head of the new model.

Following contemporary practice that favoured keeping piston speeds down, a 'square' engine was designed having bore and stroke measurements of 86 mm × 86 mm, giving a swept volume of 499 cc – 4 cc more than the original MSS model. Taper roller main bearings were used on the flywheel assembly, following their successful use on a few of the rigid-frame MSS models during 1947. To take care of the greater power output a gearbox resembling that of the spring-frame MAC but with internals identical to the earlier 500 cc model was designed and was carried in similar fashion. MAC frame design was followed in so far as the rear suspension system with Woodhead-Monroe units and the Veloce patented adjustment were concerned, but the rear wheel incorporated a 7 in. diameter brake similar to that used for the front wheel. Fuel- and oil-tanks followed the new

MAC design. Initially, the first 1954 models were destined for the export market, but later the MSS joined the range of the LE and MAC home-market models, where it proved quite popular with the solo rider as well as for sidecar use. It was no longer possible so freely to interchange engine parts with the smaller MAC model.

The great post-war interest in 'Moto-Cross' or scrambles events led to experiments with the MSS engine to improve the power output and generally to modify the machine for this type of event. It was no surprise that late in 1954 a 'scrambler' model was added to the range and that a Works-prepared machine took part in many of the larger National events. At the same time a somewhat 'detuned' version was listed expressly for the American market that demanded a less expensive model than the scrambler but which would nevertheless be suitable for competing in the long-distance 'endurance' runs that are a regular feature of the American motor-cyclist's competition calendar. As may be expected, this latter model was equipped with handlebars of the very pronounced upswept type beloved by the American competition enthusiast, which until recently found little favour with the average British rider.

Here it should be mentioned that some trouble was experienced with a few of the redesigned M-type engines from the crankcases flooding with oil which was not fully scavenged, and it was at first thought that the shape and volume of the oil-passage in which the filter gauze fitted was the cause. The gauze was accordingly replaced by a solid plug closely fitting the passage and the oil filtered by the very minute peripheral clearance of the filter-plug from the passage bore. But still the trouble persisted in isolated cases and various expedients were tried to overcome it, including the adoption of very much wider return oil-pump gears. Every once in a while individual engines would be found to smoke excessively because of incomplete scavenging, because, when the engine was running, the oil did not drain quickly enough to the floor of the crankcase. To speed up the return of the oil to the crankcase floor the crankcases were modified to cut out the drain-hole from the timing chest and substituting for it two independent passages leading to the front and rear corners respectively.

The K-type clutch that had proved so satisfactory on the unsprung 495 cc MSS models was found to be a little overloaded on the new MSS with the 86 mm × 86 mm motor. Despite the very limited amount of space at the designers' disposal, it was found possible to add one extra 'dished' plate and one extra 'insert' plate, thus considerably increasing the load-carrying capacity of the clutch. The very narrow chain-line that has for so long been a feature of the Velocettes has many advantages, including the opportunity it gives to provide a short and rigid crankshaft assembly and a means of quick and easy gear ratio changing, but it does mean that the accommodation for the clutch and its attendant thrust-bearing is strictly limited.

The excellent results from the modified engines used in the scramblers led, as may have been expected, to the inclusion of sports models in the M range during the 1956 season. With little difficulty a companion model

An unusual guise for a near-standard pre-war MSS model, stripped of all surplus fittings. The rider, Pat Whelehan, has surprised many with the performance from his home-prepared sprinter.

One of the early Venom models that enabled Veloce Limited to re-enter the sports machine market.

for the 499 cc sports model was produced by fitting a smaller bore cylinder and piston, giving an engine of 72 mm × 86 mm bore and stroke and 349 cc capacity. This in effect was a reversal of the procedure used when the original MAC model was derived from its smaller brother, the 248 cc MOV.

As there were no apt type symbols that immediately suggested themselves, and as the two new models had to be named, the practice adopted by the aircraft industry seemed to point to a ready solution to the problem. Why not choose two names beginning with the initial letter of the firm? Thinking along these lines it was not long before someone came up with 'Venom' and 'Viper', and these titles were decided upon.

The two models differed in several respects from the MAC and MSS models, particularly with regard to compression ratios, carburetters, and fittings such as imposing full-width wheel hubs with a rib exterior. Gradually the range of non-standard optional extras was extended to include larger bore carburetters, manually controlled racing magnetos, and alternative gear ratios both indirect and over-all until the eventual listing of two 'Clubman' models was decided upon. The specification of these two models included all the worthwhile 'extras' that would have been fitted if a purchaser required a Venom or a Viper fully equipped for competitions of the 'Clubman' race variety.

The listing of so many 'extras' to the standard specification constituted a major breakaway from all previous Veloce policy. Until the introduction of the sports models the sales policy had been somewhat conservative, not unlike the attitude of Henry Ford who, it is alleged, offered his motor cars in 'any colour so long as it is black'!

The question of the popularity of the traditional black and gold livery in which the Company's products had for so many years been turned out had been debated among the senior executives and the directors. The LE had shown that a colour finish had proved acceptable and it had not passed unnoticed that many scooters, the chief rivals to the LE, were mostly finished in much brighter colours. Following many discussions it was decided during the late 1950s to offer the two standard single-cylinder models in colours as alternatives to black and gold; willow green was used as the alternative in the case of the 350 cc models and a beige (known as 'dove-grey'!) for the 500s.

As far as the sports models were concerned, they broke with tradition by having part of the petrol-tank chromium plated and by using a plastic 'medallion' type of nameplate in place of the familiar Velocette transfer on the plated panel. This latter modification was later carried over to the MAC and MSS models, following yet another modern trend.

The variations that became possible from the wide choice offered by the extras and colours meant that few orders were taken for purely standard models. In consequence production methods were rearranged to permit building machines any two examples of which must seldom be similar in all respects. For example, when in 1958 a glass-fibre fairing was standardized on the Venom, Viper and MSS models which effectively enclosed the crankcase and gearbox, the outside of these components was left un-

The Endurance model, a special export version of the MSS supplied mainly to the American market. The machine shown has standard handlebars fitted.

The Scrambles model as it first appeared, heralding the Company's return to the competition sphere.

polished. But so many customers wanted machines without the fairings that it was necessary to supply machines with polished crankcases and gearboxes to meet these requirements. In such cases the price remained identical to that of the standard model; the production economy achieved by dispensing with the fairing equalled the cost of the polishing operation.

Velocette 500 cc Venom Sports, a high-performance touring mount with a reputation for reliability and good handling.

Velocette 500 cc Venom Thruxton, dual-purpose fast touring model or racer. Winner of many production machine races at home and overseas.

Following the success of the Venom model in 'Clubman' form at production-machine events such as those run at Thruxton, a special Thruxton model was listed during 1964. This was, in effect, a highly tuned Venom model with a specially designed cylinder-head, gas flowed to give the maximum power output. This model is reputed to produce a brake horsepower figure only fractionally below that of the Manx Norton when the latter was at the zenith of its post-war successes – a quite exceptional figure for a machine sold with full road equipment. As may be expected, it is not a particularly docile machine for general use on the road, as many 'coffee-bar racers' have found to their cost. But there seems little doubt that it will ultimately make its mark in events of the 'Clubman' type, for which it was specifically designed.

If proof was needed for the soundness of the engineering of the M series it is necessary only to cite the Venom's still unbeaten record of averaging over 100 mph for 24 hours high-speed running. This performance had never been accomplished before by a 500 cc motor cycle, thereby adding another entry in the World's Record Book for Great Britain. It will be interesting to see whether a similar feat can be accomplished by a Viper as a fitting sequel.

5
A new departure – the 'Little Engine'

It is probable that it was Eugene Goodman's intense interest in the problems of production, in so far as they were affected by machining techniques and the efficient use of precision equipment, that had for so many years given him the desire to plan and produce a form of motor cycle unlike any so far on the market. He envisaged a design that would lend itself more to quantity production than any of the models Veloce had so far manufactured, or in fact had been made by any of their competitors in the industry. In other words he hoped to realize his father's oft-expressed desire to manufacture a utility model that would appeal to those who had not seriously considered the conventional motor cycle as their mode of transport.

The term 'mass produced' suggests to many ill-informed people a cheap, slip-shod and somewhat badly constructed product, although in reality large-scale production is only feasible if each and every part is made with meticulous care and accuracy. One of the best examples of mass production is still the legendary Model T Ford motor car, of which more than *fifteen million* examples were made and sold. In the years during which this car was produced, machining techniques had not attained the degree of accuracy that is commonplace today. But the car could be assembled quickly and with the minimum of hand labour, even though the finished article could hardly be described as refined. Nevertheless, it brought motoring within the scope of the average family; it was no longer regarded as a hobby for the idle rich.

Using modern equipment really close limits can now be attained and what is more important, maintained. In consequence mass-produced articles can now be made much better than their earlier counterparts that needed to be assembled by skilled fitters. There is no virtue in the need for 'fitting'; indeed, it is necessary only when parts that have to be assembled will not fit without hand filing or scraping, or other manual work – a sure indication that they were not made to a sufficiently high standard of accuracy in the first place. Trouble is inevitable when components are not produced correctly to the designers' drawings and permissible tolerances.

Eugene realized that the orthodox form of motor cycle, with its separate engine and gearbox, and tubular frame built up of a multiplicity of machined lugs just does not lend itself to being made in an economical manner. To make more effective use of labour he sought a design that would enable the majority of the components to be produced accurately and in large numbers on automatic machinery. This in turn would permit more rapid assembly which would enable the price of the finished article to be truly competitive.

The basic ideas were obviously in his mind when, as far back as the early 1930s, he caused his draughtsmen to produce designs for a multi-cylinder engine that would have fulfilled his production requirements. Two 'arrangement' drawings were made, both probably no longer in existence, and so only rather vague details are now remembered. Of the first, the writers have no clear recollection, but the second was by Phillip Irving, then working at Hall Green, and was to have been a most revolutionary type of engine. Having had experience when in Australia of the Michele floating thrust-pad designs Irving drew out a multi-cylinder swash-plate engine in which the cylinders surrounded the main casing and lay parallel to the shaft that carried the swash-plate. Each piston was double-ended with the two crowns and was recessed midway to accommodate thrust-pads. In working, any one piston was at the top of the stroke at one end and at the bottom at the other since they reciprocated as the swash-plate revolved.

The early 1930s was not the time to embark on ambitious new projects, however. Business was very bad as a result of the Depression and the motor-cycle trade was at a particularly low ebb. Fortunately, Veloce Limited emerged from the crisis on the right side of the ledger but several other motor-cycle makers made heavy losses and more than one well-known make went out of production. Not surprisingly nothing more was heard of either of the designs, although there is no doubt that Eugene's opinion was unchanged. He remained convinced that if more people could be attracted to motor-cycling by offering them a machine free from the major objections to orthodox models, a huge market was available. A machine to fulfil these conditions would need to be produced in large quantities so that production could be planned to provide a steady flow which he estimated would be of the order of 300 units per week. He had ever before him the example of the overhead-camshaft models; excellent machines undoubtedly, but disappointing from the profit-making aspect. The engines necessitated highly skilled labour, which even in those days commanded high wages, and in the light of his experience in producing the two M models (the MOV and MAC) both with the much simpler push-rod overhead-valve arrangement, he was anxious to include a model in the programme that would appeal to a much larger volume of customers than any of the single-cylinder types that the firm had so far offered.

During the period before the Second World War it is probable that the most profitable model made at Hall Green Works was the MAC. Engine assembly was much easier, and consequently could be done quicker, than construction of overhead-camshaft models, and labour capable of doing it efficiently could be trained without difficulty to attain the high standard required by Veloce.

The MAC particularly became an exceptionally good seller; offering a road performance very little below that of the KSS and KTS types at a substantially lower purchase price.

Of all the expenses incurred in the manufacture of motor cycles the wage-bill is the highest, and in what is a most competitive business has to be most carefully examined and kept within strict bounds if the finished article is to show any profit at all.

In connection with the two complementary smaller M models it is interesting to know that the profit per MAC machine was better than that earned by the 250 cc MOV, or the large version the 500 cc MSS. The difference in the cost of materials used in the MOV and MAC was negligible, and labour costs likewise, but because the MAC had the larger capacity engine the machine was listed at a higher price at which it sold very well indeed.

But even though considerable economies had been possible in producing the push-rod overhead-valve models by comparison with the costs of the K types Eugene was convinced that a design that lent itself more readily to economical quantity production must be evolved if his ambitions in this respect were ever to be achieved.

He and the other Directors had been aware for a long time that rear suspension must soon become part of the standard specification and the firm had already evolved a satisfactory swinging-arm design which formed an integral part of the Mark VIII KTT racing model. The 500 cc supercharged racer, known familiarly as the 'Roarer' was similarly equipped and there was in prototype stage by 1938 a 600 cc vertical twin and also a 500 cc single, both of which had adjustable rear suspension to a design patented in the names of Veloce Limited and P. E. Irving.[1] By 1939 the Company had installed a Lake Erie hydraulic press upon which large pressings could be produced and the well-equipped tool-room housed a Pratt and Whitney jig-borer. These two machines were of the latest type and the latter was capable of working to within small fractions of a thousandth of an inch. Thus equipped, Veloce were in a position to make all the accurate jigs and tools with which to put an advanced design of motor cycle in production. The hydraulic press would have been available to provide the pressings for a non-tubular frame or chassis and their conveyor-type enamelling plant could handle all the work that could be fed into it. But again circumstances over which the Company had no control stopped civilian motor-cycle production when war was declared in September 1939.

For many years after the installation of the huge hydraulic Lake Erie press it remained the only example in the possession of any motor-cycle manufacturer in the United Kingdom.

In addition to the production of all LE-type main-frame pressings and mudguards upon it, it had the capacity to enable Veloce to accept orders from some of their competitors to press components destined for use in the construction of other makes of motor cycle.

During the war much thought was given to the evolution of new designs that would follow the eventual return to civilian motor-cycle

[1] British Patents Nos. 511,875 and 521,106 dated 25 August 1939 and 13 May 1940 respectively.

production. With their heavy commitments with all kinds of war work, the majority of which was directed towards aircraft production, Charles Udall became the Company's Chief Inspector responsible for the inspection of all such products as had to meet A.I.D. requirements and in consequence he had to relinquish all motor-cycle work for the duration of the war. No projects could be started until Irving was free to devote some time to a projected post-war design. This opportunity occurred quite by chance after he was injured when tackling an explosive incendiary bomb that fell on the factory during one of the not infrequent enemy raids on Birmingham. While recovering, but still confined to his home he roughed out an arrangement drawing for Eugene of a lightweight motor cycle embodying some of the requirements to be included in a post-war machine planned to sell in large numbers. In the light of what was eventually made a brief description of the layout may be interesting.

The keynote was simplicity and chain drive was selected for the final drive from a small-capacity power and transmission unit. The former comprised a twin-cylinder engine, the cylinders of which lay across the centre-line of the machine at an obtuse angle to each other. In other words almost but not quite a 'flat' twin. To obviate the need to break water-joints when decarbonizing and grinding in the valves, only the cylinder-barrels had water-jackets to deaden ring and so lower the mechanical noise level. They were fitted with finned heads of light alloy. A three-speed gear-box was bolted to the crankcase in unit-construction, driven through a plate-clutch in the flywheel. Behind the gearbox a bevel-driven cross-shaft carried the final-drive sprocket.

There was no rear springing. A light-alloy casting formed a casing for the rear chain and carried at its extremity a form of stub axle upon which the rear hub and brake-drum were mounted. The casting was fixed at the front end and would have formed part of the frame. A spring-loaded tensioner inside the casting would have kept the chain in correct tension and obviated the need for messy periodic adjustments. The lubricant would have been retained by a flat steel plate fixed to the side face of the casting, providing total enclosure of chain and rear brake.

It was intended to employ a simple lightweight front fork with sprung fork-ends carrying the wheel-spindle. This presumably would have been made by Messrs H. C. Webb and Company, who had supplied forks for Velocettes over the years. The proposed design was very similar to a dirt-track type of fork that Webbs had listed many years previously.

Some time later Charles Udall underwent an operation for appendicitis and while convalescing at home undertook to carry on with the design and was accordingly provided with a drawing-board, the necessary other equipment, and Irving's drawings, at his home. Thus some more preliminary work was done without hindrance to the Company's war work.

In due course Udall prepared another design that embodied many of the ideas that had been talked of, but differed from Irving's layout in several respects, and was much more elaborate.

The cylinders of the horizontally opposed twin four-stroke engine were now shown with bores at exactly 180 degrees to each other. The separate cylinder-heads were water-cooled as well as the cylinders.

The engine unit consisted of a large cast-aluminium crankcase with flat machined faces front and rear, and at the bottom to carry a pressed-steel oil-sump as in motor-car practice. Provision was made to thread the built-up crankshaft in at the front, and the cylinders were attached to machined side faces. They were deeply spigoted into the crankcase so that when in place only the water-jacketed parts were visible and the valve-stems and springs were hidden.

A circular flywheel housing was bolted to the crankcase front face and carried two ball-races supporting the front mainshaft of the crank assembly. At the rear was attached the reduction-gear housing that enclosed two pairs of gears driving the camshaft and clutch respectively. The mass of the clutch, etc., rotating in the opposite direction to the crankshaft somewhat offsets the accelerative torque reaction.

Udall took great care to design the water-passages in the cylinders and head to ensure that there were no blind ends in which steam-pockets could form, and by setting the radiator much higher than the water-outlets the natural circulation of the water was very rapid and the cooling efficient.

The over-all width of the engine, always a problem with transverse horizontally opposed designs, was kept down by the deep setting of the cylinders but this reduced clearances within the engine and the mouths of the cylinder spigots came very close to the crankshaft balance-weights and centre-disc. By employing balance-weights opposite each crankpin it was possible to counteract the rocking cross-couple associated with this type of cylinder layout in which the latter are staggered.

Side-by-side valves each carrying a single spring, retained by a collar and split cotter, were operated by flat-sided tappets radiused to bear on cams formed on a shaft running between the cylinders supported upon two ball-races. By steeply inclining the valves towards the cylinders a compact form of combustion space was obtained. The adjustable tappet-screws were accessible through openings in the crankcase above them, normally closed by two small flat plates.

Some difficulty arose for a time because no ignition apparatus was commercially available, and similar trouble was to occur later when a carburetter of small-choke bore diameter was required.

In the first setback the problem was solved by the British Thompson Houston Company producing a combined generator and coil-ignition unit to fill the bill. This consisted of a main body of an insulating material of circular outline that matched the front of the engine's flywheel housing to which it was attached by four long threaded studs.

This BTH generator was a marvel of compactness as the main body contained an armature for the DC generator, three field coils, one ignition coil with condenser, and three commutator brushes.

The armature was fitted to a parallel length of crankshaft mainshaft immediately ahead of the flywheel. Access to the brushes and other electrical items of the generator was gained from the front which was covered by a flat circular steel cover. The flywheel fitted upon the tapered part of the mainshaft that protruded beyond the front one of two ball-races in the flywheel housing, an oil-seal being provided next to the ball-race, sealing on a centre-boss. Beyond the flywheel the mainshaft was parallel to receive the generator armature. Beyond this again the extremity of the shaft was tapered to receive a compact centrifugal automatic advance and retard unit. This mechanism included the single-lobe cam that operated the contact-breaker, and a gear-wheel integral with the unit engaged with a 'half-time' Tufnol gear carrying a metal segment from which high-tension current arced across in turn to the two leads to the sparking-plugs; thus forming a very simple distributor. The fixed spindle for the 'distributor' gear-wheel was attached to the generator housing.

Inside the flywheel housing, between the ball-races, the mainshaft carried a worm driving the upward-pointing spindle of the oil-pump that was directly below submerged in the oil supply in the sump.

A fine-mesh wire gauze above the pump protected it from damage should impurities be introduced accidentally. The main supply was directed by a jet in the pump body to the periphery of the centre-disc of the crankshaft so that oil was carried to the big ends from the recesses machined in the disc. A further supply was piped off to the reduction-gear plate bolted to the rear wall of the crankcase. Drillings in the plate supplied the outrigger bearing in which ran the centre-boss of the camshaft-driving pinion, and an outlet directed a feed to the teeth of the reduction gear where these intersected.

A two-plate dry clutch was carried behind the reduction-gear housing on the shaft carrying the reduction gear. Upon the same shaft a starter-pinion was carried which was driven by two spring-loaded pawls from a toothed segment. It was operated by a system of levers from the starter-handle mounted on a short shaft working in a bushed bore in the side wall of the gearbox casting, on the offside.

The driving and driven clutch-plates were all assembled with the compression springs on the shaft, the rear end of which was supported in a bearing in the reduction-gear housing between the reduction gear and the clutch. The starter mechanism was thus enclosed in the crankcase and the clutch in a separate compartment.

A pressed-steel clutch-bell splined to the gearbox primary gear shaft fitted over the clutch friction-plates engaging with slots cut into the edges to transmit the drive. Clutch operation departed radically from Velocette usage by being arranged by means of a thrust-rod operated from a lever behind the gearbox that ran through the hollow primary gear shaft and exerted pressure upon a thrust-button in the centre of the pressure-plate, thus freeing the steel and fabric plates.

Within the gearbox the three primary gears meshed with three wheels on the secondary shaft, the appropriate pair required, to give the ratio selected, being engaged by means of the manual gear-lever on the right side of the machine.[1] At the rear end of the secondary shaft the front element of a universal joint was fitted over splines and the drive was taken thus to a propeller-shaft running through the left-hand tube of the swinging fork to the rear bevel-drive casing.

The new machine was intended to sell to a market to which orthodox motor cycles did not appeal; a section of the public that would include many females, elderly folk, and even those who had become tired of the noise, dirt, and discomfort of the sort of machines that the motor-cycle makers had offered so far. Considerable thought was devoted during the design stage to eliminating those features that had given rise to criticism on the grounds quoted.

With their lengthy experience of foot gear control, and knowing the objections to it, i.e. the difficulty in selecting neutral and the undoubted harm that the pedal does even to male footwear, a simple manual gear control was considered essential. Much the same reasons prompted the elimination of the kickstarter, a means of engine-starting that is far too demanding of physical strength to be popular with the fair sex and a principle that is disliked by many males no longer in their prime. There was every likelihood that customers would be attracted from the car-owning population who would want to buy a two-wheeler upon which to run short shopping errands, etc., for which it would be quicker, and much more economical than getting out a car; in effect its suitability as second-string transport was foreseen. The hand-starter and fully selective gear control were therefore seen to be valuable assets and were adopted. With a manually operated starter-lever and gears two objections frequently lodged against orthodox motor cycles were eliminated.

In the first, and discarded design, Irving had provided for a bevel drive from the engine to a cross-shaft and a final drive to the rear wheel by totally enclosed chain. The drawings showed a cast-aluminium chaincase that carried a kind of stub axle for the rear-wheel hub but the work had not proceeded far enough for the 'frame' arrangement to be seen. It is understood that no rear-wheel springing was intended.

Udall elaborated the project by providing a sprung rear wheel the suspension of which was to be capable of adjustment to cater for variations in load, i.e. the carrying of a pillion-passenger. To achieve this he utilized an arrangement of variable mountings for the rear-spring units. This scheme was the subject of a patent[2] held by Veloce of which they had, until then, been unable to make any use of because of the outbreak of the war. He also specified shaft drive to a bevel-box through a propeller-shaft running through the left-hand side tube of a fabricated tubular swinging-fork assembly. A steel lattice cross-member bolted to the back of the gearbox was folded back to provide the mountings for two fixed pivots upon which bushes at the sides of the tubular cross-member of the swinging fork could work.

[1] British Patent 576,454 by C. W. Udall and Veloce Limited (4 March 1946) special mounting.
[2] British Patent 511,875 by P. E. Irving and Veloce Limited (25 August 1939).

The whole power unit, comprising the generator, flywheel housing, crankcase, reduction gear and clutch housing, and gearbox formed one bolted-up unit to which were attached footboards, a tubular radiator support, and leg-shields. The rear-drive assembly consisted of the bevel-drive housing attached to the rear end-flange of the left-hand side torque tube of the swinging-fork assembly, so that by offering this up to the rear cross-member on the gearbox the pivots could be inserted and the swinging fork retained in position prior to the whole power and transmission unit having a pressed-steel 'frame' mounted above it.

In this the whole design followed the principle of a supercharged racing machine that Udall had designed in 1939; as in the case of that highly original design the whole tubular frame with front fork and front wheel could be removed from the engine and transmission unit for attention in a matter of minutes.

In referring to the generator it was mentioned previously that there was some difficulty in obtaining commercially suitable apparatus and no carburetter that would meet the somewhat different requirements of the new engine was available from those manufacturers upon whom it had been customary to rely for supplies. The engine was much smaller in cylinder bore (44 mm with a 49 mm stroke giving 149 cc capacity) than motor-cycle makers had employed hitherto and the small choke-bore carburetters that were listed were mostly intended for industrial engines, such as mowing-machines and similar equipment. On such things a low and regular idling speed is not as essential as it was deemed to be on the new Velocette and they were unprovided with efficient pilot systems.

With the sort of customer to whom the new model was to appeal ever in mind it was essential that when the throttle was closed at traffic halts the little engine must continue running slowly, evenly, and reliably. It must not race noisily, nor must it stall unexpectedly and require restarting before the machine could proceed.

Being unable to obtain a 'ready-made' carburetter that fulfilled their somewhat exacting requirements Udall set to work and prepared a design for a carburetter suitable and eventually this was produced for Veloce to Udall's design by Amal Limited of Birmingham. The instrument was a multi-jet one and was fitted as standard for some years after the little twin motor cycle went into production as the model LE. Owing to the necessarily minute bore diameters of the carburettor jets it was necessary to prevent them from becoming obstructed by impurities from the fuel and a special filter was included as an integral part of the carburetter.

By this time the war had reached the stage when it became possible to spare a little time to produce a few pieces from which to build up a prototype machine for test. One of the first parts to be made was the front lug for the swinging fork that carried the pivot bushes and was brazed into an assembly of tubes and lugs to form the swinging fork. Enthusiasm for the new machine was such that members of the staff gladly spent much of their leisure-time in helping to get things going and the lug just cited is one example. The roughly machined piece was painstakingly filed to the desired outline, working from a detailed drawing supplied for the purpose. The work took many weeks to complete working during lunch-breaks and at other odd times when circumstances allowed. The rear lattice cross-member, an item that all LE Velocette users will know quite well, was also cut and filed out by hand, and the scrolls that hold the springs to the front-fork sliders were all mostly hand-made from sleeves turned in the Tool Room. Charles Udall had discarded the idea of a proprietary front fork and had designed a lightweight telescopic type that was better but more elaborate (and heavier) than the type originally proposed.

The gathering together of the items needed to produce even the engine, so that this could be run in the Works, was by no means an easy proposition. Had it not been for the assistance of many business friends it would have proved impossible. For instance, most bearing balls and rollers were very scarce by 1945 and applications to almost every manufacturer of them drew a blank when it came to getting rollers for the connecting-rod big ends. At last a supply of some that were of the correct length but too large in diameter were obtained. These were ground to the correct diameter by a friend of Eugene Goodman's, who had access to suitable roller-grinding equipment.

Motor-cycle connecting-rods are normally produced from blanks that are forged upon drop-hammers using specially prepared steel dies of the required shapes. There were no dies for the connecting-rod blanks that Veloce required, but because of good relations between Veloce and a firm of drop-forgers in the Black Country, the latter agreed to 'hand-forge' a small number of blanks upon receipt of a drawing of the part. Needless to say a print was run off as rapidly as possible and posted to them that evening to confirm the verbal order to supply!

It should be explained that when such orders were sent out it was the practice to include on the carbon copy a note to indicate the purpose for which the items had been requisitioned. The new model had no title but had become known to all concerned with it as 'The Little Engine', presumably because nothing else had been thought of and also because by previous standards it was such a small-sized job. As is usual when something has to be written very often it becomes abbreviated and just initials are frequently substituted for full words. Hence the note soon read 'for LE'. It is possible that nobody had seriously thought about what the new model would actually be called when at last it was made and became available to the buying public, but when it was listed it was as the model LE. It is perhaps nice to think that the letters stand for 'Light Experimental', but as has been related, the true reason is more mundane!

The prototype was subjected to intensive road testing for which an allowance of the then severely rationed Pool petrol was granted. Had it not been for this, any long journeys would have been out of the question. The very meagre quantity that was obtainable with coupons even for some years after the war ended would not have been sufficient to allow a sufficient mileage to be covered in which to find out much about the behaviour of the LE.

A photograph taken when the news about the new LE model was first announced in Birmingham. Note the 1913 two-stroke, before it was restored to its present condition.

Percy Goodman (right) and his brother Eugene, with one of the 1913 two-stroke models and one of the first production 149 cc LE models.

It is germane to the history of the makers to place on record that Eugene Goodman had intended to cease manufacture of all single-cylinder models and to organize the factory for the quantity production of just the one model. He considered that the demand for the machine would easily keep the works fully occupied turning them out at the rate of some 300 per week, and that there would be no spare capacity available to make others.

In the event it was impossible to get the new model in production right away when the demand for vehicles was at its height. The first post-war Velocette was the GTP two-stroke model of which a batch of 250 was produced, and all exported. Road testing of the LE continued under the control of the Experimental Department now with Charles Udall in charge. A further very limited number of them were built to try out equipment and machine tools that were being prepared in the reorganization of the factory for full-scale production.

As may be expected, when the machine was first announced towards the end of October 1948, it aroused intense interest, even among those who had previously eschewed the thought of using a motor cycle as a mode of utility transport. It is interesting to look back to the reaction of the late Geoff Davison (winner of the 1922 250 cc TT) when he first encountered one of these strange, silent machines while riding in his open Jeep. After chasing the machine and ascertaining the make from the pillion-passenger, he telephoned Veloce Limited the following day and was invited to visit the Works to see and try the new model. He ordered one on the spot and afterwards claimed it gave him so much pleasure that he even preferred it to his car. And this was typical of the reaction of many others, who were not so familiar with two-wheel transport.

The selling points apart from economy and reliability were the silence of the machine, the built-in weather protection, and the ease of starting which held no threat to either shoes or clothing. There was a small compartment in the top of the 'frame' for gloves or small parcels and panniers at the rear for any larger items that needed carrying. Above all the engine was smooth and vibrationless with final shaft drive to eliminate the usual messy chains. Yet with all these attributes, this revolutionary 'Everyman's' model failed to fulfil the promise of success that had been so elusive in the past.

Two factors seem to have militated against the attainment of this objective. The delay in getting the machine into full-scale production had permitted a new threat – the imported scooter – to gain a substantial foothold in the rapidly expanding market for lightweight machines. Few will recall that the motor scooter is a British innovation, dating back almost thirty years before this sudden post-war boom and can be regarded as one of the first serious attempts to break away from the traditional motor-cycle design in order to create a utilitarian mode of transport acceptable even to those normally allergic to motor cycles. History shows that the first attempt at marketing such a product failed miserably, yet it is ironic that a second, foreign-dominated attempt should have succeeded so many years later, at the very time when an entirely fresh approach by a British company was about to be launched. The acceptance of the scooter is all the more remarkable when it is realized that it was designed primarily to overcome the shortage of civilian transport in post-war Italy, where the climate is better suited to this class of vehicle.

A further setback was the discovery that despite all the road testing that had been carried out the new model was by no means as free from mechanical troubles as the designer or the Directors had intended or expected. Like many other entirely new designs, defects that had not been evident before came to light when the public began to use their purchases and foremost among these were lubrication failures, caused by heavy condensation within the engine unit. Machines used for a series of short runs (one of the uses for which the LE had been stated to be specially suitable) were particularly susceptible to this malady and as one may expect a whole series of engine modifications proved necessary before the trouble was entirely eliminated. There was even some question about the reasons for fitting such a small-capacity engine as the power available in relation to the over-all weight of the machine (245 lb) was somewhat inadequate for the purposes for which the machine was sold.

Moisture is inimical to ball- and roller-bearings and Eugene resolved to eliminate them from the LE engine and replace them with plain bearings as soon as circumstances allowed. For this desideratum he also had in mind the fact that much better alignment of the four bearings supporting the crankshaft could be ensured if the ball-races upon which it ran could give place to plain bushes. He did not omit the camshaft bearings from his plan.

Such a far-reaching plan could not be accomplished all at once and more than one bite had to be taken at the cherry! Eventually the crankcase and crankshaft were modified to provide plain main bearings and the change-over enabled the Engine Building Department to be provided with a massive fixture upon which all four crankshaft bushes could be reamed out to the exact diameters required to accept the crankshaft journals. Furthermore the bores were bound to be in line. It therefore follows that a crankshaft that is built up accurately, and is true to within the very close limits that could readily be maintained, would work freely when fitted to such a crankcase.

Another incidental, but nevertheless valuable, outcome of the change-over to plain bearings is that it became possible to fit an oil-gauge by means of which the supply of oil to the bearings can be verified at all times when the engine is running.

The last engine component to be equipped with plain bearings was the camshaft, but for some time now all LE engines have had the oil fed under pressure to all places requiring it, and have included large, full-flow oil-filters.

In one respect the LE was successful; that of bringing back into the ranks of motor-cyclists many who had given up motor-cycling in favour of other means of transport. They could travel in comfort and in almost

The two-tone Mark III LE model of 192 cc capacity. The two-level dual seat never achieved popularity and was eventually abandoned for one of more conventional design.

A fully equipped LE 200 model as used by the Hertfordshire Constabulary. These models that were allocated for police duty had a special high-output generator for the extra electrical equipment fitted.

complete silence with a freedom from the vibration inseparable from singles and to a greater degree from the undoubtedly popular vertical twins. Those who did revert to the two-wheeler in this form did not regret the chance that it afforded them to recapture at least part of their youth.

Unfortunately, due to the distinctly unsporting specification and possibly because of its silence the LE failed to appeal to the younger motor-cyclist, even though it was a machine upon which quite surprisingly high average speeds can be maintained on cross-country runs. Because the over-all sales never justified a large production, it was never possible to achieve the high output figures that had been expected. As a direct result, it was not possible to get down to the competitive selling price that was intended. In circumstances such as these a vicious spiral exists from which it is difficult, if not impossible, to break free. The only ready solution was that of compromise and in November 1950 a new version was announced with an engine capacity of 192 cc by increasing the bore size from 44 mm to 50 mm while retaining the original stroke of 49 mm.

Outwardly, the new model appeared identical to the original version, but numerous internal modifications had been incorporated. The crankshaft was now modified and was more robust. The clearance volume in the cylinder-head castings had been enlarged to compensate for the increase in swept volume and to maintain the original compression ratio. The tappet faces and the cam profiles were modified to give increased acceleration in valve lift and a longer dwell. The oil-pump capacity was increased by some 40 per cent. In the clutch assembly, stronger clutch-springs were employed to cope with the greater torque of the larger capacity engine. The reduction shaft between the engine and gearbox now operated in a pair of plain bearings, as distinct from the combination of plain and ball-race bearings used previously. To the rear of the gearbox, a Hardy-Spicer universal coupling replaced the earlier Lay-rub coupling in the final drive shaft and a spiral tooth formation was used for the crown-wheel and pinion. The changes increased the basic price of the LE but only from £116 16s. to £125.

The announcement about the new larger capacity model was favourably received by owners of the 149 cc models, who fully appreciated the benefit of greater reserve of power than 149 cc provided. Judging from the correspondence in the technical Press at that time there were many who hoped the capacity would be increased to at least 250 cc, but unfortunately this was not practicable. The capacity limit was 200 cc, beyond which the engine unit would have had to be completely redesigned to enable the requisite changes to be made.

One notable attribute of the 192 cc model (listed as the LE "200") was the improved petrol consumption, the average figure being close to 120 mpg. The top speed of 53 mph was approximately the same as that of the smaller model and the smooth, silent qualities of the machine remained unchanged. Even if the original marketing objectives of Veloce Limited were not fully realized, the LE had proved there was a place for the utility machine. The 'Everyman's' machine that had once been only a cherished dream was much nearer realization than ever before.

In keeping with Veloce tradition, the gradual improvement of the LE continued without any significant changes in the basic design, from 1950 to 1958. As mentioned earlier, most of the modifications related to the lubrication system and the bearings, so that ultimately plain bearing big ends and main bearings were specified. The small increase in power of the 192 cc engine necessitated an extra friction-plate in the clutch.

It will not be irrelevant here to recall that some trouble was caused to owners of some of the earlier models by electrical failures. A DC generator made by the British Thompson Houston Company had been fitted to the first batch of machines produced. The whole of the equipment that included the generator, a cut-out, a condenser, an ignition coil, and a contact-breaker with automatic advance and retard mechanism was all contained in a surprisingly small space ahead of the flywheel.

Dust from the three brushes, also included with their attendant commutator in the enclosure, was prone to coat the internals and gave rise to short-circuits by causing 'tracking' of the current across the main housing of the unit that was made of an insulating material.

It was decided to use a simpler arrangement and H. Miller and Company who had supplied Veloce with their lighting equipment for many years produced an AC generator-ignition unit.

This was no larger than the BTH unit but had the advantage that it required no commutator or brushes and so obviously would need less maintenance. One possible disadvantage was that in order to charge the battery a rectifier had to be included in the circuit.

For a short while before the new equipment was produced the Miller generator had included a protective device to prevent damage to the equipment should the battery leads be inadvertently connected incorrectly – a somewhat desirable precaution as the Miller generator had the Positive terminal connected to 'Earth' (frame) a state of affairs unlikely to be expected by most motor-cyclists who in those days would be more accustomed to earthing the negative terminal.

Perhaps the most significant change was the use in 1955 of a gravity die-cast aluminium-alloy pivoting-fork assembly in place of the earlier tubular structure which had shown a tendency to crack after extensive service. This gave a much cleaner appearance at the rear of the machine and helped streamline production still further. The two-colour models, first available in 1955, looked particularly attractive when compared with the somewhat drab grey colour that had been used since the model's inception in 1948. This effect was further enhanced by the introduction of a two-level dual-seat and streamlined pannier-cases in 1956 and smaller diameter wheels in 1957.

Mention has been made elsewhere to the heavy condensation of water from the air in the large crankcase of the LE, an effect worsened by the large mass of metal in the whole unit that makes up the engine, reduction-gear housing, and gearbox, all of which requires a lengthy period of running to get really hot. As the cylinders and heads are water-cooled this takes even longer than would be the case if air cooling had been employed.

In consequence when an LE was used for one of the purposes for which it had been expected it would be required most frequently, i.e. short trips to the local shopping area, etc., the unit never got thoroughly warmed up and the conditions were the worst possible in that they were exactly those in which condensation would be greatest.

The moisture that separates out of the air within the crankcase became churned round with the oil and formed a sludgy emulsion. Apart from the bad effect this had upon the ball- and roller-bearings, with which the original design was generously equipped, the supply of lubricant to the big-end bearings and other internal parts was cut off. This resulted from the central oil-jet upon which their lubrication depended becoming obstructed by the sludge.

Without wishing to be unduly critical of the original layout it must be suggested that to rely upon a single central jet to provide the main supply of oil to a high-speed engine was, to say the least, unwise, particularly as the rotation of the crankshaft against which the jet was directed tended to throw off the oil. No means had been provided through which easy access to the jet could have been gained to clear it in the event of it becoming choked.

The improvement of the engine-lubrication system thus was one of the first items that was tackled and a great improvement was made by modifying the crankshaft assembly and discarding the oil-jet system of supply.

Accordingly, the full output of the oil-pump was taken by a pipe to a drilling into the outrigger bearing in the reduction-gear plate from which it entered a bore in the rear mainshaft, and thence it was directed into a cup formed in the back face of the crankshaft centre-disc. The cup thus formed a small reservoir of oil and two small-diameter drillings let oil out into the front big-end bearing on the other side of the disc. A single drilling provided a similar feed of oil to the rear big end.

In the rear bob-weight of the crankshaft opposite to the crankpin a circular opening was made to form a sludge-trap. A radial drilling from the bore in the mainshaft led into this recess which was sealed by two light-steel pressings secured by a central rivet.

The chief advantage of this modified oil-feed system was that the oil was all fed under pressure into the bore of the mainshaft and was centrifuged outwards by the rotation of the crankshaft into the big ends. Any sediment in the oil was thrown outwards and was collected in the sludge-trap. An extension of the oil-pipe from the pump fed oil to the reduction gears and plain bearings that carry the reduction-gear shaft.

This system, that was standardized almost as soon as the model LE 200 (192 cc) was started, proved a big improvement upon the first type and remained in production right up to the time when the more far-reaching alteration was made and plain bearings finally superseded the crankshaft ball-races.

It must be recorded that, good as the lubrication system now was, Eugene Goodman was still determined to get rid of the ball-races from the crankshaft mainshafts, and the rollers from the connecting-rod big ends.

Although it was satisfactory to employ plain bushes instead of rollers, the somewhat small bearing area was all that could be obtained due to the small width of the big-end eyes. He wanted to adopt wider bearings as soon as possible as a means of increasing the life of the bearings.

The very narrow eyes were of course a legacy from the original conception in which the width had been kept to an absolute minimum and roller-bearings had been employed to achieve this, in the interest of reducing the

The 200 cc Valiant model, an OHV horizontal twin design that owes much of its origin to the LE.

This photograph shows how easily access is gained to the engine and gearbox unit as the prelude to a major overhaul.

amount of 'stagger' between the opposed cylinders. In consequence there was very little room to spare, but as an interim measure it was found possible to gain a little width by slight alteration to the flywheel housing, and the crank-cheeks.

In case our readers may think that we are denigrating the LE let it be thoroughly understood that the mechanical history of this epoch-making model is dealt with very fully because it has been the authors' desire to show the perseverance and determination of Eugene Goodman to over-come all the snags and unforeseen difficulties that cropped up in connection with the little machine. Had it not been for his almost fanatical desire to produce a real 'Everyman's' motor cycle it might never have been made at all, or it might have been given up before its full potentialities had been brought out. Such a radical departure from the orthodox noisy, dirty, and unprotected motor cycles that, until the LE was produced, were all that motor-cyclists could buy, would have been miraculous if it had had no 'teething' troubles. But it is an indication of the faith in a sound project allied to much patient unremitting work that the LE now has thousands of satisfied owners, many of whom are members of a club devoted to the interests of the model.

Towards the end of October 1956 Veloce Limited made a surprise announcement, about the introduction of the Valiant, a new air-cooled OHV flat twin lightweight that appeared to owe much of its ancestry to the LE. In principle this was true, to the extent that certain components such as the forks, pivoting rear fork, and electrics were common to both models. But there the similarity ended. Although the crankcase closely resembled that of the LE it had been extensively modified to accept a new crankshaft that would withstand the increased stresses of this higher performance model. The opportunity was taken to increase the width at the big ends very considerably, the objective which Eugene had for so long been aiming.

The same bore and stroke measurements were used (49 mm × 50 mm) to give a cubic capacity of 192 cc. But the pistons were of new design and had domed crowns with valve-cutaways to give a compression ratio close to 8:1. The cast-iron cylinder-barrels, which were air-cooled, had pierced fins into which light-alloy push-rod tubes had been pressed. These mated up with cast-iron push-rod tunnels in the light-alloy cylinder-heads. With hemispherical combustion chambers the heads carried shrunk-in austenitic iron valve-seats. Single springs were specified for the valve gear and the pillar-mounted rocker assembly incorporated eccentric rocker-pins to facilitate ease of tappet adjustment.

Valve timing was different from that of the LE, although the cam assembly was similar in appearance. As may be expected from the more sporting specification of the 'Valiant' the overlap period was considerably extended. The crankshaft was stiffened by widening the circular crank-disc member and split lead-bronze liner-shells were used for the big ends.

Engine lubrication followed a similar pattern to that of the LE, although the oil-filter unit was mounted beneath the engine unit instead of alongside the offside cylinder. A supplementary feed was taken to the rocker gear by an external pipe, with additional external return-pipes so that the oil would drain back to the sump by the most direct route from each cylinder-head.

The gearbox had four gears and contained a positive-stop gearchange mechanism mounted in the top of the gearbox casting. As may be expected, a foot-change lever was fitted. A new friction material of Ferodo origin was used for the clutch-linings to give additional grip. The kickstarter, which was of very light construction, employed a rubber-snubber stop to limit the length of travel.

A radical departure from LE practice was evident in the frame design, which was of the full-cradle type of tubular, all-welded construction. Rear suspension was by specially manufactured Girling units, which were not adjustable for rake.

The top half of the engine unit was encased within a pressed-steel cowling that contained the forward-facing horn. The prototype model had a single Amal Monobloc carburetter within the cowling, which fed each cylinder-head through a long induction-pipe in a manner reminiscent of the LE. The production models dispensed with this arrangement and employed twin carburetters, each bolted directly to the inlet-port of the cylinder-head and connected by a balance-pipe. A further enclosure contained the battery and the Miller headlamp was mounted within a nacelle. The complete machine was finished in the traditional black enamel, with a gold-lined petrol-tank and plastic tank medallion. A green-coloured version was also available. On both versions, all bright parts were chromium plated, including the wheel rims and the centre-tank strap that surmounted the $2\frac{3}{4}$ gal petrol-tank. The tank was quickly demountable from the two rubber buffers mounted on the top frame-tube. A twin exhaust-pipe system was used, terminating in a pair of slim, torpedo-like silencers that gave the machine a pleasant exhaust-note. Both wheels had full-width hubs and were quickly detachable.

The Valiant weighed 255 lb unladen and sold for £146 10s. plus Purchase Tax. It aroused great interest upon its début at the 1956 Earls Court Show, especially from many of the younger generation who had previously eschewed its elder brother, the ubiquitous LE.

Despite the small capacity, the Valiant had a surprisingly good performance, which placed it in the sports machine category. The maximum speed was not far from 70 mph and it is alleged the engine produced 12 bhp at a maximum of 6,000 rpm. At 40 mph the average petrol-consumption figure was no less than 120 mpg – very good for a twin-carburetter layout. As may be expected, the exhaust-note was much more prominent than that of the LE, although it could not be classed as objectionable.

For 1959 a second version of the Valiant was announced, known as the 'Valiant Vee-Line'. This was, in essence the standard Valiant model fitted with a fibre-glass dolphin-type fairing that added some 15 lb in weight. The price of the new edition was £191, as compared with £164 of the standard model, both figures exclusive of Purchase Tax. The fairing gave only a minimal increase in performance, the main advantage being that of improved weather protection. But the 'Vee-Line' version was not a success and it was withdrawn from production towards the end of 1960. The standard version of the Valiant continued until 1963 when it too was quietly withdrawn from the production programme.

Meanwhile, the LE continued virtually unchanged until 1958, when a four-speed gearbox was fitted, with a foot-change lever in place of the original hand-change control and a conventional kickstarter in place of the old hand-starter, using Valiant components.

The choice of manual control for the gearbox had been a deliberate one when the LE was first projected in the interest of preventing the damage to footwear inseparable from the use of a pedal, however well protected the pedal is made.

The positive-stop foot gear control, as nearly all enthusiastic motor-cyclists know, was evolved by the late Harold Willis for the special requirements of a road-racing machine to obviate the need for the rider to release the handlebar-grips when changing gear, so enabling better control to be maintained. In planning the LE the Veloce designers expected that a large proportion of buyers would be ladies who could be expected to wear more delicate footwear than that usually affected by the male sex. Probably they also had in mind the undoubted inconvenience of selecting neutral position with the positive-stop pedal-operated mechanism, some-thing that most riders accept as a matter of course but a feature hardly likely to appeal to the inexperienced, ladies, or car-drivers changing over to two-wheeled transport.

Much the same objections can be lodged against kickstarters, and so the original LE model was started by hand.

But experiments carried out by various members of the Company's staff, many of whom rode to and from the works daily on their LE models, had shown that a pedal substituted for the manual starting-lever worked very well indeed and did not damage even a quite light shoe. When it was decided to incorporate a four-speed gearbox in the LE there was only the consideration of the gear control that prevented the Valiant model gearbox being used for a modified LE.

It was clear that despite the undoubted advantage of being able to select neutral from any other position on the three-speed gearbox of the LE many customers preferred foot control and so the four-speed LE, which was designated the 'Mark III', was built with the crankcase, and gearbox assembly almost identical to the corresponding items of the Valiant; a factor assisting production to no small degree! The LE was now taking on a much more modern look, a feature accentuated by the enclosure of the headlamp within a neat nacelle. Today, the model is still virtually identical with this 1958 specification, representing an unbroken span of production of the first reasonably successful 'Everyman's' model over twenty years – surely a quite amazing record.

Possibly it is for police duties that the LE has been most successful, and at one time more than fifty forces in the United Kingdom alone were LE-users, some forces having fleets in excess of one hundred. The shortage of manpower has compelled the walking of police beats to be drastically reduced in some areas, but it was found that beats could be patrolled more efficiently on an LE. The ability to run at low speed let the public see the police patrol going by and the silence of the running enabled a citizen to hail the rider in the event of his services being needed. It was found that

The Velocette Vogue, virtually a 192 cc LE model with a fibre-glass body. The specification includes twin headlamps and built-in traffic-indicators.

one rider could do the work of three men on foot, a welcome aid to the manpower shortage.

In standard form the LE was well suited for these duties and it became more useful when it was fitted with a two-way radio. For such work H. Miller and Company produced a larger generator to provide the bigger output to enable the battery to be kept fully charged when the radio was kept on almost continuous stand-by duty. Not unexpectedly, a few other modifications were found desirable for police work and some of these have been incorporated in the normal civilian specification, thereby improving the design.

The rather severe and unorthodox outline of the LE has been criticized in some quarters, perhaps because it was never Veloce practice to fit embellishments that served no practical purpose. But it is doubtful whether these criticisms were valid. In 1963 Veloce Limited announced the Vogue, a specially restyled version of the LE achieved by fitting a fibre-glass body made by Michenhall Brothers, with twin headlamps and built-in direction-indicators. Presumably it was the intention to produce a machine more in keeping with the current trends in design but it is no secret that the new design did not prove a bigger seller than the standard LE, despite a slight increase in power from the engine. There is room for both models and both have continued in production.

It was only to be expected that after the LE model became a fairly common sight on the roads some people began to think that such a nice quiet and refined little engine might be used for purposes other than propelling a motor cycle. These people were not all interested in the engine

114

being used in other forms of transport and one of the first inquiries that can be recalled was one relating to the use of LE engines to drive the generators for the refrigeration plant in refrigerated vans carrying food-stuffs and other perishables.

It seems that many of these vehicles carried small cooling plant that relied upon air-cooled motors as prime movers, and as the vibration and noise inseparable from such engines were considerable it was desired to find a quieter and more vibration-free source for driving the dynamo.

As the motor-cycle trade is of a somewhat fluctuating nature any means of keeping the factory constantly and steadily occupied upon profitable work was naturally of great interest to the Directors but although some correspondence passed between Veloce and firms running refrigerated vehicles nothing materialized. One of the difficulties in the way of supplying the LE machine as a separate workable unit was the fact that the design does not provide a suitable point at which to separate the engine from the transmission without the design and production of special new parts.

For instance, the crankcase cannot be separated from the rest of the unit because it leaves the clutch, reduction gears, and starting mechanism in another casting that, in its turn, is bolted to the gearbox. Separation at the front face of the gearbox leaves most of the clutch with the reduction gears, etc.

However, there were some who saw other possibilities in the LE and at least one car-like two-wheeler was built and used by an enthusiastic designer. As a 'one-off' vehicle he must have found it reasonably satisfactory. But it suffered from the defect that the handling was dis-concerting to those accustomed to orthodox two-wheelers as not only was it somewhat difficult to handle until well on the move, but the very low and almost fully enclosed seating made those accustomed to riding open motor cycles with relatively high saddles somewhat disconcerted. Apart from the single example no other similar designs were known.

Some friendly discussion took place about the qualities of the Ner-a-car two-wheeler that had been marketed during the 1920s and which had been extensively demonstrated and shown to have remarkable steering qualities. These machines, which were highly unorthodox, had the front-wheel hub supported upon a car-like swivel-pin lying within the front hub, coaxial with the wheel's diameter; the whole assembly being supported within a loop member pivoted in the front end of a pressed-steel main frame that carried the engine, and gearbox, and supported the tank and seat. As a Velocette dealer within a few miles of Hall Green owned one of these remarkable machines it was possible to borrow it and try it on the road.

Even though the machine tried was no longer new, or in fact in very good order, its handling qualities surprised some of the younger members of the Veloce staff who rode it, and there is no doubt that Eugene Good-man was extremely interested in the problems that would have been involved in producing a machine with a similar form of steering con-struction. Eventually the Ner-a-car was returned to the owner and work upon a new scooter proceeded.

Among those interested in using an LE engine for road use in an enclosed vehicle was a Naval gentleman who was an expert upon helicopters but was for some reason toying with the idea of building a small three-wheeler to be fitted with an LE unit. After the exchange of some letters, an appointment was made, and he visited the factory to see the units being built and to discuss the problems likely to be encountered in endeavouring to incorporate an LE unit in his proposed chassis. In this case it was understood that the project involved the supply of units in quantities to allow a three-wheeled car to be put into production. But once more, and regrettably, nothing came of the project.

Although, as far as the authors know, no three-wheeled or similar vehicles were built powered by LE engines the use of the design for an industrial prime-mover came to fruition in so far as Veloce produced and listed an 'Industrial' engine that owned a lot to the LE in its conception.

It went into production during 1964; the list price was £90.

Not having had the opportunity of inspecting an example of this engine it is necessary to rely for much of the following specification upon the illustrated Spare Parts List provided by the makers for purchasers of the unit, and upon information given by Veloce Limited.

Points of similarity with the LE engine are the horizontally opposed layout of the two water-cooled cylinders, the pressure-feed lubrication system, and the measurements of the bore and stroke (50 mm $\times$ 49 mm) and capacity.

Here the similarity can be said to end, as the Industrial engine's camshaft was supported in two needle-roller bearings and the crankshaft upon journal ball races. The connecting-rod big ends were provided with a single row of fourteen bearing-rollers each contained in orthodox cages. In this respect perhaps the Viceroy design seems to have been followed as a similarity between the Industrial engine connecting-rods and those of the Viceroy is detectable even from the line-drawings of the Parts List. The crankshaft speed was governed by an Isospeedic governor and the power take-off was through a centrifugal clutch.

Some hundreds of these engines were sold but to all intents and purposes production has now ceased.

6
The Racing Models and the Isle of Man

The name 'Velocette' is synonymous with the Isle of Man, the home of what is alleged to be the most gruelling yet the most exhilarating of all the International road-racing events. Their début was made as far back as 1913, when Cyril Pullin rode a Works machine in the Junior TT and finished last after his machine had been plagued with oil leaks. Thereafter, the name 'Velocette' was only to appear among the Lightweight entries during the early and middle 1920s since the two-strokes constituted the whole production programme after the end of the First World War.

In 1921 Velocette two-strokes took third, fifth, and seventh places in the Lightweight event, with only one retirement. The year following they again took third place, with two retirements. There were no entries in 1923 and in 1924 the sole entry gained tenth place. This was the classic occasion when the rider, Fred Povey, was mystified by erratic ignition despite the fact that a cursory glance at the magneto contact-breaker showed that nothing appeared to be broken or even out of place. It was not until Percy Goodman examined the machine after the race that it was discovered that the contact-breaker pivot had broken away at its root from the arm – a very rare fault. Probably in machining, the arm and pivot of the parallel portion of the latter had not been properly radiused at the root. This would leave a point at which such a fracture could easily occur. The pivot was, of course, formed as an integral part of the arm in the EIC magneto used.

For the 1925 event there were three Veloce entries, one in the Lightweight class and two in the Junior event, the latter being the first appearance of the as yet untried K OHC models. Fortunately, RWB was able to arrange his holiday to coincide with the 1925 TT and it is appropriate that he should describe the scene from his vivid reminiscences of this and subsequent events.

'It was in 1925 that two of the new OHC models were entered for the Junior TT to be ridden by Fred Povey (Veloce's Tester) and Gus Kuhn, and a 250 two-stroke was to be ridden by Phil Pike in the Lightweight race. As an ardent Velocette fan I arranged to holiday in the Island and went over with a friend who was also the owner of a Velocette model H.

'We arrived late on a Friday afternoon and, after a meal, set off uphill from Governor's Bridge to see the famous course. It had been a hot day but the evening was cool and with only ordinary suits we began to get cold as we got higher up the mountain until at Windy Corner our enthusiasm was thoroughly cooled off and we decided to turn back. On the return journey the sobering discovery was made that with their

Brampton Biflex forks our two machines were quite unmanageable at even the quite low speeds that we could have reached downhill as compared with what we knew the racers must do.

'Next morning after breakfast we located the Veloce racing-stable and watched work being done to the two 350s and Pike's 250. This we noted had been fitted with an orthodox cylinder with normally mounted carburetter and the poppet inlet-valve was not being used.

'On most mornings trouble developed with the 350s and the two-stroke's piston seized with depressing frequency. When the two Junior riders had not returned one morning we went up the course to see if we could find them; eventually coming upon them pushing home from near the thirty-third. We joined them and the idea occurred to us to have a race in neutral, pushing off once only, to see who could travel the greatest distance. We lined up across the road and started by each giving a hefty shove with one foot. Reducing wind resistance as much as possible by crouching down over our tanks we gathered speed and after what, to me at all events, was a hectic ride got as far as Hilberry after which all machines began to slow, with Gus easily the winner as his weight carried him much further towards Cronk-ny-Mona than any of us.

'The results of the Junior and Lightweight races were a sad disappointment to us and must also have been a setback for the designer, but nothing is truer than the statement that lessons are learned from failures. In what seemed to me a very short time the new OHC model (the K type) was in production. I received mine just in time to have the pleasure of using it over the August Bank holiday week-end. I shall never forget the delight that this machine gave me. After the vibration of the two-stroke GCS model the K was so smooth and quiet, and was so deceptively effortless, that one did not realize how fast one was moving. It is a good thing that the 7 in. brakes were really adequate!

'The TT two-stroke had employed K-type hubs and brakes and a Druid fork, but the 350s had been fitted with Webbs, which I learned long after, it had been intended to standardize on the production models. However, my K arrived with Druids which were standard wear on the first batch.

'Among the Dealers handling Velocettes was the Southampton firm of Alec Bennett Limited, and Alec Bennett himself was so impressed with the outstanding qualities of the new model that he told Percy Goodman that with such a machine, modified in detail for road racing, he could win the Junior TT. His contract with Nortons, who did not produce a 350 at that time, did not prevent him racing the Velocette in the 1926 race.

'The 1926 racing machines were greatly improved by having Ferodo lined seven-plate clutches, the hinged thrust-cup spherical-washer-operating mechanism, and a spring-loaded gear-selector indexing arrangement. The tank-side gate was deleted and the gear-lever worked without one. From first-gear position with the lever brought right up, a smart downward movement to a stop on the pivot engaged second. To change to top the lever had to be pressed sideways to clear the stop and then moved right down as far as it would go. It was all very clever no doubt and probably worked quite well, but for some reason, a missed gearchange perhaps, Bennett took a dislike to it and wanted his machine to be fitted with the earlier type lever and gate. The only parts on the Island were those on my K model upon which I had arrived on holiday, and as there was insufficient time to get new ones from Hall Green by the next day, I volunteered to lend mine in a good cause. Bennett's non-standard racing-tank was hastily fitted with threaded "pummels" (possibly $\frac{1}{4}$ in. nuts) soldered to the sides to hold the gate, the new lever, etc. were taken off and with my gate practising was continued without interruption next morning.

'In 1926 there was no regular air service to the I.O.M. and only by telegraphic communication could spares be ordered rapidly. Racing Managers had to make sure that they took with them everything that they were likely to require. I recall that some years later a German firm went all over the Island trying to obtain a graduated glass measure (burette) with which to check compression ratios. Phil Irving remarked at the time: "So much for that much-vaunted German thoroughness"! Veloce always took one!

'For tactical reasons Bennett stopped at the pits at the end of his first lap in the Junior, thereby giving us spectators some anxious moments, but he soon restarted, getting away to a loud pinking noise from his engine. The compression ratio was absolutely as high as it was then possible to go with the 50/50 petrol-benzol mixtures that was then generally used. Alcohol had been banned for the 1926 season, and the distance increased

Alec Bennett being congratulated by George Denley on his win in the 1926 Junior TT. The bent footrest bears testimony to his fall at the Nook during the last lap of the race.

Alec Bennett and Percy Goodman, after the 1928 Junior TT.

to seven laps. These changes possibly caused many entrants to err on the side of over-cautiousness, and the Velocette win by over ten minutes was most creditable. During the race incipient pre-ignition had caused Bennett to ease up a trifle, and a fall at the Nook on the last lap also wasted some time. Had it not been for his intentionally free-working throttle-lever which shut off as his hand left the grip the race might have been lost.'

The win must have convinced lots of potential customers that Veloce really 'had something' as more and more K models were seen about the roads, and the OHC engine had begun its phenomenally long run of successes.

For the 1927 TT hopes were high that the 1926 success would be repeated. Saddle-tanks were standard wear for 1927 and the new racers were much improved in appearance. Believing that there was a slight increase in power to be obtained by reducing oil-drag in the camshaft-drive casings the 1927 engines employed much larger rounded top-bevel housings that did not confine the oil so closely. These also improved the appearance.

But another modification, seemingly of but slight importance, had been made which, as things turned out, was to prove disastrous and cost Bennett the Junior race.

The item slightly modified was the threaded tappet-sleeve, a part that in those happy days sold ex-Works for about 1s. 3d. The sleeves screw into the rocker-ends and are split so that as the tappets are drawn into them by the lock-nuts they expand and lock the tappet adjustment. After some use quite a considerable effort was needed to free a tappet that required readjustment, and apparently the modification had something to do with this, but, whatever the reason, the decision was made not to carry the split right down the full length of the sleeve. Harold Willis had now joined the Company and was entered for the Junior but must have had some doubt about the wisdom of the modification and although the engines being used by the other members of the team had modified sleeves Willis split his right across.

Quite early in the race a tappet on Bennett's engine worked loose, the clearance increased rapidly, the sleeve broke up, and retirement was inevitable.

Willis's pit attendant accidentally wrenched the oil-tank filler-cap during the first pit stop and the bent hinge prevented the cap being refitted. Very hurriedly Willis snatched the cap right off, breaking it free from the hinge, threw it away, and stuffed his handkerchief into the neck to reduce loss of oil as much as possible.

Even after the time lost through this incident, and with the natural anxiety about his oil supply, he was runner-up to Freddie Dixon (H.R.D. – footboards, back-rest and all!). A Junior race almost certainly lost by the failure of such a small item is surely a similar case to that of the traditional loss of a kingdom for want of a horse-shoe nail! Later Willis showed RWB his cheque for the Prize-money, remarking characteristically, 'This'll deal the overdraft a nasty crack.'

Despite the disappointment of not seeing a Velocette first past the post that year RWB made arrangements very early on to see the 1928 races by getting in an application for his 1928 summer holidays in good time.

June came round eventually and he arrived in the Island to take in both practice week and the races. In addition to their usual workshop in Derby Square Veloce now had space at the Nursery Hotel Onchan. Some more power had been obtained during the 'off' season as the Hall Green Experimental Department had now acquired a Strobotak. By means of this stroboscopic equipment a succession of phases in a periodic motion can be observed by intermittent illumination which makes it possible to see rapidly moving parts in 'slow motion'. The movement of the valves and rockers for instance can be seen as it actually happens at high speeds; first the take up of the clearance, then the opening, dwell, and closing of the valve, and finally the restoration of the clearance. Should the valve bounce after reaching the seat this clearly shows, and among other things disclosed by the Strobotak was the fact that the rockers were flexing under load. By stiffening them and so enabling the valves more closely to follow the correct timing of the cams a small but still most useful increase in power had been obtained. The viewing of engines running on the test-bed in darkness, but for the intermittent light from the equipment, naturally suggested the term 'séance' for the observation period.

A special spring-frame machine was tried in practice in 1928. Only one was built; under Bentley and Draper patents. The frame, as far back as the gearbox bracket, was normal K. Abaft the gearbox a triangulated tubular swinging-fork assembly worked in a trunnion-bearing. From the rear fork-ends two seat-stays were pivoted and were connected to the sprung part of the frame below the saddle by a system of links and spindles incorporating two coil springs. Friction-dampers were fitted to these links and there were also two more at the bottom pivots at the fork-ends. A stand, then considered necessary in the TT, was fitted at the lowest point of the pivoting fork.

Practising showed that in certain conditions the lower front ends of the swinging-fork assembly grounded and the model was not used in the race. Because there was no provision for adjusting the suspension for a possible pillion-load it never went into production as a normal roadster either.

Christened 'Spring-Heeled Jack' by Willis it was known as such ever afterwards. The engine was a standard KSS type (KSS 932) fitted with a KTT cam-box oil-pump. Hand gearchange was retained.

When RWB borrowed it a little later he was warned that the crankcase was liable to become flooded with oil, and that it was advisable to carry a suitable coin with which to turn off the supply when parking for more than a few minutes. Taps in the main oil-feed were standard then but were deleted after it was found that far too many owners were forgetful about turning on the oil. The Veloce design had a slotted head, rather like a screw. It was operated by inserting the edge of a coin in the slot to turn the cock through 90 degrees.

It was during the week preceding the 1928 TT that he was privileged to see Alec Bennett's figures that he had written down as a guide to the speeds and times that he would have to do in order to win the Junior. During the same week he was present when a friendly argument took place between him and D. R. O'Donovan who was practising on a Raleigh under a Reserve number. The point at issue was the speed at which certain corners were taken coming down off the Mountain. Bennett maintained that speeds were much slower than O'Donovan estimated, but the latter stoutly stuck to his opinion that after the high speeds on the stretches before the corners, for instance the very fast approach to Creg-ny-Baa, speeds were greatly underestimated by riders. After being unable to agree upon the speed at which any of the corners after and including Creg-ny-Baa were taken,

A 1929 Mark I KTT model owned by B. J. Goodman. Engine number KTT 51.

Ivan Rhodes riding the ex-Mike Tomkinson KTT in practice for the vintage machine event at Mallory Park. The 1929 Works four-speed gearbox fitted to this machine is clearly visible.

Bennett, knowing that O'Donovan's Raleigh was fitted with a speedometer, reminded him of this and asked: 'Well at what speeds do you take them, Don?' The matter in dispute was to remain unsettled, however, as the reply was: 'Man – I was afraid to look!'

The results of the Junior showed how amazingly accurate Bennett's forecast of the winning speed had been, and demonstrated what a great tactician he is.

Following the 1928 success the search for still more power was continued, and Willis decided that time could be saved by other means than increases in power. He realized that quicker and more certain gearchanges would save seconds per lap, and that if a hand did not have to leave the grip to operate a gear-lever 'navigation' would become much easier. Despatch riders in France during the war had been accustomed to lowering the gear-levers of the Sturmey-Archer gearboxes on their W.D. Triumphs so that gearchanges could be made by foot. The selector mechanism was arranged so that first gear was engaged when the lever was in mid-position. Thus a 'certain' change from first to second could be made simply by pressing down the lever as far as it would go. Bringing it right up to the limit engaged top. Thus when motoring in top pressing the lever right down through first engaged second. Thinking of the wartime despatch riders' expedient, and getting an idea for the working of a suitable mechanism from a German Pfauter shaping machine in the Hall Green Works, he designed the first positive-stop gear-control mechanism.

The prototype was not followed exactly in the production models that were fitted as standard equipment on KTT models, and sold as optional extras for many years afterwards, as instead of two enclosed centralizing springs only one external one had been fitted to the original design. This pressed an internally splined two-lobe clutch into engagement with face cams at the back of the control unit.

Although perhaps not as neat as the commercial control unit it worked very well and did not seem to wear so much or become sloppy on the pivot. One that was seen only a very few years ago, long after it had first been made, was in excellent order.

The 'changement de pied', as Willis called it, was patented, but very soon after it had been described in the Press, and examples had been seen fitted to Velocettes, a whole host of other foot controls appeared. Once provided with a workable idea it is not difficult for designers to evolve schemes that will perform the same duties without actually infringing the patented specification, and in the event of any action on the part of the original patentee it is very often possible to show that the alleged infringement is an improvement upon the original. At all events there seems to be no record of any proceedings being taken to restrain any of the 'imitators', and by the next year positive-stop pedal gear control became standard equipment on nearly every TT motor cycle. Willis and Veloce certainly started something!

It was during October 1928 that the Works announced their intention to market a replica of Alec Bennett's Junior TT-winning machine to be known as the 'model KTT'. The first of the new models were made for the 1929 season (which began on 1 September 1928) and they could be regarded as a more potent version of the KSS incorporating ideas and features found desirable from racing experience. This was, in fact, the first serious attempt to market an over-the-counter replica of the Works racing models; for once a manufacturer could fully justify the claim that his racing successes were gained on standard machines 'the same as you can buy'.

At a casual glance the KTT engine was similar in appearance to that of the standard KSS model, except that the crankcase was heavily ribbed to give a more rigid assembly. A closer look showed that the cam-box was fitted with a small reciprocating oil-pump in an extension of the end cover with an oil-return pipe taking the oil drain-off direct to the oil-tank. The pump was driven by a miniature Oldham coupling from a slot machined in the end of the camshaft and its use obviated the need for the non-return disc-valve normally fitted to the nearside crankcase half. The over-all benefit was an engine that was much more oil-tight, particularly in the region of the cam-box.

Internally, a new double-row roller-caged big-end assembly was used, although a few of the very early KTT engines had the thirteen-roller single-row type. The gudgeon-pin diameter was increased to 13/16 in. by the simple expedient of dispensing with the phosphor-bronze bush in the small end of the connecting-rod. The flywheels were of polished steel and not cast iron, since the latter have a tendency to crack at very high rpm. Although the cylinder-head appeared outwardly identical to that of the KSS model, it had a smaller exhaust-valve and a different hemisphere, which improved scavenging and allowed higher rpm without fear of the valves tangling.

In standard delivery form the engine was fitted with a piston giving a compression ratio of 7·5:1 for a 50/50 petrol-benzol mixture. If it was desired to use alcohol fuel, an alternative piston giving a compression ratio of 9:1 was available. As may be expected the KTT had a long, open exhaust-pipe that terminated well beyond the rear wheel-spindle. Ignition was by a square section ML magneto, specially selected for high-speed work. A standard Amal carburetter and single-float chamber supplied the correct mixture.

The gearbox had the new positive-stop foot-operated gearchange and so-called 'TT ratios' in which the middle and first gears were higher than those of the previous 'close' ratio set. The sleeve-gear, layshaft, and the first gear (driven) were different. No kickstarter was fitted. Rear-mounted foot-rests were supported on stout steel strips running from what was the original foot-rest bar position back to the front end of the gearbox lug of the frame. The brake pedal was also fitted further back. A kickstarter could be supplied to special order and also touring gears. If the former was fitted, it was necessary to have the foot-rests in the standard touring position.

A different design of petrol-tank was fitted, with twin taps and an enlarged junction-pipe joining the two separate halves – essential modifications since alcohol fuels demand a more rapid flow. The filler-orifice was raised and had a hinged filler-cap of the quick-action type. The oil-tank was basically similar in outline to the standard 1 gal design, but had the filler-cap, also of the hinged, quick-action variety, on the left of the machine. An extra oil union, fitted high up on the left face of the tank, accepted the return feed-pipe from the cam-box oil-pump.

In order to obviate the possibility of lateral whip, a special design of strutted Webb fork was used, with a top-fitting André steering-damper anchored to a stud inserted into the top of the petrol-tank. These strutted forks were unquestionably of sturdy construction as more than one repairer found when attempting to straighten them after an accident. The extra strut made the task of straightening almost impossible!

The KTT model sold for £80 exactly. It weighed only 265 lb and on petrol/benzol mixture with an open exhaust-pipe had a guaranteed maximum speed of 85 mph. If alcohol fuels were used in conjunction with the higher compression piston it was possible to obtain speeds in the region of 100 mph.

A young rider who had become very well known for his racing successes on Velocettes prepared and ridden by him at Brooklands, F. G. Hicks, joined the Velocette racing team for 1929. His machines were always meticulously assembled and he spent a tremendous amount of time in careful lightening of any components from which unwanted material could be pared. It has been stated that 'genius is the infinite capacity for taking pains', and if that is so Hicks was a genius.

He convincingly won the 1929 Junior and was one of the riders of the record-breaking Velocette that was the first 350 cc model to cover more than 100 miles within an hour, a much more difficult feat than reaching a maximum speed of 100 mph which had already been achieved by Dougal Marchant on a Chater-Lea 350.

It is possible that the great run of successes had made Veloce a little too complacent, but it was demonstrated very clearly in the 1930 Junior that they could not regard winning as their prerogative. The radial-four-valve Rudges made it obvious that much more power must be extracted from the now by no means new OHC Velocette engine. Meanwhile, the production KTT models continued virtually unchanged.[1] They made amends by filling the first eight places in the Manx Junior Grand Prix of that year.

Experiments by Willis for that elusive 'urge', as he called it, included all kinds of modifications to head and ports, etc., even twin inlet-pipes leading in to one inlet-valve; apparently unproductive of more power as it was soon discarded. A 'long-stroke' 350 had been tried but cannot have been an improvement upon the usual 74 mm × 81 mm engines. This 'one-off' engine was later fitted with a special 80 mm cylinder and assembled, retaining the long-stroke flywheel assembly. The resulting 'oversize' capacity engine was fitted into a roadster machine which was sold.

[1] As a guide to vintage enthusiasts KTT engine numbers closed at 271 for the 1930 season. There are, however, one or two exceptions.

To set out even a small number of the experiments tried and discarded in the unceasing search for improvement would be quite impossible, particularly as most work carried out in the Experimental Department was of necessity kept secret and not mentioned to those outside the confines of the 'holy of holies'. A four-speed gearbox must be mentioned, however, as it was produced at a time when three-speed gearboxes were standard on all Velocettes including the KTT, and four-speed boxes were only just beginning to come into use for racing.

Willis designed a gearbox with four ratios operated by selector forks moved from snail-tracks on a revolving drum or cylinder. The drum was in turn worked through a rack and pinion by an external positive-stop foot gearchange mechanism that had a greater range of travel. When RWB saw it first he was rash enough to comment that its end cover resembled the contemporary A.J.S. gearboxes and this was rather resented by H. J. Willis. Because the gearbox was intended solely for racing it had no provision for a kickstarter. It should not be confused in any way with the type of four-speed gearboxes that were introduced later and which were fitted to KTT, KTS, and KSS production models, the first batch of which were made to be hand or foot operated and which in the latter event employed the external positive-stop control mechanism with modified ratchet-plate to give the required control of an extra gear.

During the somewhat barren period, in so much as TT wins are concerned, the introduction of a few modifications are worthy of mention. Some breakages of gearbox brackets occurred and enforced a change of material for the bracket from malleable castings to steel drop-forgings. The improved parts were fitted first to the Company's racers, next to KTT models, and finally to all K-type frames. KTT and racing valves had hitherto had three grooves per valve-stem for the cotters, but some instances of stems breaking just below the cotter indicated that the reduction in stem diameter at a point where there was a concentration of stress was responsible. A remedy was found by modifying the stems to employ only the top groove, and producing cotters to match, so that the full stem diameter was continued almost to the top of the cotter which gripped it over a much larger area than before. The modification was also made to the valves of all K engines.

Among other expedients to obtain more power the supercharging experiments must be described. Despite the undoubted difficulties in supercharging a single cylinder Willis began the construction of a supercharged machine mounting the 'blower' ahead of the crankcase of a racing K engine and driving it by a chain from a sprocket alongside that of the primary transmission sprocket. At first, attempts were made to get forced induction by pressurizing the atmospheric side of the carburetter which makes it necessary to equalize the pressure on the fuel in the tank and float chamber. The resulting essential pipework can be imagined.

The chief reason for going to so much trouble was to eliminate the need for a 'storage' chamber that would be filled with an explosive fuel-air mixture close to the rider. The completed machine ran, after a fashion, but after a brief trial was presumably considered wanting, and the induction arrangements were changed so that the supercharger was put between the carburetter and the inlet-port. A large chamber or 'receiver' was made up of welded steel and fitted in the triangular space between the seat-stay and chainstay-tubes on the offside of the frame. This was situated far too adjacent to the rider's right leg for his peace of mind or safety and was a potential source of danger in the event of a blow-back. Fortunately, it was possible to obtain the use of a special, and at the time very secret, flame-trap through the kind offices of Amal Limited, and by special permission of the Air Ministry.

All this work took place on an engine with a cast-iron cylinder-head and barrel; aluminium-bronze and light-alloy materials were not being used for such components at that time, and so dissipation of the extra heat resulting from the forced induction became a serious problem. Piston-crowns showed the ravages of what Willis called 'The Deathwatch Beetle' or alternatively just 'Mice'!

As was only to be expected such an unusual motor cycle acquired an affectionate nickname: Willis called her 'Whiffling Clara' by which name she has gained a place in motor-cycle racing history. She was about the scene for some years and at one time was ridden by Les Archer.

It was for the 1931 season that Veloce began to use a big-end bearing of their own design and manufacture on the KTT and later in all four-stroke engines. Big ends had been supplied previously by outside specialists such as Hoffmann or Ransome and Marles. The KTT engine was also modified in other details when the new big end was fitted.

To improve the wearing qualities of the cams the base circle diameter was greatly reduced which lowered the surface speed. Overhead rockers were strengthened, and after some cylinder-barrels had broken off above the bottom flange, on engines using methanol with very high-compression ratios, the base flange was considerably deepened and four longer crank-case studs fitted to suit. Although no official 'Mark' was allotted to this 1931 type it became necessary later on, when the Mark IV had come into the range, to have some title by which to know it, and quite unofficially the Service Department staff called it the 'Mark III'. This apparently got known outside the immediate confines of the Works and 'Mark III' it now is to many Velocette-owners and enthusiasts.

For the 1932 racing season great hopes were placed in a much-modified version of the K basic design, which, for the first time in its seven-year-odd existence was changed in appearance. To obtain greater reliability the valve-springs, hitherto coil type, were superseded by the hairpin type which were being used on Sunbeams and Guzzis. Sunbeams apparently owned the patent on springs of this type as the first Veloce bottom fixings for the springs were stamped with the patent number. Probably a royalty had to be paid for every set fitted.

Apart from alterations to the head-finning the sparking-plug hole was brought nearer to the centre of the combustion space and the opportunity was taken to supersede the hitherto almost universal 18 mm size plug by one of 14 mm. This enabled it to be brought closer to the top and left more metal in the head, which enforced changes to the cam-box and the replacement of the original scavenge-pump by one that did not get in the way of the sparking-plug. A new pump was designed which was very 'thin' and consisted of a cast phosphor-bronze body that held two gears, one of which was driven by a small coupling that engaged the camshaft. The driven gear had no spindle but ran direct in the pump body. The cylinder-head was cast iron.

The camshaft ball-race retaining-ring was discarded too and the race retained by a steel plate between the cam-box and pump body, shims being provided to permit adjustment during initial assembly.

The frame was slightly changed but the tank-lugs were lowered to enable the tank to be slung much lower than previously, a change that improved the machine's appearance and brought the weight of tank and fuel into a better relation with the rest of the machine. A four-speed gear-box was fitted with pedal control.

After his Junior third place on the Velocette, and second place on a Sunbeam in the Senior races of 1929, Alec Bennett had retired, but was prevailed upon to ride a Velocette in the 1932 Junior, and hopes ran high that the combination of his skill and the new engine would turn the tables on the Norton opposition.

The actual result was a disappointment as a sixth place was the highest achieved, and that by L. J. Archer – with Alec Bennett eighth. There were complaints of excessive vibration and shortly afterwards the frame was reinforced by fitting a tubular sub-frame that ran back from the bottom of the crankcase to the rear fork-ends, and was braced to the front of the gearbox-lug by steel plates that were used to carry the foot-rests and brake-pedal.

Very few production KTT Mark IVs were supplied before the cylinder-heads were produced in aluminium-bronze that greatly improved cooling, although at first valve-seat wear was critical. A modification to the top valve-spring collars and cotters was made to allow the valves to turn relative to the seats and this disadvantage was eliminated.

The Junior results of 1933 were not too discouraging and showed that at least another win was within striking distance, but as before this eluded Willis and really gave some grounds for belief in his theory that there would be no win as long as the production models bore the tank transfers advertising the wins of 1926, 1928, and 1929; what some of the Hall Green staff irreverently called '1066 and all that'!

Experimental work went on year by year and if the results are studied it will be seen that a slogan adopted for the Company's advertising during the war, 'Always in the Picture', was no exaggeration.

The idea that more power could be obtained by reducing oil-drag persisted and in 1935 the KTT engine was modified so that the bevel-gears, cams, and rocker-ends were lubricated by oil from strategically placed jets. The redesigned lubrication system represented a radical departure from the pressure feed used on all the previous models. Although the crankshaft and big end were lubricated in the conventional manner by the gear-pump in the crankcase, the main oil-feed to the cam-box was taken by an external pipe to the upper bevels. Another short external pipe delivered part of this oil-feed to lubricate the camshaft and rockers. A gear pump driven from the end of the camshaft returned the oil direct to the oil-tank and the oil from the upper bevels drained down the vertical coupling-cover to the lower bevels and timing gear and then to the enlarged sump where it was returned to the oil-tank by the scavenge section of the main oil-pump.

The bore and stroke measurements were retained at 74 mm and 81 mm respectively, but the cylinder-barrel was now a little shorter to compensate for the greater height of the crankcase round the spigot joint. The aluminium-bronze cylinder-head was bolted direct to the crankcase, via the iron cylinder-barrel, by using long bolts. An Amal TT 34 carburetter was used for the first time since it was considered the use of a metering needle ensured finer control of the mixture than could be obtained with the track-racing instrument used previously.

Other modifications included the use of a full cradle frame with a single down-tube and a vertical seat-tube. A new type of four-speed gearbox was necessary as a result. This pivoted at the bottom to facilitate primary chain adjustment and had the operating mechanism located at the back.

The Mark V KTT had a maximum speed of 90–95 mph using 50–50 petrol-benzol and an open exhaust-pipe. Speeds in excess of 100 mph could be attained if an alcohol fuel was used and the compression ratio was increased to 11·5:1. The over-all weight had increased to 299 lb, but the price of £89 was still very close to that of the earlier models.

For the Works Team an almost entirely new engine was designed that was perhaps the most radical departure from the original K engine that had been made up till then. Some of the features new to Velocette engines were: fully enclosed rockers that operated the valves through short tappets, and the aluminium-bronze head employed a pronounced down-draught inlet-tract. It was surmounted by a quite new cam-box that carried a neat circular cover over the upper pair of bevels. The whole assembly with its tappets was secured to the head by a number of bolts fitted horizontally through the cam-box and cylinder-head lugs. To allow for expansion and contraction two steel plates were fitted between the head and the cam-box. Valve-clearance adjustment was by means of eccentric rocker-spindles in the manner that was to become familiar later on in the production Mark II and KTT Mark VII and VIII engines.

The whole engine was rather reminiscent of certain contemporary continental racing jobs; so much so that Willis was heard to refer to it as the 'Velosacoche or FNocette'! But despite any similarity that it may have had to any other designs the 'dog-kennel'-type cam-box engine was not copied from any other designer's board, which perhaps could not be said quite truthfully of certain other engines that powered TT machines during the immediate pre-war years.

The new engine was produced for racing in both 350 and 500 cc sizes and the placings in the 1934 Junior were uncannily like those of the year before, good but not good enough, but the Senior placing of Walter Rusk; third on one of the new 500s was very cheering.

In contrast to what the Press are so fond of describing as 'Wizards of Tune', who are said to have the ability to improve engines' performance by 'breathing on them', Willis stoutly maintained that if an engine was 'designed right, made right and put together right' it would 'go right'. 'And when it is doing so; leave the b----y thing alone', he used to say! Improvements so often attributed by the Press to almost supernatural powers he regarded as the results of alterations, modifications, or rectifications to faults in design or construction, that ordinary common sense showed to be desirable. He was also intolerant of suggestions that he should go to the length of using hollow bolt-heads and the like and he said that such minute savings did not amount to enough to justify the time and labour expended.

It seems that such riders as Handley and Rusk did not contribute to the improvement of the Velocettes in so far as 'navigation' was concerned and it is a matter of conjecture as to whether had the Velocettes been handled better at the time, the years between 1929 and 1938 would have been quite so lacking in real success.

After the Mark V there was a gap in KTT production and the idea came to Willis that it might be a good thing to produce a new model for private-owner racing that would, outwardly at least, more closely resemble the standard machines than would a replica of the 'dog-kennel' engine, bearing in mind that the Mark II was on the market. He therefore grafted a modified Mark II top end to the bottom end of a Mark V. The result closely resembled a production job as the larger inlet-valve and racing-cam profile were obviously not discernible to a casual observer. This machine was the only example of a Mark VI and was known by the name Willis gave it: 'The little rough'un!' Although not used in a Junior TT it won races in the hands of Ted Mellors and Austin Munks, the latter winning the 1936 Manx Junior Grand Prix with it.

The double-overhead camshaft Velocette racing engine was a logical development of the 'dog-kennel' type that was running very reliably but was perhaps short of that little bit extra required to win. Stanley Woods had been recruited to the Works Team and it was expected that with the more efficient method of valve operation the machine would do his undoubted riding ability full justice.

Unfortunately, early in the 1936 Junior, one of the vertical-shaft couplings sheared, putting him out of the running. In the light of the later successes of the opposition with a very similar double OHC motor it is interesting to speculate on yet another 'what might have been' had Willis been willing to continue development of the engine instead of dropping it right away. The explanation of the failure was given as the extra load of the camshaft drive imposed by the additional gears that are necessarily used when rockers are replaced by duplicated camshafts. At all events no attempt seems to have been made to overcome what seemed to many at the time a defect that might have been eliminated had the problem been tackled.

But mention of Stanley Woods must include a reference to the great assistance that he was able to render Veloce in 'navigational' matters. With his help during a series of protracted tests over the TT course, the frame layout was modified and improved until a very high standard of road-holding and steering was obtained. The swinging-arm rear-suspension system was incorporated and when the engines were redesigned to employ rockers in conjunction with a single camshaft, success was achieved again.

No account of the between-the-wars period would be complete without some mention of the rotary-valve interlude. As most motor-cyclists know, there have been many designs of engines in which poppet-valves have been dispensed with. On paper most rotary-valve arrangements look extremely attractive. The rotor runs continuously and has not to stop and restart, together with its operating mechanism, every two revolutions of the crankshaft. Usually great things are claimed for such designs of which the ability to employ very high-compression ratios and burn low-grade fuel are but two.

Veloce obtained the sole rights to use a patented rotary-valve design for their racing engines during a specified period, and work began on a few examples in preparation for the 1937 season.

To normal racing bottom halves new cylinder-heads with the rotors were grafted, the latter being driven by the usual form of Velocette vertical shaft. Inlet- and exhaust-ports were cut in the head close to each other with just a narrow wall between them. The rotor was externally conical with an extension to which a driven gear was fitted engaging with a smaller one at the top end of the vertical drive. Some of the inner space of the rotor was filled by a light-alloy block that left a part of the wall of the cone exposed to enable an opening to be cut in it.

The working cycle started when the rotor turned in the head until the opening in it began to uncover the inlet-port in the head. As the piston descended, the port was opened further until the full area was exposed. When the rotor had moved and the port was covered, compression began, and when the charge was fully compressed the combustion space in the rotor was brought opposite the sparking-plug. Following ignition the movement of the rotor brought the opening round to the exhaust-port which was progressively uncovered.

Week after week the Works resounded to the beat of open exhausts that only too often stopped very suddenly as a seized rotor or some other mechanical trouble interrupted the tests. Poor Willis became more and more despondent as time went by and he was no nearer getting a reliable power unit. On one occasion he said dispiritedly, 'Perhaps if we ran it with a "crock" plug on paraffin we might get some sense out of it!' This was prompted by the inventor's claims relating to the engine's insensitivity to plugs or grade of fuel. By 'crock' plugs Willis referred to those with ceramic insulation which was then almost exclusively used for low heat-resistant types – mica insulators were employed for nearly all high-grade racing-plugs!

The Velocette rotary-valve engines were never reliable and gave no more power than their contemporary poppet-valve types and so a costly experiment only resulted in delaying development of more orthodox, but certainly more profitable designs.

The engines that followed were the square-finned type with single overhead camshaft and two rockers mounted on eccentric spindles. The very large size of the head was brought about in part by the enclosure of the hairpin-type valve-springs, but there was also a desire to extend the fins to reach into the machine's slipstream and so benefit the cooling. The Works machines of both 350 cc and 500 cc capacity had swinging-arm rear suspension, of a design not unlike that employed today. It was not until the 1938 Junior TT that Veloce Limited achieved their next win. Stanley Woods, now the star rider of the Works Team, rode an unchallenged race, closely followed by Ted Mellors on a similar mount. In the Senior event, Woods narrowly missed the double, after a gruelling scrap with Harold Daniell on a Works Norton. This was the highest position the 500 cc model had yet achieved in an Isle of Man Senior TT event.

Graham Walker, as Editor of *Motor Cycling*, took the opportunity to test Woods's Junior mount. He recorded no less than 109 mph on the run down to Brandish, with a tachometer reading of 6,700 rpm. According to Harold Willis peak revs were 7,000 rpm, representing a maximum speed of 116 mph in top gear – not bad for a single overhead-camshaft engine of 348 cc capacity! In the lower gears it was even possible to go up to 7,400 rpm for a short period.

RWB recalls three interesting sidelights on the 1938 TT that are worth relating.

The petrol hoses and nozzles for the pit fillers were delivered by the petrol company during practice week, but very shortly after they had been left at the Veloce 'stable' at the Nursery Hotel, Onchan, an apologetic tanker-driver arrived and asked for their return. Naturally they were handed back in exchange for another set, but not before Willis had ascertained that the originals should have been delivered to Castle Mona.

Willis had checked them over in the very short space of time that they had been with him and had seen that the normally rough brass castings of the nozzles had been smoothed and internally streamlined to hasten the flow of liquid through them. The name of the real destination to which they would have gone had an error not been made told Willis all he wanted to know, and his great sense of humour allowed him to appreciate the astuteness of the Norton establishment who had been issued with these particular items in previous years. As he was heard to remark later 'Old Joe even tunes the fillers', as it was obvious that Joe Craig had taken every possible opportunity to gain even the slightest possible saving of the valuable seconds lost during pit stops.

During the preceding winter, the period when most of the effort was exerted to find more 'urge' for the forthcoming year's racing programme,

Willis had been experimenting with exhaust-valves cooled by the introduction of sodium to specially produced valves with bored-out stems. The procuring of the special forgings and the production and filling of the valves had been conducted in great secrecy.

It seems that quite accidentally Willis met his rival, Joe Craig, at some function that they both happened to attend or at some early season race-meeting. Willis afterwards related how Joe sidled up to him and with head characteristically on one side in a typical Craig manner quietly breathed into his ear, 'What have you been doing, Harold, cooling the exhaust-valve?' Willis could imitate the Joe Craig manner most accurately.

Although racing rivals (Willis always referred to Nortons as 'The Opposition') it was almost headline news in the motor-cycle Press when Willis invited Joe to see over the Hall Green Works. Needless to say, before the visit Willis got his two faithful mechanics Jimmy Owen and Tommy Mutton (both sadly no longer alive) to 'tidy up' the Experimental Department and when Joe came round there was nothing remotely secret to be seen. But it is very doubtful that Craig was fooled for an instant!

One of the items included in the consignment of spares, tools, and equipment taken over to the Isle of Man for the TT was a toy telephone comprising two hand-sets, a length of wire, and a battery. Although originally made as a child's plaything this was of great use to the Veloce racing-stable which was housed in a long wooden shed or building erected in the Nursery Hotel grounds, above the bowling-green. It probably housed chickens for the rest of the year!

Ivan Rhodes in the process of winning the August 1968 post-vintage event at Mallory Park. The machine is a standard 1934 Mark IV KTT model fitted with a small petrol-tank and a Mark VIII KTT front wheel.

Obviously those working on racing machines, whether those belonging to Veloce or to private entrants, require some degree of privacy and it is necessary to limit admittance to those genuinely on business. This was particularly so when the stable housed an experimental machine.

One of the hand-sets was housed in a small wooden box fixed to a tree conveniently growing at the gate to the ground in which the shed stood. A notice alongside directed visitors to ring up and state their requirements but not to enter until requested. Those at the receiving end could then invite the caller to enter or the person asked for could go to the gate to interview them.

Ted Mellors, who understood such things, used to get the 'phones' working when the personnel arrived at the start of the proceedings. Although a toy, it is surprising how well the set worked and what time it saved, in addition to saving those inside who had important work to do from being interrupted and from having to get rid of unwelcome intruders.

The new production KTT model, known as the Mark VII, employed a similar type of engine but retained the unsprung frame. A sprung rear end was not available to the public until the Mark VIII was introduced the following year, although the Works machines had used rear suspension in 1936. The Mark VIII engine was also improved in detail by increasing the diameter of the shanks of the crankpin which enabled a higher compression ratio to be used safely. Pistons that had been produced to burn alcohol fuels in the Mark VII were then fitted to use 50/50 petrol-benzol mixture in the Mark VIII. More of this later.

Although the 1938 Junior TT was won by Stanley Woods it was quite clear to any follower of racing that a very strong foreign opposition was growing in the form of multi-cylinder machines. The V-twin Guzzi had shown that the continental manufacturers were capable of putting in contenders that just had to be taken seriously. There were four-cylinder designs that were knocking at the door in no uncertain manner.

It is perhaps difficult for those who have not actually lived through the pre-war period to picture a scene in which a win by a foreign motor cycle was almost unheard of. That favourite weekly, *The Motor Cycle* and its equally popular rival *Motor Cycling*, did what they could to shake the manufacturers out of their complacency, but the former journal still brought out annually a 'British Supremacy' number. The directors of Veloce had no illusions, however, and their draughtsmen were started on designs for a new machine with which to counter the menace. This design resulted in the now well-known Velocette that has been exhibited at Earls Court and on the premises of many dealers throughout the British Isles: the twin racer that so many people think was designed specially to contest the 1939 Senior TT. An appropriate summing-up of the situation was that by Willis when he said 'Delete British Supremacy; for British Supremacy read "Had it"', and this very regrettably is just as true today!

There had been some friendly controversy at Hall Green about the effect of accelerative torque reaction upon a machine's road-holding and steering when shaft final drive was used with a transverse-mounted engine and

Charles Udall, the late Tommy Mutton, and Stanley Woods discuss the 'Roarer' supercharged vertical twin during its assembly at Hall Green.

crankshaft in line with the direction of travel. The different theories on the subject were put to a practical test by the new racer. The engine is a twin cylinder with two crankshafts geared together to rotate in opposite directions; best visualized by imagining it as half of an Ariel Square Four. The two alloy-jacketed cylinders and their light-alloy heads are bolted to a large crankcase that carries the engine oil and is bolted up in unit construction with a clutch housing and gearbox. The drive is taken from the left-hand-side crankshaft to the four-speed gearbox which is controlled by pedal and is indirect in all ratios. A supercharger is carried immediately behind the right-hand crankshaft from which it is driven and it lies alongside the gearbox. The rear-suspension swinging arm is controlled by two Dowty

Oleomatic struts and the bevel drive is contained in a housing attached to the rear end of the left-hand torque-tube through which the drive shaft is led forward to the gear-shaft, which drives it through a special constant-velocity universal joint.

The frame is of particular interest as being of welded construction mainly of tubes, believed to have been the first example of this form of motor-cycle frame construction. It is constructed so as to be readily detachable from the power and transmission unit; in fact after the removal of a few bolts and the uncoupling of the fuel-line and some controls the frame with front wheel and fork can be lifted off. The same underlying principle was used later in the well-known LE model which also may be dismantled in a similar manner.

The racer was also the first motor cycle to employ full-width hubs in both wheels. Apparently it had been intended at first to liquid-cool the cylinders but air-cooling was employed for the sole example built, and light-alloy deflector-plates were attached to the sides of the cylinder-heads to direct air along the outer fins. The long induction-pipe was fitted with a release-valve and divides just as it rises over the engine to reach the inlet-ports which were at the front.

The length and volume of the tract ensured that pulsations from the supercharger are largely damped out before the charge reaches the valves.

Valve operation was by a single overhead camshaft and rockers and only two valves per cylinder were fitted. The vertical-drive shaft went up between the cylinders.

To anticipate somewhat: the machine was dismantled during the war and as the constant-velocity universal joint, which had been obtained from the U.S.A. and was the only one in Great Britain, was urgently required by a Government department this was removed. After the war the model was rebuilt for exhibition but when shown at Earls Court lacked some of the details that had been included when it was first built and tested on the TT course. The air-deflectors were omitted and a normal KTT Mark VIII front wheel, hub, and brake were fitted instead of the full-width ones.

RWB's graphic description of the 1939 TT more than adequately conveys the uneasy atmosphere that prevailed.

'Reverting to the TT, the 1939 series was run in an uneasy atmosphere as we all knew in our hearts that this was most likely to be the last of the series for some time. Personally, I tried not to think about war, but however one tried, the thought of it intruded; there was too much talk of war to disregard it. For instance, the motor-cycle Press were taken to task by some Germans over in the Isle of Man because they described the exhausts of the DKW racers as being "As noisy as a Nazi Congress", and a member of the trade entering the "Snug" of a Douglas pub surprised a group of Germans in a discussion in which he heard the word "Krieg" just before the Germans very suddenly, and suspiciously, stopped talking when they saw him.

'Willis had been away from work for some time before the usual party

A close-up of the offside of the 'Roarer' engine showing the aluminium shields that were fitted to aid cooling. The adjustable rocker gear is very reminiscent of that fitted to the Mark II KSS models.

Flat out and not giving an inch! Stanley Woods on his way to yet another win in the 1939 Junior TT.

left for the Isle of Man and as the responsibility for getting ready the new twin racer was on Charles Udall's shoulders he was unable to be released to go over until the machine was completed. Accordingly, I was detailed to take over the machines for Stanley Woods and Ted Mellors with the usual stock of spares and equipment with which the stable was provided. In addition to maintaining the machines that our two riders were to use there were numerous private entrants using Mark VIII models to be catered for, including Les Archer, Billy Tiffen, and Jock West. The twin racer was not ready when we sailed and Charles Udall was left at Hall Green with one of Willis's mechanics, Tommy Mutton to finish it, while Jimmy Owen, Harry Harrison, and Len Udall (Charles's younger brother) travelled with me to Douglas.

'At the Nursery Hotel we found the shed that was to be our workshop just as it had been left after the 1938 TT. Behind one of the work-benches there was still a card on which Willis had written directions for the use of some insulated cables near by indicating that they were aerial and earth leads respectively for the radio that was always brought over. The message concluded, "Do not remove – it is well arranged." When I read these it was just as though he had spoken to me as so very often I have heard him use the phrase "Well arranged" in referring to anything that had been done satisfactorily.

'The radio was soon working and we also fixed up the toy telephone set from the workshop to our gate. Although just a cheap toy this was most useful and worked well; making it possible to intercept those callers whom we wished to exclude from the workshop.

'In 1939 one of the popular tunes that we heard so often from our radio was "Deep Purple", and even now after the passing of so many years I have only to hear it again to be taken right back in spirit to that wooden shed in Onchan. I little realized that sad, and uneasy, June just before the TT was to be the last before the war stopped all pleasurable activities and an era that to me represented a Golden Age. We did not foresee that the wonderful new 500 racer would never be used for the purpose for which it had been produced.

'Charles Udall and Tommy Mutton arrived with it one afternoon and very soon afterwards Stanley Woods was able to take it out up the course for a run over 'open' roads – it is very handy to slip out of the Nursery up the road to Signpost without going through populous districts. Woods said of it after this ride that it was the best steering motor cycle that he had ever ridden; high praise for an entirely new design right off Udall's drawing-board! It was almost impossible to get near the model when it was in the pit area during evening practice.

'The Junior win by Stanley Woods was not unexpected as there was no real opposition. Returning to my lodgings after the race I read of Harold Willis's death, and I am afraid that the remainder of the week had but little interest for me; a respected and very likeable person had gone and we all felt a sense of personal loss. He died from meningitis, a complication that followed a relatively minor operation.'

After the war racing was resumed, but the International Racing Regulations now banned the use of supercharging, which effectively precluded the racing twin from competing as designed. Apparently it was considered that it would not have operated efficiently if set up for atmospheric induction. The single-cylinder models were however taken out of storage and overhauled for a resumption of the struggle against the opposition. It was indeed fortunate that these old warriors had been well kept as there was now Purchase Tax to be considered. This tax was levied on all new motor cycles and so had it been necessary to build two new 'teams' of machines to run in the Junior and Senior classes, a very considerable additional expense would have been incurred which would have increased very greatly the cost of racing.

The well-known brands of fuel had disappeared during the war and only 'Pool' petrol was available when the 1947 TT races were run. This universal grade was of low-octane rating and quite unsuitable for the high-compression ratios of pre-war racing engines. Fortunately, there was quite a good stock of Mark VII pistons at Hall Green and these were taken into use for Mark VIII and other racing engines as they provided a ratio that was sufficiently reduced to use 'Pool'.

When June came round RWB was sent over once more to look after the private entrants' machines, but this time was quartered in the basement of the Velocette dealer's premises in Fort Street, Douglas. Charles Udall had a workshop 'somewhere in Onchan' where he and Tommy Mutton took

A rare sight! A batch of Mark VIII KTT racing models awaiting dispatch to their lucky recipients.

care of Frith's and Foster's racers; both single OHC motors of pre-war design. Not having been present there RWB cannot write about what went on but a trial was made by Freddie Frith of a Dowty Oleomatic fork that was fitted to one of the machines. As far as he has ever been able to ascertain, the result was unsatisfactory and no more was heard of the scheme to use telescopic forks with the racing frame. Webbs continued in use until a special 250 was built some years later with a quite different frame.

Frith was prevented from riding his Velocette in the 1947 Junior following an accident when practising on his Senior Guzzi, but Bob Foster gallantly brought his machine into first place and Velocettes filled the first four places, ridden by David Whitworth, Jock Weddell, and Peter Goodman in that order.

When Graham Walker, Editor of *Motor Cycling*, had the opportunity to road test the three TT-winning machines, some unusual aspects of Bob Foster's mount became apparent. The engine, number KTT 498, had started life as far back as 1935 when it was used for development purposes at Brooklands. Les Archer, Senior, had used this engine, fitted into a rigid frame, in the 1938 Junior TT and again in 1939 when the spring frame was used, what the railway folk call 'Accountants rebuilds'. In essence it was still in 1939 trim, apart from a lowered compression ratio to tolerate 'Pool' petrol. Les now performed the role of the successful entrant.

It was alleged that Bob Foster could attain 114 mph on the approach to Brandish, with peak revs at 6,700 rpm. Handling was impeccable and is

Bob Foster, who finished second in the 1948 Junior TT. Ken Bills, Bertie Goodman, and Les Archer Junior are to the right.

perhaps best summed up by Graham's description that the machine had the easy handling of a Lightweight but potency of a Senior motor.

As may be expected, the price of the production Mark VIII KTT had escalated somewhat steeply after the war to £330, although £70 of this total was represented by the infamous Purchase Tax that now applied.

At the start of the 1948 racing season there were signs of increasing opposition from other manufacturers who were busy developing new designs. Associated Motor Cycles had announced their new 350 cc racer, the 7R AJS, earlier in the year and for the 500 cc class there was the new Grand Prix Triumph twin based on Ernie Lyon's successful 1946 Manx Grand Prix winner. Perhaps more ominous, the Italians were already showing signs of their forthcoming dominance, particularly in the Lightweight class.

Velocette hopes were pinned on Freddie Frith and Kenneth Bills, entered on two new Mark VIII KTTs by R.M.N. Spring. Four specially tuned engines were prepared at the works, the other two being allocated to Bob Foster and David Whitworth who represented equally good prospects. A number of standard Mark VIIIs were also produced and purchased by riders of International repute such as Ernie Thomas and Fergus Anderson.

Freddie Frith set the pace by leading the Junior TT from start to finish, closely followed by Bob Foster. There were no Works entries in the Senior event; no 500 cc models were manufactured in 1948.

Graham Walker's customary road test of the TT winning machines was somewhat dampened by the gale-force winds that persisted while he rode Frith's machine. Even so, he was able to reach 109 mph on the approach to Brandish, with peak revs of 7,200 rpm in the intermediate gears. For once he was at a complete loss of words adequately to describe what he considered to be a superb piece of machinery.

Although the range of standard production models had been seriously reduced in 1949 to permit full production of the LE model, racing enthusiasts were delighted to learn that the Mark VIII KTT would again be produced in limited numbers for the 1949 season. Just prior to the TT the excitement increased when it was learned that the Works had produced seven very special engines – two each of 350 cc and 500 cc capacity for the Spring equipe (Frith and Bills) and the remaining three, all of 350 cc capacity, for Bob Foster, David Whitworth, and Ernie Thomas through their respective entrants. All seven engines were of the double overhead-camshaft design, similar in many respects to the original 1935 pattern. In order to reduce weight, Elektron was used for the crankcase and rocker-box castings and the cylinder-head and barrel were of light alloy.

Freddie Frith won the Junior TT but only after a tough struggle with Bill Doran on a Works 7R AJS. Ernie Lyons, who substituted for an injured Ken Bills in the Spring team, took second place. In the Senior event, Ernie Lyons took one of the new 500 cc models into third place; Freddie Frith had retired on the third lap when part of the camshaft drive failed. According to Nigel Spring, the new 350 cc engine would peak at 7,500 rpm representing 116 mph in top gear. It is interesting to learn that this same machine carried Freddie Frith to victory in every major Grand Prix that year, earning for him the 350 cc World Championship and bestowing the same honour on the Company.

In 1950 the Spring equipe was reorganized to include Reg Armstrong and Frank Fry, since Freddie Frith had decided to retire while at the zenith of a long and successful career. For the 350 cc class, virtually the same machines were used, although there had been some attempt to reduce the weight still further by employing additional alloy components. Some winter development work had slightly increased the power output from the engines.

This can be regarded as the first year of very serious challenge for it heralded the introduction of the 'featherbed' Norton with Works riders of the calibre of Artie Bell, Harold Daniell and, a rising star, Geoff Duke. As far as the Junior TT was concerned, the Velocettes were never in the hunt after the early retirement of Bob Foster. Ken Bills was the first man home, in ninth position. In the Senior event, Reg Armstrong tied with Bob Foster for equal sixth place, the latter riding an Italian Guzzi twin. Fortunately, the results from the continental Grand Prix were more encouraging. Once again the Company were awarded the 350 cc World Championship honours, with the individual title going to Bob Foster – a fitting reward for the 'Cheltenham Flyer'. Happily, it was during this year that the award of the OBE was made to Freddie Frith for his services to motor-cycling. Very appropriately, the announcement in the Birthdays Honours List was made just prior to the 1950 TT.

Despite the ever-increasing costs of development work and the fielding of Works-sponsored machines in racing events of International status, it should not be assumed that Veloce Limited were staking all on what was a basically pre-war design. While it was unfortunate that the 'Roarer' project should have terminated so abruptly as a result of the Fédération Internationale Motocyclette's post-war ban on superchargers, other possibilities were being explored. Perhaps the most ambitious was that for an in-line four, a project that is alleged to have started from a chance conversation between Bertie Goodman (then Veloce Racing and Development Manager) and Joe Craig of Nortons in a Berne Hotel prior to the 1949 Swiss Grand Prix. It was no secret that Joe was planning a Norton four-cylinder racer in an attempt to meet the increasing challenge from the Italian MV and Gilera factories who were close to perfecting their own four-cylinder designs and were already notching the occasional win. Bertie jocularly asked Joe how the four was progressing, and added that Joe should wait until he saw the Veloce counterpart. Needless to say, nothing whatever existed within the Hall Green Works at that time, but Bertie afterwards became preoccupied with the thought and put the proposition to his father. He must have proposed a convincing case, for Percy Goodman took up his drawing-board after deciding there were distinct possibilities in a liquid-cooled four mounted transversely in a duplex frame and having a 'unit' gearbox. After the customary 'arrangement' drawing had been produced, the decision was taken to proceed with the design of a complete machine. Work on the project commenced in 1950 with Percy setting as his target the 1953 Senior TT.

The project started well and by 1951 the initial layout had been completed. Sadly, Percy was in failing health so Bertie took over the project to complete the detail work by the year following. It was decided to construct an experimental 125 cc engine from which test-bench data could be extracted, the engine being virtually one of the four cylinders with the full-scale overhead-camshaft drive. The light-alloy castings were made, but before they could be fully machined Percy Goodman died and there was a radical change in Company policy. By this time most of the British manufacturers were finding it increasingly difficult to justify racing as an economical form of advertising. A family concern such as Veloce did not have the financial backing from outside sources that was now virtually essential for a continuation of these activities. Every effort had to be deployed to maintain their unbroken record of independence if they were to retain full control and not follow the course of other manufacturers who 'merged' to become part of large combines. In consequence, the project was abandoned at this early stage – a prelude to the later complete closure of the Racing Department.

We are indebted to Bob Currie of *The Motor Cycle* for what little information remains about the four-cylinder design for during 1960[1] he published a full report on the project together with a cut-away drawing of the proposed engine unit and main cycle parts. The results of his research can be summarized as follows.

As mentioned earlier, the engine unit was to have been transversely mounted in a welded duplex-tube frame having a unit gearbox and shaft drive to the rear wheel. The capacity was 498 cc, each of the four cylinders having 'square' bore and stroke dimensions of 54·1 mm. The camshafts were driven by spur-gears mounted within a casing in the offside of the engine, and each had an additional centre-bearing to maintain rigidity. The cylinder-block was fitted with wet liners and the coolant was circulated by an impeller through cored passages. A radiator of small dimensions completed the system, which was fully pressurized. It was conveniently mounted just below the nose of the petrol-tank.

Space limitations necessitated the use of coil valve-springs that were conical in shape to eliminate surge. They were encased, in the fashion of the Jaguar car engine, within large-diameter tappet-cups running directly in the light-alloy cylinder-head.

The transmission was similar in its broadest aspects to that employed in the LE and the Valiant models, for it was necessary to use a counter-shaft arrangement in order to permit the clutch assembly to be more centrally disposed. It is anticipated that a constant-velocity joint would have been used at the forward end of the final-drive shaft which ran through the nearside swinging-fork tube according to Veloce practice.

Projecting rearward from the offside crankcase assembly was a car-type replaceable-element oil-filter. Oil was carried in an integral crankcase

[1] *The Motor Cycle*, 5 May 1960, pp. 552–5.

144

compartment. The four carburetters were provided with a cross-shaft arrangement to operate the throttle-slides, in a manner identical to that of the MV and Gilera 'fours'. Surprisingly, a magneto supplied the HT current, driven by one of the spur-gears in the camshaft train. It was located transversely, to the rear of the cylinder-block.

It is alleged that the design had provision for the incorporation of a supercharger in the hope that the Fédération Internationale Motocyclette would ultimately relax their ban. But the truth of this will never be known. The project never reached fruition and the hope for a British 'world-beater' died with it.

There was no mention of the production KTT model in the 1951 programme, and had there been an Earls Court Show for 1950 they would not have been evident on the Veloce Stand. The long line of 'over-the-counter' replicas was now broken and although it was not to be known at the time, 1949 was to prove the last Isle of Man TT win for this handsome black-and-gold racer.

Interest was now directed towards the Lightweight class which had been so badly neglected in the post-war years by British manufacturers. In an attempt to break the stranglehold in this capacity class, Veloce Limited decided to field a team of three double overhead-camshaft models of 250 cc capacity, to be ridden by Bob Foster, Bill Lomas, and Cecil Sandford. Basically these could be regarded as 'cut-down' KTT models with the bore and stroke dimensions reduced to 68 mm × 68·5 mm. Although the most obvious departure from the original specification was the use of telescopic front forks, closer inspection showed that an entirely new frame was used

The late Les Graham with one of the post-war Works 250 cc KTT models.

Adrian Richmond riding his ex-Ernie Thomas 1939 Mark VIII KTT in the August 1968 meeting at Mallory Park.

An unusual combination! Ann Haydon Jones, Wimbledon lawn tennis champion at a New Zealand Tennis Championship organized by Velocette main distributor Bill White. Bill won a Gold Star on this machine at Brooklands.

with a detachable top tube that also acted as the clamp for the redesigned fuel-tank. The rear-suspension units, still of the Oleo type, were adjustable for rake by means of a series of holes drilled in the top anchorage-plate of the sub-frame. Mention has already been made of the telescopic front forks; they were outwardly similar to the type fitted to the MAC road models, apart from the top shrouds. Internally they had a modified damping system that also acted on the recoil.

A new 350 cc model was also built to the same broad specification, but with a five-speed gearbox. This machine was allocated to Bob Foster, who was again supported by Bill Lomas and Cecil Sandford. In the Lightweight event the Veloce hopes suffered an early setback. The machines did not arrive until after practice had started and they were plagued with so many 'teething' troubles that it was not possible to complete the machines for Lomas and Sandford by the deadline. Bob Foster's luck was out too; he retired on the second lap before the machine could show its paces.

The Junior event proved a little more promising. Bill Lomas finished in fifth place with Bob Foster just behind, riding the new model. Cecil Sandford managed to complete six laps before he retired, after a lengthy earlier stop to rectify some gearbox trouble.

It was now obvious that the old, pre-war single-cylinder designs had reached the limit of their development as far as racing was concerned. The multi-cylinder engine, of predominantly Italian origin, was offering formidable opposition, especially since a long period of development under racing conditions had greatly improved mechanical reliability. Some British manufacturers had no new designs on which to pin their future hopes and the general air was one of depression with a tendency to withdraw what slender resources existed from the continuation of racing support in view of the ever-increasing costs.

Veloce Limited were as badly affected as any other manufacturer for their revolutionary four-cylinder design was still only at the drawing-board stage. Their total support for 1952 was a lone Works 348 cc KTT to be ridden by Cecil Sandford and a 250 cc KTT for Les Graham, who had shown remarkable consistency on a privately owned KTT in last season's events.

The Works models were virtually modified versions of the machines used during the preceding year. One significant change in specification was the reversion to girder forks, although a concession was made towards modern advances in suspension by incorporating a hydraulic damper within the conventional, centrally disposed spring. Higher speeds were anticipated, as evidenced by a new 8 in. twin leading-shoe front brake that is alleged to have been designed with the four-cylinder racer in mind.

In the 1952 Junior TT the Velocette entry had dropped to 19 (including the Works entry) out of a total of 95. This was proof indeed that the KTT model was no longer available to private owners for in 1949 the total Velocette entry in that year's Junior event was over one-third – 34 out of 101 entries. As expected, the opposition swept the board and Cecil Sandford was never on the leader board.

The double overhead camshaft cylinder-head used on the post-war Works 250 cc KTT models. Note the provision for a second sparking-plug to the rear of the vertical coupling.

Another view of the cylinder-head showing the spur gear casting that encloses the valve mechanism.

As far as the Lightweight event was concerned, it was obvious that the 250 cc KTT now had the reliability but was sadly lacking in speed. Les Graham did well to clinch fourth position, after a spirited duel with Sid Lawton. As luck would have it, this was to prove the best result for an International event during the year. It was now obvious that the Company could no longer support racing and these activities were terminated at the end of the year. The Racing Department was closed down and the machines and spares were put up for sale. Thus ended another chapter in the history of the Company and the development of the British racing motor cycle.

7
The War Years 1940–46

After the 1939 Isle of Man TT races in which Stanley Woods had won the Junior race once again for Veloce there was far too little time in which to develop the racing twin-cylinder machine, even though the design clearly had great possibilities. After the declaration of war all the racing machines, spares, and equipment were packed away until, at some date then not even to be guessed at, happier conditions might prevail.

Charles Udall, who had taken over control of the Racing Department following the tragic death of Harold Willis in June 1939, was appointed Chief Inspector and was approved in this capacity by the Aeronautical Inspection Directorate to pass out all components and material produced under Air Ministry contracts. With their long experience of the production of parts to very close limits of accuracy, and their long insistence that their products should always be of excellent quality, Veloce were ideally suited to undertake sub-contracts for aircraft components.

The 1940 models had been announced but need no particular mention here. Apart from such minor details as slightly modified attachment brackets for the rear registration-plates they differed little from the previous season's types. The programme consisted of six models – the GTP, MOV, MAC, KTS, KSS, and MSS – but only a few examples of each were manufactured and sold before all production of the familiar black and gold finished motor cycles ended.

To those of the staff and workpeople whose main interest was motor cycles it was good news when a contract for military machines was awarded to the Company by the French Government. The 350 cc MAC was the model selected and preparations began to produce these finished in khaki with those items that had been normally polished and chromium plated finished in dull chromium plating. A few alterations and additions were made to conform to military requirements, these being a reduction in compression ratio in the engine, lower over-all gear ratios with a specially low first-gear ratio, a K-type clutch, and the addition of a steel plate undershield bolted to the frame below the crankcase.

Among the other things that had to be done for the French contract was the printing of an Instruction Book in French, and so a translation of the standard book was made. An officer from the French Army on a visit to Hall Green stated that 'his blokes' would be quite happy with the translated instructions. This was a great relief to those whose duty it had been to produce them as some of the personnel at Hall Green had memories of an instruction leaflet that had been issued with the racing two-stroke DWK motor cycle in 1939. Ernie Thomas had ridden one of these machines in races and had considered the Roneod leaflets so humorous that he had given a set to Harold Willis. Many were the laughs at the expense of the writers who had translated the German directions absolutely literally into English. The pitfalls of entrusting translations of such things to people who are obviously devoid of all technical knowledge were very obvious to the Hall Green staff, and therefore it was a great relief to learn, from a Frenchman who spoke English like a native of these shores, that it all made sense.

In the conditions of wartime secrecy it was not possible to find out what happened to the first shipment of machines to the French contract but it is generally believed that the ship carrying them was sunk by enemy action on the way over. Before more machines were produced the French surrendered and motor-cycle production ceased again.

Having much material on hand for making more MAC models the Directors naturally wanted to make use of it, but permission to produce civilian models for export was not forthcoming. With no definite programme in view that would utilize the materials in stock, or the production capacity to make motor cycles, an increasing number of aircraft and other wartime jobs were taken on. The Enamelling Plant was employed in spray painting thousands of steel helmets and so was found useful employment for a while.

In the light of subsequent events it is interesting to recall that the British Government were not at first in the slightest interested in taking over the balance of the French contract but at long last were prevailed upon to accept the Velocettes. They made it clear in so doing that when the outstanding balance of some 1,200 machines had been supplied they would certainly not require any more.

In the quite justifiable belief that they would not be called upon to produce any more motor cycles after the 1,200-odd had been made, Veloce took on more and more sub-contracts for aircraft, army material and components. All these were classed by the authorities as of much higher priority than the motor cycles and so production of the latter was not as rapid as it would have been had that been the only work upon which the Company was engaged.

But then the picture changed, and after the retreat from Dunkirk it was found that many more motor cycles were needed, so much so that the Government impressed large numbers of used civilian machines. It was also given out that after the completion of the contract for the MAC still more would be required. Training establishments were set up in different parts of the country at which soldiers, including officers, were taught to ride, and the usefulness of motor cycles was at last realized by the War Office, presumably largely because of the extreme mobility of the German Panzers before Dunkirk.

The military version of the MAC as produced for the French Army was reasonably satisfactory but there were points that required alteration and improvement, and so an example was taken off the production-line and put into use as a mobile experimental model. As RWB then lived some twenty-three miles away from Hall Green and was making the return journey every day, the machine was entrusted to him so that items included upon it could undergo continuous road tests. Fortuitously, the ex-TT rider Tommy Spann, then a Major, was Officer in Charge of a Training School near Wolverhampton, and an opportunity was taken to visit the establishment with the experimental MAC. This was ridden in various test-runs over rough country in company with men undergoing training.

By these expeditions, and through the good offices of Major Spann, Philip Irving, then working for Veloce, and RWB were able to try other makes of army motor cycles. The information and experience gained was soon put to good use in the preparation of a prototype of the new 350 that it was proposed to offer for any further batch of military machines that would be produced to a new contract.

A few of the changes that were made included the redesign of the lower part of the frame to eliminate the separate undershield by replacing the bottom horizontal tubes with a malleable 'cradle' lug thus considerably strengthening the structure and simplifying manufacture. The brake-pedal and its pivot, having been found to be somewhat vulnerable, were re-designed and brought to positions in which they were unlikely to suffer damage over rocky ground, or in a spill.

The anchorage for the rear brake-plate had been considered to be capable of improvement for some time and the chance was taken to anchor it by means of a torque arm running from the bottom of the brake-plate, which was suitably extended for the purpose, to the prop-stand pivot-lug. The improved parts were all capable of being fitted to existing machines,

The war-time WD/MAC model, specially manufactured for use by the armed forces. Note the headlamp mask, crankcase shield, and unusual design of silencer.

a valuable asset from the 'service replacement' angle. In producing the MAC gearbox for military use with a reduced first-gear ratio it had been necessary to use a sixteen-tooth ratchet-gear meshing with a larger-than-standard twenty-eight-tooth loose low-gear wheel on the mainshaft. As the kickstart-ratchets are all cut with eighteen teeth, which matched the standard eighteen-tooth first gear, it follows that when the gear had only sixteen driving teeth it was impossible to produce 'full' kickstart ratchet-teeth all round. And so as some teeth were incapable of giving full engagement for the kickstart-ratchet the starting arrangements were not entirely satisfactory. Irving devised an eighteen-toothed gear that he meshed with a suitably cut driven gear that gave the requisite ratio but overcame the ratchet difficulty.

It became necessary to give the much-modified model that was to be supplied under the new contract a different 'Type' designation, and 'MAF' was chosen, a decision for which there were valid reasons. The first inclination had been to call the machine the 'MAD'; 'D' being the next letter to 'C' alphabetically, but for obvious reasons this was vetoed! 'MAE' was suggested but it was thought that over the telephone this might be mistaken for 'MAC' and so the next letter alphabetically 'F' was finally chosen and 'MAF' is after all quite apt as the machines were for the use of H.M. 'Forces'!

The new contract was duly received and the 'MAF' was put into production including the modifications previously mentioned but also with an important change in the gear operation. All Velocettes had hitherto employed a control mechanism that gave an 'up for up' movement which had always proved quite acceptable in peacetime, but unfortunately all other makes that were issued to H.M. Forces worked the other way. The Velocette was therefore considerably outnumbered by the Nortons and BSAs, etc. with the result that riders were inclined to accelerate up to quite high speeds in second or third gears, and then stamp hard on the gear-lever to change up which of course on a Velocette engaged, or tried to engage a lower ratio. The result was that several instances of broken lay-shaft gears came to light. Rather than be 'the only man in step in the parade' Veloce decided to 'change step' and Irving designed a much simpler gear-lever arrangement that gave the desired 'down for up' movement without making any internal alterations to the gearbox.

The Japanese invasion of whole tracts of territory in the Far East caused considerable complication to manufacture as they overran those places from which tin and rubber were habitually obtained and it became essential to obtain substitutes. The motor-cycle specification had to be denuded of everything that was produced from rubber wherever possible and among those items that were affected were the twist-grip and dummy-grip rubbers and the rubber buffers from the Webb front fork. Canvas grips and Neoprene hose were used in place of the original materials, and experiments were carried out with cast-iron bushes in as many locations as possible as tin is a major constituent of the normal phosphor-bronze that is used for these parts. Those parts that were produced in cast iron were the oil-pump driving worm and all gearbox bushes except that in the sleeve-gear, which it was judged to be unsafe to produce in iron because of the risk to a rider in the event of seizure. To economize in the use of aluminium alloy (also scarce during the war) the gearbox end-covers were modified to include the kickstart-spring housing, and timing covers in cast iron were used. It was even found possible to use cast-iron timing-gear bushes and malleable-steel selector forks were employed.

But as this is not intended to be a technical description of the motor cycles produced during the war it is not proposed to detail further the many things that were done to improve the MAF for its duties. It will suffice to conclude this part by mentioning briefly that as it was expected that the machines would be used in sandy desert conditions provision was made for the fitting of a huge and ugly, but most efficient, air-filter to the top of the fuel-tank entailing a cut-away at the rear to accommodate the hose connection to the atmospheric side of the carburetter. To give better steering qualities in sand the front fork was modified to increase the trail considerably.

In addition to the motor cycles the contract called for the supply of a huge number of spare parts and the production of all this material in a factory already taxed to the utmost by the other contracts for bomb-slips, bomb-hoists, filter components, air-screw feathering pumps, etc., all of the highest priority, became exceedingly difficult. A dispersal factory, or at least part of one, was obtained and most of the fitting and assembling work was transferred to a part of a toffee factory at Greet (Birmingham). This was adjacent to a fireworks factory, too close for peace of mind in wartime conditions! At this place the welding of parts for Sten-guns was carried out in addition to the assembling of the bomb-slips, the bomb-hoists, and the feathering pumps, the last being rig-tested on the premises. Later a sub-contract was taken on to produce and test cabin-blowers.

This last contract was welcomed by the Company as it was work that was likely to provide them with experience that might come in useful in the production of superchargers for post-war racing. (The fact that the use of superchargers would be barred by post-war racing regulations was not of course foreseen!)

There were some compensations for being separated from the parent factory, as with toffee rationed, the opportunities that many of the Veloce workpeople were afforded of obtaining supplies of a most delightful toffee, not only 'off the ration', but quite often as a gift, were much appreciated. The toffee people were only too pleased, in return, to avail themselves of the services of skilled labour in attending to mechanical bothers that occasionally occurred with their equipment.

It may be of general interest that when working at the toffee factory, of which ground-floor area Veloce had taken over half, it was quite impossible to detect the smell of anything but the toffee – at least that is what the Veloce workers thought. But the work carried on by Veloce required the installation of a trichlorethylene degreasing-tank which was located against the brick partition wall between the two workshops of the now divided factory. The Manager of the toffee firm had frequently to complain that the fumes from this installation were pervading his territory and spoiling the toffee, and RWB, the resident Veloce Manager, was called in to take a sniff, to confirm that the complaint was justified. Once inside the toffee factory part of the building however nothing but the smell of toffee could be detected by him. As the complaint was obviously well founded it was essential to take their word for it and the degreasing equipment was moved away from the wall to a place further inside Veloce territory, after which the complaints ceased.

Both the toffee factory and the Hall Green Works escaped hits by bombs during the frequently heavy raids upon Birmingham but one bomb fell just in the middle of the road outside the front gates of the latter but did not explode, and was removed safely afterwards. A Coventry-Climax fire-pump was purchased and installed in a specially built shelter adjacent to a heavily sand-bagged shelter for the squads that undertook fire-watch duties. There were in addition several underground shelters in the ground adjoining the Great Western Railway line that runs past the Works.

While on the subject of air-raid precautions a special look-out tower must be mentioned. This brick structure was built at the corner of the Main Works building over what was later to be the Designs Drawing Office, the roof of which was suitably strengthened by the inclusion of steel girders to carry the weight. Access to it was by means of an external staircase. Certain members of the staff were detailed off to be in readiness to man the tower when the air-raid sirens sounded. In such circumstances the works kept going and it was the 'Jim Crow's' job to sound an electric hooter inside the factory by pressing a switch in the tower when danger threatened so that workers could run to the underground shelters.

Although on many occasions during daylight hours it was necessary for watchers to rush upstairs and man the look-out post it was not necessary to bring the workers out to shelter although on one memorable afternoon an enemy aircraft was observed over Birmingham. Fortunately it circled well away from the Hall Green area and flew away in the direction of Longbridge where it is believed that a few bombs were dropped doing insignificant damage.

As was inevitable with so much Air Ministry work on hand it became increasingly difficult to maintain a steady output of the model MAF and the Company fell behind with deliveries, but by this time the war had taken a more favourable turn for the Allies and the urgent need for motor cycles was past. The Ministry of Supply accordingly cancelled their contract for the balance outstanding leaving Veloce to supply only the remaining spares on order. The resident Government C.I.E.M.E. Inspector was sent elsewhere but before leaving instructed RWB, as the Veloce Executive responsible, that henceforth parts would be accepted on delivery notes signed by Veloce personnel.

There remained, with the spares to be supplied, a number of complete engines which had been bench-tested in the presence of the Government Inspector who stated that they were satisfactory and could be forwarded when suitably packed. The contract stipulated special cases that had to carry a panel of specified size with certain specified information. Special stencils were obligatory to produce the required lettering on the panel. Despite the ordering of all this special material, as soon as the exact requirements were known, it was a very long time before it had all arrived and the engines could be dispatched to their destination.

On arrival at the depot they were promptly refused on the grounds that the notes accompanying them did not carry the signature of an authorized Government Inspector. Veloce explained that they no longer had a Resident Inspector and that the last one had seen the engines tested and had instructed that after his departure dispatch could be authorized by Veloce personnel. His verbal agreement was repudiated by the 'powers that be' and the whole batch of engines was returned at Veloce expense.

No attempt was made to get the notes signed by a Government nominee and when the engines came back they were taken into stock. As matters turned out they were most useful to fit into post-war civilian motor cycles when the production of these was resumed. The engines of course were fitted with the wartime cast-iron timing covers but it was a simple matter to change these and to raise the compression ratio a little. As 'Pool' petrol was still the only fuel on sale this did not amount to much.

By this time there were indications that the war was coming to a favourable conclusion. The production of motor cycles had been stopped and the problem of disposing of all the spares and surplus machines was under consideration. The Company agreed to buy back a number of both military and impressed civilian models, and to accept all 'non-warlike' parts for which they would have an outlet.

In due course used motor cycles began to arrive at Hall Green in batches. Most of these were WD Type MAC and MAF models with a sprinkling of ex-civilian MSS type, all usually very much the worse for wear and neglect. A condition of the purchase of them was that they were to be reconditioned for resale and a price was fixed that was based on pre-war catalogue figures for the equivalent models. Having space at the Greet factory, the reconditioning was at first done there, but such work as frame repairing and enamelling (in black this time) was done at Hall Green.

The whole undertaking was carried out systematically and all machines lost their original identities when they were dismantled. Every one was stripped right down and the main components, after reconditioning, received new numbers that followed the last of the pre-war numbers of their respective types, but these were prefixed by a letter that indicated a Works rebuild. This action was taken because batches of surplus machines were sold to various retailers who also reconditioned them for subsequent resale. The wisdom of so marking the components was demonstrated later when some complaints were received from purchasers who had assumed that 'Works Reconditioned' in dealers' advertisements meant that Veloce had rebuilt them. Perhaps there was no intention to mislead but it certainly appeared not unlikely!

All Veloce rebuilds were restored to standard specification using only

Velocette-type parts, something that could not be said of some of the examples that came to light where mudguards, etc., of other makes had been fitted. For such discrepancies and mechanical faults arising after purchase it was obviously unreasonable to expect that Veloce should accept responsibility.

Despite their main preoccupation with the production of the many aircraft sub-assemblies the directors had not overlooked the fact that plans must be formulated for the post-war working of the factory and some time previously, during convalescence following injury from an explosive incendiary bomb, Phillip Irving had prepared an 'arrangement' drawing of a projected new model.

Nothing much more seems to have been done about it until Charles Udall had to undergo an operation for the removal of his appendix and while recovering from the effects he undertook to take over the post-war design project. He worked quite independently of the ideas that had been put on paper by Irving and in due course produced a much more complete layout. His design became the now well-known LE model more fully described in an earlier chapter.

When the war ended the necessary alterations to the factory and the special equipment upon which production of the LE depended were not completed, and in fact it was to be some time before it was possible to 'launch' the new machine. For the time being therefore a batch of 250 GTP models of 1940 type were produced, all with magneto ignition, and all of them were exported to overseas Agents who had received no new Velocettes for several years. After these machines had been manufactured and shipped a further programme was started that included all the pre-war types except the Mark VIII KTT, and the KTS.

Once again the assembly-line carried motor cycles finished in the beloved and traditional black and gold, and gradually things settled down to a happier and more normal state of affairs. Unfortunately, it was still difficult to get supplies of materials and proprietary equipment as promptly as the firm would have wished in the period of scarcity that existed then, and production had the greatest difficulty in meeting the demand for new motor cycles.

8
Experimental and Limited production models

For obvious reasons what goes on in the Experimental Departments of motor-cycle makers' factories has to be kept secret, and it is difficult even for a firm's employees to get to know anything much about the designs with which experiments are being carried out. All sorts of ideas are tried out; sometimes in the form of modified components fitted to standard models before they are known to be desirable, or even worth while, to be adopted in production.

When there were more independent manufacturers in and around Birmingham as was the case until quite recent times, particular care was essential to keep new developments from the knowledge of rival firms in the vicinity. In order to produce even a prototype machine for road tests at least a few items of ancillary equipment must be obtained from outside suppliers: patterns and core-boxes for the casting of new parts, the castings themselves, electrical items, and perhaps tyres that differ from those with which the firm are normally supplied. Such things are seen by the suppliers' employees and many others and so, to the curious, and to anyone interested in possible future developments, it soon becomes evident that something new is afoot.

Road-testers from different firms cannot avoid meeting on the roads radiating from a centre of motor-cycle production, and such men are usually interested in the models issuing from other factories. Seeing a model differing radically from those to which they are accustomed, a tester may ride up alongside the experimental machine in order to get a better look at it, and as trips into the country to get to unfrequented areas require the rider to travel along roads near the factory when going out and when coming home concealment is most difficult.

It was usual to leave off all means of ready identification such as badges and transfers on petrol-tanks, etc., and before a new design is finalized it is not customary to have the maker's name or trade-mark included in the patterns or dies from which the first set of castings are produced. If a new motor cycle is registered, in order to avoid the use of trade number-plates, which always have the licensee's name on their licence, more people can ascertain that a new model is on the stocks. All of which serves to show that the keeping dark of any new project is by no means easy.

The motor-car makers are able more easily to disguise a new design during the road testing by cloaking it in a form of 'body' that gives nothing away to prying eyes, but with cycles, upon which the major assemblies are all exposed, identification is much easier.

While wishing to include something about experimental Velocettes that have never been put into regular production the authors have realized that their information on the subject is sparse. But as those designs that for some reason or other have never got further than the workshop, or perhaps under one brief road testing are often interesting examples of motor-cycle design an attempt has been made to give at least a few details of activities of the Veloce 'holy of holies'.

Elsewhere in this work reference is made to a two-stroke machine that was experimental but got much further than preliminary road testing. This very interesting machine included an engine having a mechanically operated poppet inlet-valve and avoided the limitations of timing imposed upon the induction period by the conventional piston-controlled port of the normal two-stroke engines. Previous to this a two-stroke Velocette engine is understood to have been fitted with two carburetters, one at each side of a cylinder modified to provide two inlet-ports, but it has not been possible to get further details after such a lapse of time since it was used.

The machine with the poppet inlet-valve was ridden in the 250 cc class of the Isle of Man TT by Fred Povey who was then Veloce Chief Tester. The object of constructing this engine was to obtain greater power in order to compete on more even terms with the four-stroke engines that by then were using overhead valves and had overcome the valve troubles with which they had previously been plagued.

Still less is known, however, about an interesting single-cylinder two-stroke engine of some 250 cc which was to be supercharged from a separate pumping cylinder that was situated behind the working cylinder approximately in the position normally occupied by the magneto of the contemporary models. The piston within this cylinder was reciprocated by an articulating-rod from the normal component.

After the two designs mentioned Percy Goodman realized that if greater power was required it would be better to design an up-to-date four-stroke motor, and not to add expensive complications to two-strokes, the consensus of opinion then being that two-stroke engines had reached the practical limit of development.

During February 1928 a new form of motor-cycle sport known as 'dirt-track racing' hit the headlines when a crowd estimated at 20,000 attended a meeting held by the Ilford Motor Cycle and Light Car Club at High Beech, near Epping. Historically, this was the first successful large-scale meeting to be held in the U.K. and with the almost complete absence of any professionals (apart from a few Australian nationals who had contributed to the birth of the sport in their home country) this was clearly the province of the amateur. The wave of enthusiasm that swept throughout the country as a result led to the rapid growth of many tracks in the London area and the provinces. It was not long before manufacturers added a special dirt-track model to their catalogue in an endeavour to capture their share of this promising new market.

Veloce Limited were not so favourably placed, since they did not manufacture a standard 500 cc model at that time. But they could not resist the temptation and during July 1929 they introduced their own dirt-track model, virtually an overbored KTT engine driving via a countershaft and mounted in a specially constructed frame.

The main requirement for this type of racing was a short wheelbase frame that would not be subjected to the 'whip' that could be tolerated in a normal road model. Apart from the effect that this would have on the handling of the machine, frame whip would often cause the final-drive chain to leave the sprockets and this would be most liable to occur when the machine was subjected to the stresses of cornering round the small, oval-shaped circuit associated with most dirt-track events. A more rigid frame assembly was therefore an essential requirement.

The Works overcame this problem by constructing a special frame having a vertical saddle-tube and torque stays carried from the rear fork-ends to the base of this tube. They joined the tube at differing heights, the nearside stay being much higher to give adequate clearance for left-hand cornering. A small combined petrol- and oil-tank was suspended within the space between the top frame-tubes, with long, flexible leads to the engine. The front forks were of the telescopic type with the braced tubes arranged so that the spring-loaded inner tubes would slide within them and have the 22 in. brakeless front wheel attached to their lower extremities. The main tubes were bridged at their upper ends and were braced by small-diameter girders to give them greater rigidity. Between the top bridge and another fixed to the head stem was a single coil spring to form the main suspension unit. The forks were specially manufactured for dirt-track use by Messrs H. C. Webb.

Transmission was by chain via a countershaft and conventional clutch, this being a modified gearbox. It occupied the space between the normal gearbox lug and the torque stays, to which it was bolted. The rear wheel was also of 22 in. diameter but a 2·50 section dirt-track tyre was fitted in contrast to the tyre of only $2\frac{3}{8}$ in. section used for the front wheel.

There has been much confusion about the true capacity of the over-bored engine, especially after the original Veloce announcement erroneously gave the capacity of the 80 mm $\times$ 81 mm engine as 415 cc. Reference to the capacity tables shows that the correct figure is 411 cc, although even today there are still some references to a 407 cc engine!

In order to accommodate the overbored cylinder-barrel, the cylinder-head (of standard KSS design) had a double-diameter stepped flange joint to match up with the very narrow spigot of the cylinder-liner. No gasket was used. The inlet-port was enlarged to accept a large-bore track-racing carburetter manufactured by Amal, which was fitted with an air-cleaner. An ML racing magneto supplied the sparks. The polished steel flywheels and ribbed crankcase were identical with those of the KTT model, apart from slight relieving of the crankcase-mouth.

The compression ratio of 10·25:1 was achieved by using a specially forged piston with a steep-sided crown and deep valve cut-aways. A $\frac{13}{16}$ in. diameter gudgeon-pin was clearly essential under these conditions, which necessitated the use of alcohol fuel. The cam-box was of standard KSS design and it was not considered necessary to employ the cam-box oil-pump of the KTT model. Performance was enhanced by the use of a special cam (K17/3) that gave the engine the much-needed spread of bottom-end power.

It is alleged that about fifty of these machines were completed, all the engines having the KDT engine number prefix. Not all of them were sold and of those taken back by the Works, the engines were removed and converted into standard 348 cc KTT models. Sad to relate only one complete engine (KDT 149) and one set of cycle parts appear to have survived, although they are in the hands of separate owners with little chance at present of a marriage of convenience being arranged.

For some time after the K model was marketed experiments with many different cams were carried out until satisfactory profiles were obtained, and for the KSS engines the No. 24 in the Maker's List was adopted. Profile No. 23 was used on other types including in later years the KTP.

During the 1930s at least two revolutionary designs of multi-cylinder engines were on drawing-boards at Hall Green but neither of them got beyond the paper stage. The writers have but hazy details of them but give what is remembered to indicate that whatever may be said about Veloce designers being too conservative in their outlook, by those who have not had close contact with them, they have never been without originality of thought, or unwilling to try out ideas by which their products might be improved.

The first design that can be recalled, from occasional peeps over the designer's shoulders, is that of an engine that was to have two banks of cylinders in 'V' formation.

The second was more unconventional, however, and was to have no crankshaft. There were to be two sets of cylinders opposing each other set radially round the driving-shaft. Upon this central shaft there was to be a 'swash-plate' and the double-ended 'pistons' drove this as they reciprocated and operated the swash-plate through the medium of thrust-'slippers' of the type used in the large thrust-blocks on marine propeller-shafts.

This design originated in the fertile brain of P. E. Irving who was then working in the Veloce Designs Drawing Office but had at one time worked for the patentee of the type of thrust-pads that it was proposed to use in the engine. Preoccupation with other more urgent matters apparently prevented the design proceeding beyond the drawing-board.

During 1938 two further experimental designs occupied the attention of the Experimental Department staff. Both of these interesting machines utilized patents[1] taken out in the joint names of P. E. Irving and Veloce Limited.

The first of the two patents, and as things turned out, probably the more important, was that covering the use of movable upper mountings for rear-suspension units by anchoring them in arcuate slots in the frame structure in such a manner as to permit of them being moved along the slots to alter the inclination of the struts or spring units. The effect of

[1] British Patents 511,875 and 521,106, dated 25 August 1939 and 13 May 1940 respectively.

The Velocette model O of which only one example was made. The Second World War and other factors caused the project to be abandoned, but the machine has been preserved at Hall Green and exhibited on various occasions.

An offside view of the model O showing the shaft drive to the rear wheel and the adjustable rear suspension.

setting the units nearer to the vertical position is to increase the load-carrying capacity and so the rear suspension can be adjusted in a matter of moments to cope with a change in load, e.g. a pillion-passenger, or of riders of different weights. Possibly through an oversight the patent is worded to cover the application of the design to motor-cycle rear wheels and in this connection did not preclude a firm of sidecar-makers from using the idea to provide adjustable load-springing for the wheel of one of their chassis. The same principle is used in the Vincent Girdraulic front fork so that Irving was able to use his original idea again without royalties being chargeable!

The system was tried out first upon a 500 cc machine that consisted of a new frame with a 'stressed-skin' rear portion and a swinging-fork rear-springing system incorporating the patented adjustment. As far back as the seat the frame was normal MSS with a 650 B and D Webb fork and MSS engine and gearbox.

The swinging-fork construction was interesting as the pivoted member was fabricated from sheet steel welded up, the actual arms being square in section and of course hollow. But further interest was to be found in the pivot itself which was made so that the axis of the supporting spindle was eccentric to the fixing threads at each side of the pivot where the spindle was secured in the frame structure. This construction enabled the swinging fork to be adjusted relative to the mounting in the frame and permits the centre distance between the rear wheel-spindle and the driving sprocket to be altered by turning the pivot-spindle in the frame.

This simple and most efficient method of adjusting rear-chain tension is the subject of another patent[1] in the joint names of P. E. Irving and Veloce Limited. The method of adjustment has the advantage of better fixing for the wheel-spindle which is always held parallel to the gearbox mainshaft, a condition difficult to maintain with slotted rear fork-ends.[2]

This model was completed by late 1938 but the outbreak of war in 1939 prevented very much being done with it. Such running as it did have showed that a machine that was adequately sprung at the rear end immediately showed up imperfections in the suspension of the front ends. Designs for a telescopic fork had been produced by the Designs Drawing Office some time before but had not gone further than the paper stage.

The 'stressed-skin' frame portion consisted of steel pressings (actually manually produced in the absence of press tools) welded together to form a component from just behind the engine to form a seat-support, and rear mudguard. It included the arcuate slots for the rear suspension units and at its forward end included a tool-box and mounting for the oil-tank. The machine was used quite extensively as a Works hack for sundry business trips during the war but nothing further was done with the design in the direction of producing a model for sale along these lines, although the experience gained with it no doubt helped when designing the LE.

The other machine that was built immediately prior to the war in 1938–9 was the one-off model O, another project that was abandoned, possibly on the score of expected high cost of production and probably limited demand for a machine of its type.

The model O was designed by Phillip Irving and was a 600 cc twin with vertical cylinders, air-cooled, and set side by side on a light-alloy casting to which a four-speed gearbox was attached in unit.

The two crankshafts were geared together and were set transversely in the frame, the right-hand-side one driving the gearbox through a dry-plate clutch. The overhead valves were operated by four push-rods running up the centre of the monobloc cylinder-casting. The one-piece cylinder-head in light alloy was surmounted by a detachable cover over the rockers and valves. Removal of this cover disclosed four rockers lying in the form of

[1] British Patent 521,107, dated 13 May 1940.
[2] This assumes no 'whip' in frame or swinging fork.

The late Tommy Mutton testing a Mark VIII KTT engine in the Test House. It is interesting to note the continued use of a near-vintage oil-tank.

a large 'X' above the head. There was one carburetter. A DC generator mounted parallel to the gearbox provided current for lighting and ignition and a contact-breaker and distributor were at the rear of the camshaft.

Final drive was by exposed propeller-shaft to a bevel-box fixed to the rear end of the tubular built-up pivoted fork, the latter controlled by spring units held at their upper ends in arcuate slots in the 'stressed-skin' frame member. Front suspension was by this time the usual 650 B and D Webb fork.

First impressions of the machine's handling indicated that all was not quite right with the steering geometry as there was an unpleasant tendency for the machine to 'fall' round sharp turns at slow speeds, but at the time no steps were taken to eradicate this defect. The Company's preoccupation with Air Ministry and other wartime contracts prevented development proceeding until happier times returned.

When the opportunity came after the war to carry out some further trials with the model O Eugene Goodman decided that the rake of the steering head-lug was incorrect and he chose rather drastic and unorthodox means to alter the angle with a view to improving the steering characteristics. Removing the tank he cut through the single top-tube of the frame and removed a very short section of it. Drawing the two sawn ends of the tube together by means of a length of steel cable looped round a point behind the cut and the steering-head and a turnbuckle he aligned the ends and had them butt-welded. Additionally, he later had the front fork-girder lengthened. Whatever the wisdom of such unusual means of modifying the angle or rake, or the safety of the machine afterwards, it can be stated truthfully that the steering was very much improved by the process and that no trouble of any kind has been reported arising from frame or fork. Percy Goodman who chanced to come along just as his brother was wielding a hack-saw and cutting through the tube was horrified!

The next experiments were directed towards the launching of the LE model and the spring-frame MAC and MSS range, but after the LE had been in production for some years it was thought that it might be made to appeal to a wider class of customer if it could be produced with a frame

Stanley Woods officially opening the newly erected Test House at Hall Green. There is little difficulty in identifying the Veloce staff present at this ceremony.

that enabled it to be mounted without having to lift a leg over it; in other words, produce it with an 'open' frame.

Accordingly, a standard frame was modified to provide the opening desired and was used daily for some time by one of the directors. But the strength of the structure had been impaired to what was certainly an unacceptable degree and it was decided not to make the alteration standard.

This experiment led to the manufacture of a special new tubular frame to carry an LE power and transmission unit that had the requisite 'open' layout and also had smaller wheels. For reasons unknown to the authors this design was not adopted either.

Motor-cyclists of the 'what might have been' type who indulge in 'pipe-dreams' of so-called 'ideal' motor cycles may speculate upon what sort of a reception from riders a production version of a Viceroy twin 250 cc two-stroke engine mounted in a Valiant frame would have received. Such a model was actually built up and used when conducting road tests with the engine. From all accounts the acceleration was phenomenal!

9
Specials

The cult of the special builder is not as new as some may suspect, for the origins can be traced back to the very early days of motor-cycling. In some respects there is a strange parallel with the situation that exists today, for just after the turn of the century there were few manufacturers and therefore a greater desire existed to construct a machine from a collection of parts in the hope that it would more closely meet the requirements of the owner. As can be expected, the number of parts available during the birth of the industry was somewhat limited. Some of these parts originated from the Continent and were of doubtful or decidedly poor quality. Although much the same situation exists today, with regard to the number of individual manufacturers, the availability and quality of parts has improved beyond all recognition. It is now possible to purchase a number of complete, tailor-made kits that require only a basic mechanical knowledge for their successful assembly and even these can be modified at the constructors whim by a bewildering array of so-called 'customized parts' to give the completed machine a degree of individuality. Money has, to an extent, replaced the older requirement of mechanical ingenuity of the individual. It is not uncommon for any of today's home-assembled specials to cost well in excess of £150.

During the past few years an increasing number of 'marriages' have taken place in which the main component assemblies of two well-known makes have been joined to produce hybrid machines using the engine of one make in the 'chassis' of another. So commonplace have these motor cycles become that under 'portmanteau' names composed from the halves of the original makers' names they have almost become a commercial proposition.

One can only presume that the navigational properties of the model from which the 'chassis' is taken allows the full potential of the engine with which it is provided to be utilized; which in turn gives rise to the inference that the 'chassis' provided for it by its makers was not!

Such now more or less commonplace exchanges of component assemblies is seldom heard of with Velocettes which causes one to wonder whether it is the unorthodox inboard location of the clutch that discourages would-be 'Bitsa' builders, or whether the inherently sound designs produced by Hall Green engineers provide a complete machine that is entirely satisfactory as they supply it.

That the Velocette gearbox and clutch could be incorporated in another make satisfactorily was demonstrated some years ago when a Birmingham motor-cycle dealer fitted a two-stroke type clutch and gearbox to his Scott.

Older readers may remember him; his name is Phillip Cranmore and he won the Colmore Cup in two successive years driving sidecar combinations; first on a Zenith JAP and on the second occasion using a 350 cc BSA.

The term 'special' can cover a wide range of deviations from standard specification; from complete experimental machines to those equipped only with one or two items not included in the normal commercially available model.

'Spring-Heel Jack', the spring-frame Velocette that was taken over to the Isle of Man and tried by expert riders during the TT practice periods, was a 'special' but apart from the rear end of the frame was mainly a normal KSS model.

The fitting of major assemblies from other makes without careful consideration is a practice that must cause some concern to the makers of the machines undergoing such 'transplants'; to employ a word often heard nowadays in connection with surgery upon human beings. Provided the transplants do not affect the safety of the rider all is well, but not long ago many owners of older machines were anxious to exchange their girder forks for telescopics and some exceedingly risky exchanges were made. Not infrequently the effect upon the steering of a motor cycle by the rake and trail of the fork was not realized and of course a different fork designed for another machine altogether may be quite unsuited to the frame into which it is fitted. But apart altogether from these considerations many people failed to take into account that a girder fork does not rely upon the front wheel-spindle to add strength to the fork structure and that the usual spindle in a girder fork is quite inadequate to form the only brace between the two independent side-legs of a telescopic fork.

Apart from the danger aspect of inadvisable conversions and 'transplants' there is the trouble and inconvenience that may be caused when spare parts are required. Specials do not conform to the manufacturer's records of the model in its first state as delivered and therefore the confirmed special-builder is seldom popular with factory service managers.

It should be remembered, however, that the desire to modify a standard production model does not always arise from the need to construct something that has this degree of individuality. Many owners prefer to modify their present machine, which they may originally have purchased new, so that the detail improvements incorporated in later models can be applied to their own machine where there is some definite advantage to be gained. While this process of gradual modification has much to commend it, in terms of extending the life of the machine, it gives rise to problems when the machine is ultimately sold. Worse still, it is anathema to the purist and/or Vintage enthusiast who sees this as a distinct disadvantage with the necessity to restore the machine to its original specification at the earliest possible opportunity.

The more sporting machines have suffered particularly badly in this respect, as instanced by JRC's acquisition of KTT 266 – a much-modified 1930 KTT model painted a brilliant pillar-box red and fitted with such modern attributes as AMC 'Teledraulic' forks, a later-type four-speed gearbox, and competition petrol- and oil-tanks of unknown origin. It was only after much diligent research that it was finally established that this was originally the machine owned and raced by the late H. C. Lamacraft at Brooklands and other speed venues in the early 1930s. It had been raced in some form or other almost continuously until the early post-war years, when it appeared at various grass-track events in the South-Eastern Centre area of the Auto-Cycle Union. Had it not been pensioned off, registered, and used on the road, it may well have suffered the fate of many other machines with a racing history by being literally ridden into the ground and then scrapped. Fortunately, Veloce Limited has always maintained very accurate records of their production and on receipt of details of an engine number can invariably quote the matching frame number, the date on which the machine left the works, the Agent to whom it was sold and, in many cases, the name and address of the first owner. This 'service' alone has materially aided the preservation of many of the more interesting machines of yesteryear that may otherwise have passed unnoticed.

It should not be inferred that the special-builder has been solely responsible for the desecration of many standard production models, thereby contributing to their scarcity. Many interesting and highly ingenious specials have been built over the years and it is significant that the Rules of Membership of the Velocette Owners' Club have been deliberately framed to admit owners and/or constructors of this type of machine. It will be appreciated that it is possible to comment on only a few of the more interesting examples of this type of machine of which the authors have a personal knowledge. They are not necessarily outstanding examples for it is virtually impossible to take a representative sample of the infinite variations on a theme that have been constructed over the years.

The models that have probably received the least attention from the special-builder (with the possible exception of the LE) are the two-strokes. Several 'hybrids', such as that illustrated, have appeared in Vintage MCC trials, where the main requirement has been adequate ground clearance. Engines of the single-port AC type will quite readily fit into the later-type U or USS frame, to permit the use of a saddle-tank, and wired-on tyres. The single-port cylinder-barrel facilitates the use of an upswept exhaust-pipe and it is thus easy to obtain 6 in. ground clearance, even with the original 19 in. wheels. The later twin-port GTP can be used to much the same effect, in virtually unmodified form. But the essential unswept exhaust-pipes, first made available in 1932, are now almost impossible to obtain. It should be explained that the Vintage MCC has never been happy about this modification of old machines, even though it may be possible to convert them back to original specification with comparative ease. A more rigid specification for trials machines now severely restricts modifications that materially change the design of the original production model.

As may be expected, the OHC models have found the most favour with special-builders and they have appeared in all manner of guises, many of which bear little resemblance to the original design. Lest it be thought that special-building is the prerogative of the private individual, it is interesting to recall that a small number of 'hybrids' have originated from the Works. In an earlier chapter mention has been made of a special long-stroke racing engine that was specially constructed by Harold Willis and was subsequently abandoned by him when it showed no particular advantage over the standard 74 mm × 81 mm engine. This engine was eventually fitted into a road machine and if it should still survive, it will undoubtedly baffle many a Vintage enthusiast! An even stranger model appeared in Sussex only a few years ago, which proved virtually unidentifiable in view of the mixture of components used in its construction. Basically, the engine consisted of a 1930 411 cc KDT (dirt-track) crankcase from which the magneto platform had been skilfully removed, to which was fitted a standard 348 cc KTT

A hybrid vintage racing model, virtually a 1930 KSS engine in a 1930 KTP frame and cycle parts.

cylinder-barrel and head, the latter having a KTP cam-box! In short, the engine represented a cross between the KTP and KSS models, with coil ignition and with the dynamo fitted in the conventional position used by the latter model. It would be foolish to credit the Veloce directors in 1930 with the foresight of knowing that in 1968 difficulty in obtaining supplies of magnetos would force them to standardize coil ignition on their single-cylinder models but the prolonged use that this 'special' gave does show that the belt-driven dynamo was well able to provide the electricity for lighting and ignition requirements. Another departure from standard practice on this machine was the use of a Brampton bottom-link front fork together with a special front-hub assembly to suit. Here again the carefully maintained production records of Veloce Limited were consulted to good

170

effect. The entry showed the machine was first registered by the Works and that it had remained in their possession for some while. A more detailed investigation was finally resolved by RWB who recalled the model being specially assembled for one of the Veloce directors during 1930. Yet there were many who would have rejected the machine out of hand as yet another amateur attempt to marry together a miscellany of parts that happened to come to hand.

It was the policy of Veloce Limited to embark on a scheme of gradual improvement to enhance the performance of the various models, rather than to make changes for changes' sake or become involved in the present questionable practice of badge-engineering. The by-product of their policy led to a degree of interchange of parts between the various models that is

A vintage trials 'special'. A 1925 model AC two-stroke engine has been fitted into a 1929 model U frame and cycle parts to give well over six inches ground clearance.

not found in any other make of machine. The KTP model, which was never outstandingly successful on a number of counts, was quite easily converted to KSS specification, for example. There must be a number of such models that can still testify to this; they can be easily identified since the engine number will have the KA prefix. It is possible to build a Vintage racing machine on this principle, which has the advantage of being slightly lighter in weight and permits the fitting of modern racing tyres to the 19 in. diameter wheels. JRC constructed such a hybrid during 1960 which complied with the Vintage racing specification in all respects and was aesthetically pleasing, as the illustration shows. It possessed handling qualities that were quite impeccable.

In the post-war era, after the production of the KSS had ceased, there

The Douglasette, an attempt to fit a Mark II KSS engine into the frame and cycle parts of a Mark V Douglas twin.

This 'do it yourself' frame for an early LE model is made from Dexion slotted angle. Note the unusual riding position and the dropped handlebars.

was an upsurge of interest in fitting the KSS engine and gearbox into the spring frame from the later-type MAC and MSS models. This conversion is not without its problems, particularly if a post-1938 KSS engine with the crankcase suction-filter was used, thereby raising problems with frame clearance due to the close proximity of an unwanted lug. There is also the question of access to the tappets and petrol-tank clearance for the cam-box. Some opted to use the front half of the original frame in order to resolve these problems by the simplest means, but whatever course of action was taken, some very presentable versions of what appeared to be a fully modernized KSS were to be seen.

172

The novelty of owning a twin-cylinder Velocette had obviously appealed to one special-builder, who coupled together two of the early OHC engines side by side in a Norton ES2 frame. A road test by *Motor Cycling* proved none too conclusive since the machine was still being run-in, but there appeared to be some doubt about the standard of roadholding. Unfortunately, the engine came to a premature end when a later owner forgot to turn on the vital oil-tap in the main oil-feed line.

It does not follow that the interchange of parts is restricted solely to those of Veloce origin, although the Velocette special-builder seems to have a particular allegiance in this respect for quite obvious reasons. One particularly enterprising enthusiast in the London area overcame the spring-frame shortage by fitting a KSS engine and gearbox into the frame and cycle parts from one of the torsion-bar-sprung Douglas twins. It was necessary to incline the engine forwards, which caused a tendency for the exhaust to smoke as the result of incomplete scavenging. It was also necessary to fit an elbow joint in the induction system to give the carburetter sufficient clearance. Unfortunately, the finished machine handled badly, due to poor weight distribution.

In the racing sphere there has been much activity, particularly with regard to the reduction of capacity of the Mark VIII engine to 250 cc in an endeavour to overcome the immediate post-war shortage of competitive lightweight racing models. Arthur Wheeler, the Velocette dealer of Epsom, was particularly successful with his own 250 cc KTT which

JRC on his much-modified KSS model while performing the role of BEMSEE Travelling Marshal at Snetterton. This machine started life as a quite standard 1938 model.

A superb KSS/KTT 'special' constructed by Ivan Rhodes of Derby.

174

among other awards won the coveted Governor's Trophy in the Ulster Grand Prix. The now legendary 250 cc specials built by Bennie Rood and Doug Beasley are so well known as to obviate the need for further mention. And there were other lesser known examples that helped boost the lightweight entry in major road-racing events.

Mention must also be made of the 'Covel', a 500 cc racing machine built by Hedley Cox, a one-time employee of Veloce Limited. This consisted of two reduced-capacity KTT engines spline-coupled together to give the effect of a vertical twin. Sad to relate it was not the success intended even if the exhaust-note was quite delightful! Cox finally abandoned the project to concentrate on a very special twin KTT with swinging-fork suspension but this too lapsed into obscurity when he emigrated to the U.S.A. The 'Covel II' is reputed to be with Ralph Seymour, in his workshop at Thame. During recent years he has supported road racing by entering a special consisting of a KTT engine and gearbox fitted into a modern 'featherbed'-type frame. It is enthusiasts such as these who have striven to keep the name Velocette in International road-racing events, even though there is but faint chance of success. He is now constructing a number of very potent-looking 'Metisse' specials, using a Venom engine and gearbox.

The M series of push-rod models have also featured in the domain of the special-builder. One of the earliest examples originated at the Works, where what may be termed a true MSS model was specially constructed for a Works director. Basically this was a standard MSS engine and gearbox fitted into a KSS frame and cycle parts. It will be appreciated that the Velocette nomenclature, if correctly applied, should refer to the standard MSS model as the MTS.

Several Velocette dealers have been actively associated with the development of the production Viper and Venom models, including Reg Orpin of L. Stevens Limited, Geoff Dodkin, Mike Tompkinson, and Arthur Taylor. Indeed, the last had already made quite a name for himself with some very quick push-rod models long before the Viper and Venom models came into being. Mention must also be made of the very clever desmodromic valve conversion by BMG Motorcycles of Ilford that was available in kit form for a short while, until rising costs rendered it uneconomic to produce. It is interesting to note that the Works now manufacture separate engines and gearboxes for installation in other cycle parts, thereby aiding the export drive. The American Indian model is but one example of a machine using these parts as standard.

As may be expected, the smaller capacity models have, in the main, escaped the attentions of the special-builder, although a very ingenious LE model was seen in the car park at Snetterton where the main 'frame' was composed of Dexion slotted angle bolted together with untrimmed ends, and the petrol-tank was from a Valor oil-stove! There has also been a go-kart employing the same basic engine unit. No doubt some other interesting variations have been tried, for even the Works found that a quite lively 'hack' could be created by marrying together the Viceroy engine with the Valiant cycle parts. It is probably fair to say that it has all been tried at some time or another, even if the outcome sometimes failed to match up to the expectations.

In referring earlier in this chapter to 'navigational' shortcomings in certain makes of motor cycle possibly influencing their owners to seek satisfaction by mounting the more satisfactory power unit in a 'chassis' nearer their ideal, a true story bearing on the subject might not be out of place:

A party from Hall Green was at the M.I.R.A. track carrying out some high-speed tests on Vipers and Venoms, and, as is quite usual, testers from other factories were similarly engaged. During one of the pauses in the proceedings the rider of one of the machines from a rival concern stopped alongside one of the Velocettes. Naturally, Don Harrison the Veloce Tester glanced at the other machine and, noticing that one of the frame tubes leading to one of the suspension units was broken, drew the rider's attention to it. The man expressed surprise, saying that he had not noticed it.

To this somewhat surprising answer Don could not help retorting that the standard of 'navigation' of the model could not be very good if the fracture of a frame tube made it no worse!

10
Trials and Six-Day events

When reviewing the broader aspects of motor-cycle sport, the name 'Velocette' tends to be more closely associated with racing and other high-speed events where their successes have been widely publicized. In consequence, it is seldom realized that the marque has been almost as successful in other spheres, such as trials and six-day events. Admittedly, most of these successes were achieved in the period between the two world wars, when the interest in motor cycles was at its zenith and there was not the degree of specialization that is prevalent today. The machines of that era had a degree of flexibility almost unknown today that rendered them suitable for almost any type of event with only a few minor changes in their specification. It was by no means unusual for a sports model to be used for trials events during the winter or for a standard road model to be used equally successfully in much the same capacity. Furthermore, the riders, who were usually of amateur status, stood more than a reasonable chance of figuring in the awards list at the end of the event. They rode their machines to the meeting and back home again at the conclusion. In consequence they often covered a very considerable mileage on the road in addition to that of the event and they would have been mildly surprised if they experienced trouble with a minor breakdown.

Apart from the satisfaction of taking part in an event and completing the course, it was the ultimate ambition of each competitor to win one of the coveted major awards or, failing that, to win a gold or a silver medal. One of the earliest successful attempts on record for a Veloce rider is that of Eugene Goodman, who rode a 293 cc Veloce in the 1913 Auto-Cycle Union Spring Trial to gain a Silver Medal and a First Class Certificate. He was accompanied by James Ingham, mounted on a 499 cc model, who achieved the same distinction.

It should be remembered that a trial at this time was a much more severe test of man and machine than its namesake today. Invariably a very considerable mileage was involved with many steep hills and tracks that had surfaces far worse than those of the dusty unmetalled 'main' roads. Taking the 1913 Spring Trial as an example, this event started and finished at Dorking and embraced 120 miles of the Surrey lanes. Many of the notorious hills such as Pebblecombe (1 in 5), Ranmore Common Hill (1 in 4 with 6 in. of sand), and Cracknorth Hill (1 in 7 with wet sand) were included, and the entrants rode standard road models complete with all the usual accessories including acetylene lighting.

Eugene obviously enjoyed taking part in this type of event for his name, in conjunction with that of James Ingham, was included in the Register of Form, a 'league' table of the more successful trials riders that was compiled and published by *Motor Cycling* at regular intervals. In just three trials he had amassed the grand total of 200 marks; it was customary to award marks for a meritorious performance at this time and not deduct them as is common practice today.

Later in the year another name appeared as a Veloce entrant, although there is no record of the capacity of his mount. A. R. Sharp was the sole Veloce rider in the Birmingham MCC's 'Land's End Trial' in a total field of thirty-three starters. The run was exceptional by the fact that there were no stops or checks for meals so that competitors had to carry their food with them or make up time if they stopped *en route*. In consequence it was necessary to average 20 mph over the whole distance of 294 miles, a formidable task with the road conditions that prevailed at that time. Sharp is recorded as having signed off on time at Penzance, but it is not known what award he gained.

The greatest event of the year was the ACU Six-Day Trial, an annual event that on this occasion attracted a record entry of 170 competitors. Eugene Goodman and James Ingham entered their machines in the respective capacity classes, little knowing what lay before them.

The event proved to be the most arduous of the series so far held and there were numerous protests about the freak hills, appalling surfaces, and water-splashes over 2 ft deep that nearly led to a strike of the riders. Most of the machines that completed the course would not have survived another day and there were many that fell by the wayside. Eugene had the misfortune to retire on the last day of the event, but James Ingham completed the course to win a Gold Medal, after a very creditable performance culminating with a grand total of 102 marks gained. This performance was all the more remarkable on account of the severity of the event.

Clearly Eugene meant to vindicate his untimely retirement in the Six-Day event, for only a matter of a few weeks later he returned to Carlisle while taking part in the Birmingham MCC's Birmingham–Carlisle–Birmingham Reliability Trial. This time he was successful and honour was satisfied.

The major events of the year following continued in much the same pattern, with emphasis on the 'toughening up' of courses and time schedules. But on 4 August war was declared, and all events were terminated for the duration.

As far as the future of the trials type of event was concerned, the period that followed the war can be regarded as transitory. In 1914 a strike of riders had taken place during the ACU Six-Day event held in July, and this was considered by many to be the first sign that events could no longer continue in the old established manner. After the war there was even more incentive for change since it was recognized that the motor cycle had now successfully emerged from the experimental era to become a much more sophisticated device with improved suspension, variable-speed gears, enhanced performance, and greater reliability. The post-war 'boom'

178

induced many new manufacturers to produce motor cycles and those who were already well established offered an extended range of models to meet the requirements of most potential customers. Local clubs played their part by taking more interest in the sporting type of event and they promoted competitions for their members that were more parochial in nature, so that competitors would not have to ride long distances in order to take part.

A secondary factor, which should not be overlooked, was the gradual improvement of the main roads throughout the country, brought about by necessity through the increasing amount of traffic that used them. The club official, when planning a route for a forthcoming event, tended to make greater use of tracks and other routes across rough terrain in order to introduce the appropriate competitive element in what was gradually developing into more a test of man than machine. Before long, most of the smaller events were run on 'pocket-handkerchief' courses that were vastly different in nature than those used hitherto. Comparatively few clubs continued to run the really long-distance events, although there are some that continue to follow tradition and run events such as the Colmore Cup Trial and the Victory Trial that still exist today. However, it should not be assumed that the whole scene changed virtually overnight. More than a decade was to elapse before the type of event that is common today began to be generally accepted.

In 1919 Veloce Limited again supported the ACU Six-Day event. Eugene Goodman was the sole entry, now riding a two-stroke; the four-stroke models had been abandoned in the post-war production programme. The event was reputed to be the most severe of any in the series, but Eugene had a trouble-free run and acquired a Gold Medal. The 1920 Velocette Catalogue makes proud mention of this achievement and that in spite of the severity of the test no appreciable wear could be detected even after a further 3,000 miles had been covered. The actual medal-winning machine formed the centre-piece of the Veloce Stand at the 1919 Olympia Show, supported by the claim that the Company attached greater importance to this type of event since the usual club or reliability trials were of little value in proving the lasting qualities of their machines!

No doubt encouraged by their 1919 success, they decided to field a team of three riders in the 1920 event, all on identical D2 models. The riders were Eugene Goodman, George Denley, and Stan Jones who gave brilliant performances to win three Gold Medals and take third place in the Manufacturers' Team Prize. It is worth recording that the Veloce team made the fastest time on the observed hill, accomplished clean ascents of Park Rash Terror and Summer Lodge Hill, and for good measure completed eight laps at over 40 mph round Brooklands after a hard run of nearly 1,000 miles.

In 1921 the Veloce team ventured further afield. George Denley, in company with two other riders, A. Berger and Ŕ. Humphreys, entered for the Paris–Nice Trial, a long-distance event for which the President of the Republic of France was to donate a cup as the Premier Team Prize. All

E. F. Goodman, S. J. Jones, and G. Denley, the Velocette Team in the 1920 ACU Six-Day Trial. Each won a Gold Medal in this event.

Eugene Goodman pauses for a brief consultation with the late Harry Thorne during the 1920 ACU Six-Day Trial.

A. Berger, G. Denley, and R. Humphreys after their successful 1–2–3 win in the Paris–Nice Trial of 1921.

G. Denley and E. F. Goodman on a more desolate part of the Six-Day Trial course. This was probably the 1921 event.

three won Gold Medals, finishing first, second, and third in order of merit – a highly creditable performance for standard production models. Needless to say the Team Prize was a foregone conclusion and they won the President's Cup, much to the delight of the French agent.

Many of the successes recorded during the post-war period could be attributed to George Denley, a brilliant rider who had the ability to extract the very maximum from his diminutive mount. He was a good all-rounder too, for he climbed Corkscrew Hill, claimed to be the worst hill in Wales, at his very first attempt and then showed his versatility by taking seventh place in the Junior TT of 1921, riding a 250 cc two-stroke. Perhaps his most outstanding performance at this time was his success with a two-stroke and sidecar in the Victory Trial. He won a Gold Medal and conquered Wyche Cutting, alleged to have a gradient of 1 in 2·8!

His other successes of note in the 1921–2 season included a Gold Medal and a £50 prize, together with the Travers Trophy (valued at £200) in the 1921 event organized by the Newcastle and District MCC, a Gold Medal in the Lycett Trophy Trial and the Sangster Cup Trial, two events organized by the Birmingham MCC, a Gold Medal in the Leicester and District MCC's Bowerman Cup Trial, and a Bronze Medal in the West Midland ACU Open Trial for his performance with a $2\frac{1}{4}$ hp Velocette and sidecar. Stan Jones won a Gold Medal in the Travers Trophy event for the best performance by a private owner and three other Velocette riders, J. M. Philpot, G. Povey, and L. Judge, gained medals in the West Midland event.

It is worth recording that a lady rider, Mrs M. C. Jennison, figured among the award winners of the year by being awarded a Gold Medal together with the Best Silver Cup and a special prize for her performance in the Grimsby MCC's Winter Reliability Trial. She was later to achieve even greater distinction by being the first lady rider to top 70 mph at the ACU speed trials held in Grimthorpe Park, still Velocette mounted.

In the Scottish Six-Day event, a gruelling test for man and machine, M. T. Calderon won a Silver Medal and in the Scottish Open Two-Day Trial, a Gold Medal was won by W. T. Tiffen, Senior, a name closely associated with other Veloce successes in trials events. Tiffen also won a similar award in the Eskdale M and MCC's Reliability Trial held during the same year. B. Hill surprised many by winning a Certificate of Merit for his performance in the Scott Trial of 1921, a formidable annual event of which much has been written. He was the only rider to complete the arduous eighty-four-mile course on a lightweight machine. There could be little doubt that the lightweight Velocette two-stroke was achieving a measure of success that was the envy of many manufacturers of larger capacity machines.

The two brothers Cope, Arthur and Frank, were both active trials riders during this era, on occasions using the experimental poppet inlet-valve two-stroke machine that has been mentioned in an earlier chapter. It had been relegated to less exacting work after the unfortunate magneto trouble that eliminated it from the 1924 Lightweight TT; yet another example of the versatility of the post-Kaiser War motor cycle.

Corkscrew Hill, the Welsh terror, that was successfully climbed by George Denley on a 250 cc two-stroke at his very first attempt.

Several rear wheel-spindle breakages were experienced by Arthur but the substitution of a taper roller-bearing K-type rear hub and wheel satisfactorily overcame this source of trouble. Still later, and after Arthur had retired from trials riding, Frank took over the machine and fabricated a water-jacket upon the Velocette's cylinder and equipped the machine with a radiator. With the machine so modified, he attached a light sidecar and entered for the Colmore Cup Trial, then one of the chief events of the annual competition calendar.

As a customer of Copes and a friend of Frank and Arthur, RWB was co-opted to act as Frank's passenger for the Trial which, as was customary

George Denley shows his versatility with a sidecar outfit during one of the Victory Trial events.

in those days, was a whole-day run. The event started in the early morning at Stratford on Avon, took in an extensive circuit of the Cotswolds, and finished in the evening at the place from which it started.

On the morning of the start the weather was very cold, all roads were covered with frost, and the prospect of a whole day seated in a rather small and quite open sidecar was not an alluring one. However, a start was made from Hagley Road, the 'brave' passenger being handed a rubber hot-water bottle by a sympathetic Mrs Arthur Cope who had risen to see the departure. All went well until Shirley was reached on the Birmingham–Stratford road, where the engine began to show signs of the piston tightening. The crew decided that the cold oil was not running too freely down the long pipe from the oil-tank to the oil-pump on the engine – there were no multi-grade oils then! The outfit was stopped and the sparking-plug removed to permit a little oil to be dripped into the cylinder to help the piston until perhaps the temperature might rise a little and the oil flow more readily. Unfortunately, the water in the rubber bottle was quite cold by now!

On restarting and driving at reduced speed Stratford was reached safely and the engine seemed to be running much better, so that it was decided that a start should be made when the time came.

As wheel grip is improved by employing much lower pressures than the makers specify for their tyres (or so it was believed anyway) Frank had reduced the pressure in the rear tyre to a point that he judged would afford the wheel grip required to negotiate the always slippery and difficult hills that were always a feature of the Colmore. His forethought proved useful in enabling the outfit to surmount 'clean' many of the observed sections including the notorious Mill Lane hill just outside Cheltenham, which finishes with a section of deep leaf-mould between steeply sloping banks. The willing little engine simply romped up this gradient, earning the Press comment: 'On the steepest part of Mill Hill Cope's Velocette had so much power that it four-stroked occasionally!'

Unfortunately, the stony nature of the Cotswold lanes caught Frank Cope unawares and a sharp stone caused a 'concussion cut' in the insufficiently inflated rear inner-tube. The loss of time this brought about robbed Frank of a premier award, and success to a highly original engine.

As may be expected, the introduction of the model K in 1926 provided the opportunity for even greater participation in trials events, with an engine capable of providing greater power. Many famous names previously associated with the 249 cc two-strokes changed their allegiance to the 348 cc OHC model and their successes continued unabated. Only a year after the introduction of the model K, W. T. Tiffen won a Silver Cup in the Scottish Six-Day Trial and a Gold Cup in the International Six-Day event, to name but two of the more outstanding achievements of that year.

In writing of Velocettes and the interest that Eugene Goodman took in riding in reliability trials it is relevant to state that he favoured the long-distance type of competition that placed more emphasis upon the reliability of the machine to gain an award than the balancing ability of the rider to surmount some slippery, or otherwise tricky surface without using his feet to maintain balance.

And so late as the late 1920s he used to enter himself in the Midland Cycling and Athletic Club's Annual Birmingham–Holyhead–Birmingham Twenty-four-Hour Trial. This event, some 300-odd miles in length, took in many severe Welsh hills between the morning start from Holyhead and the finish in the evening of the second day back in Birmingham.

Usually he was accompanied by one or two enthusiastic private Velocette-owners who also enjoyed the rather free and easy night run to Holyhead at which place a stop of about one hour was made for breakfast.

The fact that the regulations specified a night route that allowed stops for supper and a later stop for coffee, exclusive of the running time, meant that as the timing required only the maintenance of a 20 mph average riders were not called upon to hurry during the night. The first official stop was for supper that was laid on in a café at Shrewsbury.

It was during one of these Twenty-four-Hour Trials that Eugene found out that all transmission chains were not identical. He had experienced some trouble with the rear chain of his mount on the way to Shrewsbury, and, having no spare links for the Coventry chain with which it was fitted, wished to borrow a link from one of the Velocette privateers. Their machines were older and had been built when Veloce were fitting Renold chains as standard equipment. But the two makers employed different diameter pins and roller-bushes and Renold parts would not fit the Coventry chain.

All this took place before the days of mergers, amalgamations, and take-overs and there was a choice of several makes of chain available to manu-facturers: Coventry, Brampton, Perry, and Renold to mention four only.

Eugene lost interest in the Twenty-four-Hour Trial after the organizers began introducing sections into the course that had to be negotiated during the late-afternoon run on the homeward journey, when riders were tired and hardly in good shape to excel at 'balancing acts'. Almost level sections over muddy lanes which placed no stresses on the machines but over which a rider lost marks for putting a foot down did not appeal to him at all, and he never entered the competition again.

In this connection most of the competitors of the earlier part of the between the wars period had no time for those who did not ride to and from the courses of the trials in which they competed, but then, as has been mentioned elsewhere, machines had not become so specialized and com-petitors were real motor-cyclists and not merely jockeys, or as Harold Willis so aptly described them: 'Posh Conductors'!

The advent of the 1930s brought about the beginnings of a need to design a special type of machine that was still basically a road machine yet incorporated a number of modifications that would make it especially suitable to use in 'off the road' competition events of the trials type. The main requirements were greater ground clearance, some weight reduction through the removal of all non-essential fittings such as the lighting set, and a low-compression 'soft' engine that was very responsive at low speeds. In some respects the OHC design that formed the mainstay of the Veloce production programme was not particularly well suited to these require-ments, although it was possible to modify the machines in various respects and to use some of the later optional fittings such as the high-level exhaust-pipes first catalogued in 1932. The amateur enthusiast is nothing if not ingenious and it is largely to his credit that success in the 'open' event continued unabated.

W. T. Tiffen was a regular Silver Cup winner in the Scottish Six-Day Trial, riding his 348 cc OHC model and perhaps one of his more memor-able rides was in the 1932 event when he used a machine fitted with the newly introduced four-speed gearbox. He won the George Albert Memorial Trophy and a Silver Medal and he rode throughout the whole week without ever opening the tool-box. By now his son, Billy Junior, was also riding in trials events and making a name for himself as a result. He was one of the first successful riders to make use of the 248 cc MOV model after its introduction in 1933.

Another rising star at this time was Stuart Waycott, a Bristol Velocette dealer who had already amassed several awards with a sidecar outfit. One of his first major wins was the Hosking Trophy in the 1933 West of England Trial, using an OHC engine. Thereafter his name figured promi-nently in the awards list of most of the major 'opens', usually while riding a 348 cc OHC combination. Occasionally he used an overbored version for which the varying capacities of 407 cc and 415 cc have been quoted in the motor-cycling Press. It was not until 1936 – his first attempt in the

Scottish Six-Day Trial – that he changed over to the new 495 cc MSS engine and was duly rewarded by winning a Silver Cup for his performance.

During this period many others had contributed to the imposing list of Hall Green successes. Two particularly familiar names associated with the OHC model were F. E. Bunn and T. C. Whitton, both solo riders. Sub-Lieutenant W. G. Hornby of the Royal Naval Engineering College, Devonport, won the 1934 Arbuthnot Trophy, a tough 'classic' event open only to the Royal Navy, Royal Marines, Royal Naval Reserve, and the Royal Naval Volunteer Reserve. A year earlier, a name not often associated with the Velocette marque appeared in the awards list for the Scott Trial. The rider was no less a person than H. G. Tyrell-Smith, better known for his road-racing successes with other makes. He rode a 348 cc OHC model and won the Special Prize for the best newcomer to this event. In 1935 Tiffen Senior decided to make this year's International Six-Day Trial his last. This was the twenty-second in the series that he had contested and he retired gracefully from International competition with the award of a Gold Medal. A year later he achieved the rare distinction of winning the Scott Trial outright, to become the proud possessor of the A. A. Scott Memorial Trophy. This is the only occasion on which a Velocette has won the major trophy, a truly magnificent achievement in view of the severity of the event.

By now, Stuart Waycott, in common with a few other of the more successful riders, was receiving the support of Veloce Limited. The biggest event in the calendar was the International Six-Day Trial, an event in which the Velocette riders invariably won Gold Medals. In view of the excellent performance by Waycott in the 1935 event, as a member of the Sunbeam MCC B team, he was a natural selection for the 1936 British International Trophy Team. Accordingly, Percy Goodman decided to build for him a one-off 494 cc OHC sidecar outfit that also made use of the Harold Willis 'Loch Ness Monster' dual-seat used in the 1934 TT, and what was virtually a slightly detuned 500 cc TT engine. The completed outfit, registered COF 496, performed exceptionally well and Waycott scored his first International success when the Team completed the trial unpenalized to win the International Trophy for Great Britain.

There has been much conjecture as to whether any thought was given to marketing a 500 cc OHC model as an adjunct to the current production programme at that time. It has been claimed that no production 500 cc OHC model was ever planned, but it would seem reasonable to expect that some provision was made for this eventuality when the Mark II KSS and KTS models were first announced in 1935. The crankcase was made very much larger than would have contained flywheels of the diameter for a 350 cc engine; there is sufficient clearance for the MSS flywheels, for example. Since the engine was to be used in a frame very similar to that of the MSS and since there was the precedent of the MOV and MAC models in one frame, it seems probable that the production of a 500 cc OHC model, using many parts of the existing Mark II KSS and KTS models must have seemed an attractive proposition. (It should also be remembered that the immediately preceding KSS and KTS models were virtually the same machines except for wheels and mudguards.)

The fact that Willis had produced the 500 cc racer and a production 500 cc OHC would have made a useful model to offer as a machine benefiting from the Works racing experience supports this line of thought. It should be appreciated that much of what is discussed round the Board Room table would not necessarily have been disclosed to the staff, even though Willis had a seat on the Board. In consequence it cannot be denied that a production 500 cc OHC model appeared to offer a very attractive proposition from many aspects and must have been seriously discussed, even if all of these suppositions are not well founded.

Stuart Waycott was again selected for the British International Trophy Team in 1937. In order to match the power of the 600 cc BMW sidecar outfits, Percy Goodman decided to increase the capacity of COF 496 to 596 cc during the period that preceded the 1937 International Six-Day Trial. The engine was now so tall that it was necessary to insert a 'trap-door' in the petrol-tank, in order to gain access to the sparking-plug. The Willis reference to the 'Great Pyramid of Cheops', to which he likened the pyramid-shaped form of the original Mark II cylinder-head, was probably even more appropriate! Again the British Trophy Team comprising V. N. Brittain (348 cc Norton), G. E. Rowley (346 cc AJS), and W. S. Waycott (596 cc Velocette sidecar) scored an outright win and the International Trophy remained in Britain.

It is fortunate that COF 496, the largest OHC Velocette ever built, is still in existence today, although it is reputed to have been 'modified' by the addition of an hydraulic damper in place of the girder-fork spring and the replacement of the original rear wheel by a Triumph spring-hub version. The machine is now honourably retired and its use is restricted to the road. In the early post-war days it was raced in the West Country at various grass-track events, with moderate success. No doubt many will remember its appearance at the old track, Farleigh Castle, ridden by Reg Lewis.

Another interesting facet of the 1937 International Six-Day Trial related to the entry made by Billy Tiffen Junior, who was now making an admirable substitute for his father. He used the same 348 cc engine that he had used in the previous year's Junior TT event. Even though there was an increasing tendency towards machine specialization, the pre-war engine undoubtedly possessed a degree of flexibility that is virtually unknown today. His reward was a Gold Medal, which no doubt helped compensate for his retirement in the 1936 Junior TT.

The poppet induction-valve two-stroke engine mentioned earlier was still in active service at this time, although it now fulfilled a vastly different role. Still used by Frank Cope, it had been fitted to power the rear wheel of his BSA three-wheeler. This unique double-engined tricar special was a familiar sight at many of the 'classic' long-distance events in which Frank still participated with some success.

Billy Tiffen won the Colmore Cup Trial and he was ably supported by

W. T. Tiffen Senior and Junior with the awards they have won on Velocettes. This photograph was taken in December 1937.

Stuart Waycott with his MSS sidecar outfit during the Wye Valley Trial of March 1938. The broken front mudguard stay denotes the severity of the event.

Stuart Waycott who won a First Class Award in this event and in the following Kickham Memorial Trial. Later, Waycott won the Chekko Cup in the Victory Trial and made best performance with a sidecar in the Bemrose Trial.

Waycott was a natural selection for the 1938 International Six-Day Trial team and with this in mind Percy Goodman made some further modifications to his 595 cc sidecar outfit. A new frame, of stronger section, was built having a top tube that no longer had the characteristic set to clear the cam-box. The steering-head angle was slightly modified to give lighter steering and the fork links were considerably strengthened. The compression ratio of the engine was raised and a swill-pot was incorporated in the petrol-feed to the carburetter in an attempt to obviate the tendency to cut out when cornering at high speed.

Tiffen's machine had a racing frame, tank, and front wheel since he had been selected for the British Vase A Team in the same event. A saddle-cum-rear pad was also fitted in conjunction with two sets of foot-rests – one pair further back in the frame. Obviously the speed test at the conclusion of the event was now of much greater significance.

In the preceding Scottish Six-Day Trial, Waycott won the sidecar class with his 495 cc outfit and was awarded the MacNaughton Challenge Trophy and Silver Cup. He lost only ten marks. Billy Tiffen won a Silver Cup despite the handicap of riding with an injured ankle.

Four riders made up the British Team for the 1938 International Six-Day Trial, the additional member being Jack Williams (348 cc Norton). The team achieved the hat-trick and retained the International Trophy for the third time running. As luck would have it, Waycott was the only member of the Trophy Team to be penalized; he lost nine marks through his misunderstanding of the delay card system. In the Vase A Team, Tiffen completed the event without loss of marks. The other members of this team were less fortunate and Britain emerged as runners-up to Germany in this sector of the competition.

Motor Cycling arranged to test the Trophy-winning machines and Graham Walker, who had taken on the role of Editor earlier that year, rode as passenger to Stuart Waycott. Waycott claimed he could get 68 mph in third gear (5,500 rpm) when hard pressed and 75 mph in top. This was hardly surprising for Charles Udall claimed the engine would produce over 37 bhp. Even during the initial testing period at Donington, Philip Irving with Peter Goodman in the chair, had circulated only just below the existing track record. Yet it was quite normal to change from third to top gear at around 35 mph, such was the flexibility of the engine.

For the first time tribute was paid to Waycott's passenger, V. Munday. His name and the part he played in the success of man and machine had been overlooked only too frequently in the past by the motor-cycling Press in their reports of events.

The sidecar incorporated many ingenious features, including a whole array of tools retained by aeroelastic and clips behind the seat-squab. A

190

special design of wheel brace had been included that held the wheel nuts in magazine fashion after they had been removed. The sidecar chassis was designed by Phillip Irving and it employed an unusual swing-axle suspension system with a 'live' sidecar-wheel axle. All wheels were interchangeable, using the model KSS three-bolt arrangement. A spare was carried at the rear of the sidecar body.

Access to the chassis was gained by withdrawing a bolt, which in turn permitted the sidecar body to be tilted. A rubber tube was attached into which the detachable wheel-spindle could be inserted after its removal. Waycott had once learned of a rider who lost his Gold Medal through getting dirt on the spindle threads.

When the 'open' trials season commenced in October 1938 it was announced that as from 1 January 1939 a new regulation would be introduced that would necessitate the use of standard tyres in all future trials events. The organizers of the West of England Trial decided to implement this regulation in advance and they became the first club to ban competition tyres for many years. However, Stuart Waycott rose to the occasion and showed that this change would be of little concern to him. He won *The Motor Cycle* Sidecar Trophy with the loss of fifty-eight marks.

It was now becoming evident that the whole pattern of the trials type of event was changing and that there was increasing competition from other manufacturers, many of whom were prepared to market special trials models. Out of twenty-four 'open' trials held during 1938, Velocettes had made the best individual performance twice and had won the sidecar award three times. It was no longer sufficient to rely on the devoted few if success was to be maintained in this sector of the sport.

Before much attention could be given to the situation, the political tension in Europe had increased to the point where it was of concern to all. Germany was now unified under the Nazi Party and there were many who knew that it would not be long before some form of conflict proved inevitable. The German bid for national prestige in sport could be traced back to 1936 and there had been severe criticism about the excessive military support given to German competitors in the International Six-Day motor-cycling event. Success at all costs was now vital to the all-powerful Third Reich.

It was agreed that the 1939 event would be held in the Salzburg area of Germany, following the success of their Vase Team in the previous year's event. But the support from Britain was not quite as great as had been anticipated, with a total of only sixty-one entries. Possibly the average British entrant realized that he had little to gain in relation to the expenditure involved when the chance of success was so heavily weighted against him. The German competitors would have even greater national support on their home ground and many regarded the results of the 1939 TT as a foretaste of what was to come. Perhaps even more important, there was speculation on whether the event would be held at all as the war clouds gathered.

In Britain the services were just beginning to realize the potential of the modern motor cycle in times of war and they held several closed competition events during the year. It was not uncommon for some members of the armed forces to compete in civilian events and, for the second year running, an army team took part in the International Six-Day event. Meanwhile, Waycott's run of successes continued. He won the Tythersleigh Cup for the best performance in the opposite class to that of the winner in the Kickham Trial, and the Traders' Cup in the following Wye Valley event. He was not entered for the International Six-Day Trial; the sole Veloce entry was in the name of Billy Tiffen, who again represented Britain in the Vase A Team in company with L. Heath and G. F. Povey, both of whom rode Ariels. He had entered at his own expense. Percy Goodman was convinced that war with Germany was imminent and was unwilling to risk Waycott and others being interned should it break out while they were in German territory. In consequence he decided not to make the customary Veloce Works entry.

There is little to record about the event because the whole British contingent withdrew from the Trial on the last but one day when they were still favourably placed. The political situation had now become grave and the Government had advised the early return of all British nationals. This proved to be a wise decision, for only a short while afterwards war was declared on Germany and once again all motor-cycle sport ceased for the duration.

To the credit of the organizing club there was one exception. Somehow the British Experts' Trial was held in these troubled times and Stuart Waycott became the runner-up in the sidecar class. A fitting conclusion to yet another facet of the Company's activities.

11
Records and Record-Breaking

Until the outbreak of the Second World War, record-breaking in Britain was invariably associated with Brooklands, the banked, high-speed track close to Weybridge which H. F. Locke-King had the foresight to build at a cost of £250,000 during the winter of 1906–7. Brooklands was the world's first track to be built specially for car and motor-cycle racing and almost immediately after the opening on 6 July 1907 it became the natural habitat for those closely associated with the preparation of machines to be used for both long- and short-distance events and record attempts. Many of today's successful names can be linked with their earlier exploits at this venue.

Apart from the prestige afforded by the establishment of a new national or international motor-cycle speed record, many of the more successful riders and tuners supplemented their income by means of the cash bonuses paid by the various fuel-suppliers and accessory-manufacturers whose products they used. It will be appreciated that in total this could amount to a substantial sum of money for each company involved was anxious to publicize the use of their products in the successful bid for a new record, irrespective of whether they sold petrol and oil or manufactured chains, sparking-plugs, or tyres. Indeed, these payments were not necessarily confined to the equipment and products closely associated with the machine used. Some riders were even successful in negotiating bonus payments from manufacturers of such diverse products as beverages, hair preparations, and health tonics!

As may be expected, the payment of these bonuses was exploited to the full and it was not long before a pattern was established whereby the potential record-breaker would achieve his target with only the minimal increase necessary. This permitted one of his contemporaries to raise the record a fraction higher within only a few days and gain his reward. Thereafter, the whole cycle of events could be repeated until such time as the possibilities had been exhausted! Needless to say the companies involved soon grew wise to this exploitation and gradually the bonus payments dwindled until most of the more successful riders derived their supplementary income from a 'flat' retainer payment paid as the result of a negotiable contract.

The first Velocette success in the records book was achieved by D. R. O'Donovan, a tuner/rider of no mean ability. On 9 March 1921 he set up a world record for the kilometre at 62·73 mph riding a 249 cc two-stroke. As may be expected, the machine had received considerable attention and had been stripped to the bare essentials. An interesting feature was the use of two carburetters, both of the Binks 'Mouse-Trap' design. One was located in the conventional position and the other was attached to the crankcase where it operated via a spring-loaded automatic valve that was actuated by crankcase depression.[1] Unfortunately, this arrangement gave the machine the tendency to catch fire with alarming rapidity. A blow-back from the lower carburetter would cause a flare-up which immediately ignited the second carburetter poised above it.

Quite by coincidence, a second name soon figured in the records book – that of Rex Judd, a young assistant employed by O'Donovan. The latter had prepared the two-stroke for some further record-breaking attempts but was experiencing some trouble with the lubrication system. Because the engine required more oil on full throttle than the plug would stand at low speeds, it was his practice to start off from the top of the Brooklands banking for a standing lap with the oil turned off. After completing the first lap, when the engine had warmed up sufficiently, O'Donovan would turn on the oil and proceed as planned. But the inevitable occurred. On this day he omitted to turn on the oil while his mind was distracted by other events, with the result that the engine seized quite violently and threw him off. Somewhat the worse for wear he decided to abandon the record attempts until he had fully recovered from his injuries which fortunately were only superficial.

Rex Judd told one of the authors that 'Don', as he was affectionately known, was bare-headed at the time of the accident and being of Irish descent, and proud of it, made light of the matter and boasted that no harm had come to a 'Tough Irishman' such as he was!

Rex Judd had other ideas and after hurriedly repairing the damaged machine he implored O'Donovan to let him attempt the record bid as a substitute. He was somewhat grudgingly given consent whereupon he broke the world kilometre record at 62·73 mph. Realizing Judd's riding ability O'Donovan quickly relented and gave him every encouragement to make further record attempts. By the end of 1921 Judd held the British flying mile record at 70·31 mph and the world five-mile and ten-mile records at 65·31 and 63·09 mph respectively, in addition to the British kilometre record at 71·70 mph. He later progressed to even greater fame with larger capacity machines of different manufacture.

As may be expected, the advent of the overhead camshaft model K gave fresh impetus to successful attempts at the existing records. It is appropriate that Harold Willis, in conjunction with A. P. Hamilton, should have made the first significant attempt at record-breaking for a number of years. They set up the new 500 kilometre record at Brooklands during September 1927 with a speed of 127·4 kilometres per hour, using a 348 cc OHC model. The machine obviously ran well, for they continued and also broke the existing four-hour and five-hour records at a speed of 78·86 mph and 78·93 mph respectively.

[1] It is interesting to speculate about this additional carburetter that was employed in conjunction with an 'automatic' form of valve. Some forty years later the two-stroke engine of the Velocette 'Viceroy' scooter was produced with an automatic inlet-valve in the form of thin spring-steel vanes between the carburetter and crankcase.

In terms of successful world record bids, the year following was undoubtedly the best the Company ever achieved. By the end of 1928 no less than fifty world records could be attributed to Velocettes. Freddie Hicks figured prominently in the list of riders and some of his successes at Brooklands were made with a sidecar attached to his 348 cc mount.

In 1928 what proved to be one of the best-known achievements was the new 'hour' record set up by Harold Willis at Montlhéry, a French track near Paris that had a smoother surface than Brooklands and required no silencing restrictions. His speed averaged just over 100 mph and we are indebted to *The Motor Cycle*[1] at that time for the description of how his machine was prepared for this event.

The 348 cc OHC Velocette used by Willis was virtually a stripped KTT model, with larger than standard petrol- and oil-tanks. Outwardly, the engine differed little in appearance from the production model, but this

The machine used by the late Freddie Hicks for his successful record attempts at Brooklands. Note the absence of a front brake and the retention of the hand gear-change.

did not apply to the internals. The compression ratio had been raised to 10·5:1 to obtain the maximum advantage from the use of Discol RD1 fuel, which in turn necessitated some reduction in the radius of the hemispherical cylinder-head. It was also necessary to slightly reduce the diameter of the exhaust-valve in order to maintain the essential clearance between the valves and to form a slight depression in the crown of the piston to ensure the tulip-shaped exhaust-valve (of KE 965 steel) would not touch the piston. The inlet-valve had the normal profile.

Both cylinder-head ports were polished, but it was not considered necessary to cut away the cast-iron valve-guides where they projected into the ports. A number 24 profile cam was used, the timing that was standardized on all early KTT models. The valve timing was arranged to give an overlap of 87 degrees, using a long, straight-through exhaust-pipe.

[1] *The Motor Cycle*, 31 January 1929.

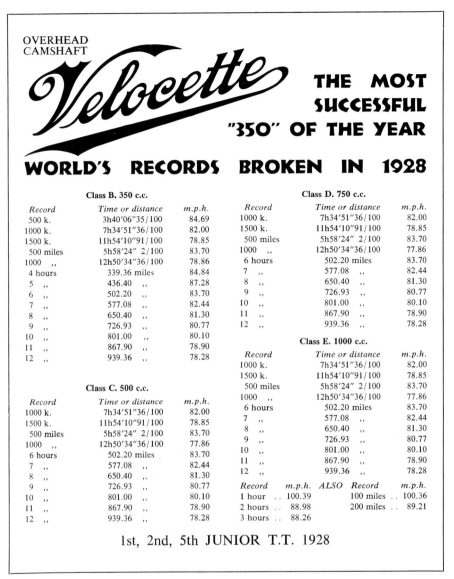

The following is a reproduction of the original publicity leaflet:

OVERHEAD CAMSHAFT

Velocette

THE MOST SUCCESSFUL "350" OF THE YEAR

WORLD'S RECORDS BROKEN IN 1928

Class B. 350 c.c.

Record		Time or distance	m.p.h.
500 k.		3h40'06"35/100	84.69
1000 k.		7h34'51"36/100	82.00
1500 k.		11h54'10"91/100	78.85
500 miles		5h58'24" 2/100	83.70
1000	,,	12h50'34"36/100	78.86
4 hours		339.36 miles	84.84
5	,,	436.40 ,,	87.28
6	,,	502.20 ,,	83.70
7	,,	577.08 ,,	82.44
8	,,	650.40 ,,	81.30
9	,,	726.93 ,,	80.77
10	,,	801.00 ,,	80.10
11	,,	867.90 ,,	78.90
12	,,	939.36 ,,	78.28

Class C. 500 c.c.

Record		Time or distance	m.p.h.
1000 k.		7h34'51"36/100	82.00
1500 k.		11h54'10"91/100	78.85
500 miles		5h58'24" 2/100	83.70
1000	,,	12h50'34"36/100	77.86
6 hours		502.20 miles	83.70
7	,,	577.08 ,,	82.44
8	,,	650.40 ,,	81.30
9	,,	726.93 ,,	80.77
10	,,	801.00 ,,	80.10
11	,,	867.90 ,,	78.90
12	,,	939.36 ,,	78.28

Class D. 750 c.c.

Record		Time or distance	m.p.h.
1000 k.		7h34'51"36/100	82.00
1500 k.		11h54'10"91/100	78.85
500 miles		5h58'24" 2/100	83.70
1000	,,	12h50'34"36/100	77.86
6 hours		502.20 miles	83.70
7	,,	577.08 ,,	82.44
8	,,	650.40 ,,	81.30
9	,,	726.93 ,,	80.77
10	,,	801.00 ,,	80.10
11	,,	867.90 ,,	78.90
12	,,	939.36 ,,	78.28

Class E. 1000 c.c.

Record		Time or distance	m.p.h.
1000 k.		7h34'51"36/100	82.00
1500 k.		11h54'10"91/100	78.85
500 miles		5h58'24" 2/100	83.70
1000	,,	12h50'34"36/100	77.86
6 hours		502.20 miles	83.70
7	,,	577.08 ,,	82.44
8	,,	650.40 ,,	81.30
9	,,	726.93 ,,	80.77
10	,,	801.00 ,,	80.10
11	,,	867.90 ,,	78.90
12	,,	939.36 ,,	78.28

Record	m.p.h.	ALSO	Record	m.p.h.
1 hour	.. 100.39		100 miles	.. 100.36
2 hours	.. 88.98		200 miles	.. 89.21
3 hours	.. 88.26			

1st, 2nd, 5th JUNIOR T.T. 1928

The impressive list of World records broken by the 350 cc OHC models in 1928. This is a reproduction of the original publicity leaflet issued by Veloce Limited.

The piston was virtually standard and had two $\frac{1}{16}$ in. compression-rings above the gudgeon-pin. Of the slipper type, it weighed approximately 10 oz. The large-diameter gudgeon-pin ($\frac{13}{16}$ in.) was retained in position by the conventional circlip arrangement. Surprisingly, an uncaged roller-bearing big-end assembly was used, although this was of an experimental design with rollers that were slightly wider and larger in diameter than standard. Outwardly, the crankcase had the appearance of that of the KSS model, but the castings had been substantially stiffened and were over $\frac{5}{8}$ in. thick in places. This can be regarded as the forerunner of the KTT crankcase, where much the same effect was achieved by the expedient of externally cast stiffening webs. The complete lubrication system closely followed standard practice.

The most conspicuous change in the layout of the cycle parts was the rear-mounted Lycett saddle that was necessary to give Willis a better riding position and to help accommodate the larger $4\frac{1}{2}$ gal. petrol-tank. It was estimated that this quantity of fuel would be more than sufficient for the hour record by about 1 quart. The oil-tank had a capacity of just over 1 gal. and contained a vegetable-base oil (Castrol R). It was clipped to the saddle-tube in the conventional manner. The front wheel contained no brake assembly; both wheels were carefully balanced and were fitted with 27 in. × 2·75 in. Dunlop racing tyres.

Transmission was via a standard close-ratio gearbox with a top-gear ratio of 4·84:1. This permitted the engine to average over 6,000 rpm throughout the record attempt. The intermediate gears were not removed. A square-type racing ML magneto provided the ignition and the carburetter was of the TT Amal design.

Harold Willis broke the hour record with an average speed of 100·39 mph and when the engine was stripped for measurement the internals were seen to be operating under ideal conditions. Apart from minor changes in specification, the same machine was successfully used by Freddie Hicks to capture the flying-start five-kilometre record at 106·98 mph and the standing-start ten-mile record at 104 mph. By the end of 1929, Veloce Limited held no less than sixty world records.

In May 1934, Les Archer set up a new 100-mile record for the 350 cc sidecar class at Brooklands, when he averaged 79·52 mph. His passenger on this occasion was G. E. Bishop. Archer had been appointed to the Veloce Team after Freddie Hicks left to join AJS in 1931. Many more years were to elapse before Veloce Limited annexed another world record. By then, Brooklands had been sold to Vickers and was lost to the car and motor-cycle fraternity for ever. There was no longer any British track suitable for such an attempt.

The story of the successful twelve- and twenty-four-hour record attempt[1] made during 18–19 March 1961 began in June 1960, when Veloce Limited decided to take from stock a standard Venom Vee-Line Clubman model and develop it to lap consistently at over 110 mph on an as yet unspecified track, with a view to achieving their objective with an average speed of more than 100 mph. Many months of painstaking development and testing produced an engine that had a power output of just under 40 bhp and appeared capable of sustaining the desired standard of performance. Plans were made and March 1961 was selected as the month in which the record attempt would be made.

As mentioned earlier there was no longer any track in Britain for such an attempt and so Montlhéry was chosen as being the most convenient location. But it was no longer the smooth banked circuit used by Harold Willis for his 'hour' attempt thirty-two years earlier. Like Brooklands, the

[1] See *Motor Cycling*, 23 March 1931, pp. 637–9 for the exclusive story by Bruce Main-Smith.

B. J. Goodman, a member of the successful record-breaking team, aboard the actual machine that secured the twenty-four-hour record in 1961.

surface had deteriorated with the passage of time and there were now huge gaps between the concrete slabs of which the bankings were composed. A yellow line defined the official measured distance and regulations forbade riding below this line. It was soon found that the line indicated the lowest point on the banking at which it was possible to ride at the requisite speed. During the actual record attempt most riders opted to stay higher up to gain the advantage of a smoother ride. Unfortunately, this incurred the penalty of increased tyre wear for it was necessary to cant the machine over at a greater angle.

Two very brief practice sessions were held on 17 March in order to select the team of riders for the attempt on the following day. One of these sessions was held in the dark, when the circuit was illuminated by car headlamps. The final team comprised Pierre Cherrier, Alain Dagan, Bertie Goodman, Andre Jacquier-Bret, Robert Leconte, Bruce Main-Smith, Georges Monneret, and his son Pierre.

The weather forecast proved inaccurate for despite earlier predictions of fine weather it was raining by 7.30 am on the morning of the eighteenth. Undeterred, Georges Monneret had the honour of starting the attempt and at 8.27 am he pushed off and commenced to circulate in the 51–2 second bracket that was essential for success. Riders changed every hour and the average speed remained well above 105 mph.

Dennis Durbridge, the Dunlop tyre representative, estimated the rate of tyre consumption at two front and four rear tyres for the session, an estimate that proved extremely accurate. At the first change, after the first six hours, the Veloce supporting team effected a complete rear-wheel change in just three minutes. Pit facilities in general were primitive. The machine was refuelled from a plastic bucket via a tin funnel, to quote but one example.

When Pierre Monneret finished his stint, during which the twelve-hour record was broken at an average speed of 104·66 mph, both tyres and the rear chain were changed. And then trouble struck. As Bruce Main-Smith prepared to start off, the gear-selector mechanism jammed. Swift action by the Veloce mechanics soon rectified the damage, but not before a precious thirty-three minutes had been lost. Undaunted, the team readjusted themselves to the new situation and slowly pulled back the lost time. Alain Dagan took over from Georges Monneret shortly after 8 am on the morning of the nineteenth and by the time the twenty-four hours had elapsed another record had fallen at an average speed of 100·05 mph.

In total, no less than six world records had been broken, for the twelve-hour and the twenty-four-hour figures also applied to the 750 cc and the unlimited classes for solo motor cycles. The results were all the more creditable when it is realized that only one machine was taken to Montlhéry, together with only one spare engine.

The machine that was used for the successful attempt on the record was much closer to standard specification than many would imagine. Outwardly it appeared almost identical with the current production models apart from the removal of the front mudguard and the complete lighting set. Closer inspection showed a number of minor modifications, each considered essential for the prolonged high speed that had to be maintained. There was one unusual addition, that of a centre-stand. This was considered essential to assist with quick wheel changes.

The engine in itself was quite standard although it had been carefully assembled and developed on the test-bench. The compression ratio was 8·75:1 and it ran on 94 octane fuel simply because 100 octane fuel was not readily available in France. A 20/40 multi-grade mineral oil was employed for the lubrication system and the oil-tank had a specially perforated plate welded to the outer face of the oil-tank to prevent direct contact by the hot tank with the rider's leg. There was a twin-pipe 'bleed' from the oil-tank to lubricate the exposed primary chain.

A manually operated BTH magneto supplied the ignition and an Amal GP carburetter of $1\frac{3}{16}$ in. bore, with a remote mounted float-chamber, looked after the carburation. It had been deliberately over-jetted to give an ample safety margin. The exhaust-pipe was of standard design, but it terminated in an open megaphone of the KTT pattern.

The gearbox was fitted with close-ratio internals and had a twenty-two-tooth final-drive sprocket that gave a top gear of 4:1. It was lubricated by a straight SAE 50 oil. A conventional blanking-off plate replaced the kick-starter assembly. The gear lever had already been reversed so that the Clubman rear-set foot-rests could be used.

The riding position had been modified by fitting a pair of non-standard 'clip-on' handlebars, which in turn necessitated replacing the customary fork-shrouds with the rubber gaiters from the scrambles model. Pillion foot-rests gave an alternative riding position; they had built-up ends to help retain the rider's feet in this position.

Both wheels were carefully balanced and had light-alloy rims. They were shod with Dunlop racing tyres. The fairing was the Mitchenall prototype used for the Vee-Line models because it had been tested and proved. This also applied to the earlier design of petrol-tank that was fitted.

Perhaps the most interesting fact was the knowledge that the machine had covered over 1,400 miles before the attempt took place, mostly at speeds well in excess of 100 mph. During this period the engine had not been stripped and it was not until the capacity was measured at the conclusion of the attempt that the cylinder-head was removed. The reason was then only too obvious, for it could be seen that the engine was running under ideal conditions.

Although the twelve- and the twenty-four-hour records were beaten by a 600 cc machine of foreign manufacture only a few days later, Veloce Limited had the honour of producing a machine that first exceeded 100 mph for a whole day, a fitting sequel to their successful bid for the 'hour' record on a 350 cc model thirty-two years earlier. In each case they topped the magic 'ton' and even today the twelve- and twenty-four-hour records have not been beaten by a machine of similar capacity. It is interesting to speculate whether the 350 cc 'Viper' model would be equally successful in setting up a similar set of records within its own capacity class.

12
The Happy Family

It may be difficult for those younger readers fully to understand the wonderfully friendly family spirit that pervaded the Veloce factories in the earlier days. In these days of huge combines and impersonal management such happy co-operation among all the personnel is probably very rare, but the Goodmans had been successful in gathering round them a small band of dedicated workers who got on well together, and shared a common interest. It is indication of the esteem in which those who helped so loyally to build up the excellent reputation the machines are held that due acknowledgement to as many of them as possible is included. A former lady Director of the Company furnished the authors with valuable notes and reminiscences of those days, that now seem so far away, when motorcycling was so much more an adventure than it is today.

Harking back to the Six Way Aston days, when the Isle of Man was not connected by submarine telephone cable with the 'Adjacent Islands' – as the Manx people so picturesquely describe the United Kingdom – communication with the Works took much longer. When riders and mechanics in the Island for the TT races required spares urgently, these were longer in reaching them, for there was not the air service that is available today.

Interest in the races was intense and one of the premier journals devoted to the pastime – *The Motor Cycle* – used to issue up-to-the-minute information from the Island to subscribers in the form of daily 'telegrams'. During the practising that, as now, precedes the races these daily bulletins gave the lap times and speeds of the various riders and machines for the previous morning's activities. Most motor-cycle dealers subscribed to and displayed the 'telegrams' in the windows of their showrooms. Groups of enthusiasts would gather round these to read of the fortunes of riders or machines which held a particular interest for them.

Like all other manufacturers Veloce subscribed to and received news of their entries in the races. On the day of the 1926 Junior TT Race the excitement that spread through the whole Works can better be imagined than described, especially when Alec Bennett's win was announced.

We are told that John Goodman and his family hastily ordered from Pattisons, the oldest Birmingham restaurant, lobster sandwiches to enjoy with their usual afternoon cups of tea, and to celebrate their first Junior TT win. Syd Stevenson, the driver of the Works transport, a long-bodied commercial sidecar outfit, was sent to get the sandwiches. The outfit was affectionately known as the 'punt'!

It is relevant as a historical note that it was not until many years later that Veloce bought a motor van to pick up and deliver material. Like most other motor-cycle firms in Birmingham they used one of their own machines to draw a huge wooden-bodied sidecar with a body long enough to carry a motor cycle. When, at an earlier date, the range of models was restricted to two-strokes of 250 cc one of these machines had to provide the motive power for this, by no means light, combination. It speaks volumes for the stamina of these small machines that the combination proved so satisfactory.

Every day Syd took his instructions from a slate that was provided for that purpose in the Buying Office; Miss Ethel Goodman's domain. Personnel requiring transport, or material, simply wrote on the slate the word 'Take' or 'Collect' (which ever was appropriate) followed by the name of the firm to which or from which transport was required. The last journey every evening was the transport of machines to the railway station for dispatch – in pre-British Rail days Kings Heath (LMS) or Hall Green (GWR).

Among the earliest to join Veloce were members of a family by the name of Ridge, a father, son, and grandson. Of these Billy Ridge was in charge of all frame-building, a job of which he is a master and an expert when it comes to cycles, motor-cycle frames, or sidecar chassis.

Another family who can claim very long service with Veloce are the Williams', as two brothers Fred and Harry have worked respectively as Caretaker/Time-keeper and Storeman. Harry Williams's son has an electrical contractor's business and his firm is that appointed to carry out electrical maintenance at the factory.

Harry Thorne, who was working for Veloce before the First World War, and whose employment was interrupted by a period of war service, looked after the assembly of all new machines. He also managed the Packing

Left to right Ernie Taylor, Mrs Ethel Denley (*neé* Goodman), Harry Thorne, George Denley, Alan Edwards, Syd Stevenson, Percy Goodman, and Fred Williams with the 'Roarer'.

202

Department in which, with other items, motor cycles were partly dismantled before crating and boxing for export; always a major part of the firm's market. He assisted Percy Goodman in the assembly of Alec Bennett's winning racer and each year he took charge of arranging the Company's exhibits at Olympia and later at Earls Court.

Harry Thorne was a founder-member of the Veloce Social and Sports Club formed between the wars. This club derived its funds from subscriptions deducted from the wages of those who had signified their wish to join and willingness for the deduction of a few pence weekly from their remuneration. Harry Thorne also organized sweepstakes on the TT races and upon major horse-races such as the Derby. Harry died during 1942 and his former deputy Len Moseley was appointed his successor. Len had joined the Company in 1923 and had worked his way through various jobs including the lacing of spokes into hubs and rims, tyre-fitting, and other jobs, during which he gained real experience that fitted him to take over the Assembly Department.

Len is justly proud that he was in the department that built the machines for the TT and those specially finished models that have graced the Velocette Stands at various Shows at Olympia, Earls Court, and latterly other venues. Like Len, and with similar long experience of motor-cycle work, is Norman Eaton who after working for the now defunct Diamond Motor Cycle Company at Wolverhampton and other jobs in the trade joined Veloce early in 1928 under Harry Thorne. He later transferred to the Repair Department under Eugene Goodman's brother-in-law Chris Lomer. His experience included work on military motor cycles, fitting and Tool Room work. After the war he was in charge of gearbox and front fork assembly.

Kenzo Tada, the Velocette Agent for Japan, with the Mark I KTT he rode in the 1930 Junior TT.

The manufacture of high-grade motor cycles demands the preparation, making, and maintenance of a huge number of jigs, tools, and other items of special equipment. This work is the responsibility of the department known as the Tool Room in which only highly skilled machinists and fitters can be employed. For many years, until he retired during the 1950s, this important department was ably managed by Jack Gale, one of the employees who had joined the Company in its very early days, and is an engineer of great experience and ability.

Another of the 'old hands' who has only recently retired after some fifty years with Veloce is Harry Perkins. He was the Engine Bench Foreman and one experienced in building all kinds of Velocette engines, having dealt with both two-strokes and four-strokes in single-cylinder and twin-cylinder form.

With similar length of service behind him Harry Ward, a machinist, has been presented with a gold watch by the directors in appreciation and as commemoration of the completion of half a century with them.

But this catalogue of long-serving members of the personnel has its exceptions that convincingly show that those established with Veloce were not unfriendly to new employees or unwilling to welcome them to the 'family'. In this context mention must be made of at least one of these who integrated happily with those who were already at York Road when he came. With prior experience of working for many of the other Midland motor-cycle makers George Wilkes had been the Chief Draughtsman at Hall Green for some twenty-four years, and has been a leading light in the affairs of the Social Club.

The black and gold finish that has distinguished Velocettes for so long and is still regarded as their traditional livery requires among other things a highly skilled worker and a very steady hand to complete the exacting job of painting the lines round the tanks in varnish to which to apply the real gold-leaf. At one time during the 1930s the high price of the real gold-leaf used in the tank lining forced Veloce 'off the Gold Standard' and for a while a bronze paint had to be used. Real gold-leaf was resumed as soon as circumstances permitted. The location of the line is marked out from a chalk mark formed by dusting the surface of the tank sides over the edges of a specially shaped templet. The line is then applied from a special brush freehand by another of those long-service men namely: Jack Kettle, the Head Enameller in charge of the Department.

Jack Kettle is also responsible for spraying the frames of the LE models and runs the conveyor enamelling plant through which all frames pass with many other parts for the stoving of the enamel at high temperature. He is the second member of his family to work at Hall Green as he took charge of enamelling when his father, who had run the department before him, died.

Many of those employed by Veloce, as is usual in any factory or similar place where many people work together, acquired nicknames and this is fortunate in this case as it is necessary to mention another of the old hands who was known only as Cockney Bill! It seems that he got a job with the

Company when his father, a Mr Taylor, moved from London with his family, which probably accounts for the nickname. At all events Cockney Bill worked for most of his time with Veloce in the Repair Department, and was exceedingly rapid in his work and at the same time a very reliable worker. To watch him assemble an engine was an experience; the parts seemed to go together into place like magic under his hands at a speed that might have been expected to be asking for trouble to develop later on – but it never did. In the course of his work Bill overhauled many KTT engines for customers. No fault in his work upon any of them was ever reported, even under the racing conditions in which they were used.

Another at Hall Green whose real name was seldom heard was Alf Griffiths who was in charge of the Tool Stores, where, as its description implies, were stored all kinds of tools, jigs, cutters, drills, broaches, taps, dies, and all the vast array of materials that a factory constantly requires.

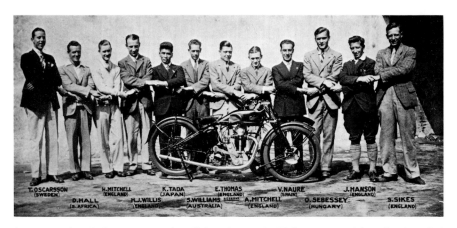

An example of the many nationalities that rode Velocette machines in the 1930 Junior TT.

Known throughout the works as 'Pagan', he was almost a universal provider – but why he was called 'Pagan' is not known to many, if any, of his colleagues!

Upon the outbreak of war in 1939 the personnel did not immediately show any changes as most persons employed were classed as being in reserved occupations, but gradually it became necessary to employ workers from other trades. Not all of these readily integrated with those who had mostly been with Veloce for many years before the war, and even before the war before that. An exception to this, however, was Bill Phillips who, with his father, ran a joinery and decorator's business not far from York Road and who had undertaken many jobs in the factory and offices. So much extra work that came within his scope was required that shortly after September 1939 he was employed full time by Veloce. He remained on the pay-roll until after the war when it became possible to release him to return to his own business.

Extra space was required during the war to accommodate the sections

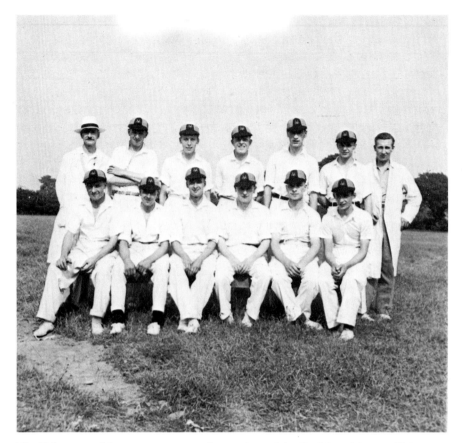

The Velocette cricket team, a very active section of the Social and Sports Club.

that had grown up for the assembly of such units as bomb-hoists, bomb-slips, parachute-releases, variable-pitch propeller feathering-pumps, and aircraft cabin-blowers. Test-beds had also to be provided for the last two. The overflow from the York Road factory was housed 'for the duration' in a portion of a toffee factory at Greet, Birmingham, as recounted in an earlier chapter and became known as Veloce No. 2 Works.

Some personnel were transferred from the York Road Works to man it, including Harry Perkins, and Ernie Taylor; the latter as Chief Welder to handle welding work on aircraft components and Sten-guns. Also at the No. 2 Works engaged upon work of the assembly and fitting-up of Air Ministry jobs were two of the other racing mechanics: Jimmie Owen and Tommy Mutton who had worked for Harold Willis in happier days before the war. The dispersal factory space was actually half of Fillery's Toffee Works at Greet, Birmingham, adjacent (too adjacent perhaps!) to Wilder's Firework Factory which caused Harry Perkins, who was among those transferred temporarily from Hall Green, to say that in the event of an air raid the 'women and children' would run a poor second to him in getting out!

Apart from the general relief when the war ended the prospect of old associates being able once more to work together under the same roof, and again upon motor-cycle work (in which they were much more interested), made the return to Hall Green a happy occasion.

Visitors to the factory cannot have failed to notice the friendly atmosphere that existed between all those with whom they came into contact. Any of these callers will first of all have been greeted by Miss Wilden, known to one and all of her many friends at Hall Green Works as Doreen; the telephonist in charge of the PBX in the Gate Office. If first impressions are important, as it is sometimes stated, Doreen certainly creates an exceedingly pleasant and happy one, with a smile for all. Visitors must have found how willing and in fact eager, workers were to show how jobs were done, how units were put together, and that they obviously took pride in their work. Many motor-cyclists, who had doubtless struggled many times to fit new tyres to their machines, used to stand, unable to believe their eyes, when the Veloce tyre-fitter used to get tyres and tubes into place without apparent effort, and marvel at the dexterity with which complex assemblies were put together. Such assemblies were quite often taken apart and rebuilt to make clear some point that the visitor had missed or not understood the first time.

The Goodmans, by some subtle and inexplicable quality, attracted to work for them a number of persons, each a specialist in a particular line. By their united efforts under the direction of gifted engineers, they produced honestly good, reliable, motor cycles of brilliant, if perhaps sometimes unorthodox design with a reputation of which any maker could be proud.

In the course of this progress friends were made on a world-wide scale and included many of the Company's agents and suppliers. In view of the current influx of Japanese-produced motor cycles to the British market it is relevant to relate that during the 1920s not a single motor cycle was manufactured in that country. K. Tada, the Velocette agent for Japan, rode a KTT in the 1930 TT in company with many other overseas riders.

The friendly family atmosphere that was such a feature of the Works extended way outside it, and what was really a large party known as the 'Velocette "Do"' used to be arranged for Veloce staff, suppliers, agents, their friends and relatives. This annual function was organized by George Denley and usually took place at the Plough and Harrow, a well-known Birmingham hotel, or at the Botanical Gardens. Many trade personalities and some Velocette-owners used to attend and the MC was usually the late Stanley Banner, at that time Sales Manager of Levis. One of the highlights of the evening was the mock sermon he used to 'preach' while dressed as a parson during which he ribbed nearly everyone present. About the model K, which was on Percy Goodman's drawing-board a very long time, he said of the forthcoming new model, 'An verily it was drawn out; some said it was long drawn out!!' As mentioned earlier, there was also a very flourishing Social and Sports Club with its own football and cricket teams, to name but two activities.

The lives of John Goodman, his two sons Percy and Eugene and his daughter Ethel were closely interwoven with the history of the Company,

A post-war party for the female staff of Veloce Limited.

as will be realized from the earlier chapters. John Goodman, of whom little has been written, was clearly a man of considerable foresight and he had the reputation for his ability to make a quick decision that time proved would be correct. He was a quiet man, who dearly loved a quiet game of snooker, but he found his greatest joys in the family circle. It was this love of the more simple things of life that gave him the feeling that those who worked for him were part of the family and that they all contributed equally to the success of the business. When he died in 1929, during the height of the Depression, it is no exaggeration to say that the whole trade mourned his loss.

Percy is best known for his mechanical ingenuity and it is no surprise to learn that his hobby was watch-repairing. There is the story about the loss of a vital part he had made for a watch repair which magnets failed to retrieve, even after a protracted search. The part concerned was eventually found in a most unexpected place – behind one of his thumb-nails! It should be remembered that Percy designed and prepared the machines that won the 1926 Junior TT, a remarkable achievement when it is realized that the total complement of the staff at that time was only forty-six. It is particularly unfortunate that ill health should have dogged him during the vital period after the Second World War, leading to his untimely death in 1953.

Eugene had an intense interest in production methods and he was responsible for the design of the very successful push-rod engine that helped boost sales in the early 1930s. They produced a greater profit margin than the Veloce OHC counterparts because they were easier to assemble. Yet their road-holding and their performance were still in keeping with the very high standards already set by the Company. Later still, Eugene became intrigued with the prospects for a utility machine that could be manufactured on a mass-production basis. The result was the LE, surely the most successful 'Everyman's' machine yet produced by any motor-cycle company. In early life he was a trials rider of no mean repute. Later, he turned his attention to boats, a hobby that culminated in the purchase of a former Douglas relief lifeboat.

Not mentioned in the text, but none the less a person who played an equally important role in the fortunes of the Company, was Percy and Eugene's sister Ethel. In the early days of Taylor Gue she came into the business to help her father. Later she became more involved with many of the other activities of the Company and to record but one example, she can remember helping Percy lay out the copy for the very first comprehensive two-stroke instruction book and spares list during the whole of one Whitsun holiday. In due course she became Secretary of the Company and was also in sole charge of the buying, working closely with Percy on such matters as quality. She also served on the Board for many years.

The Sales Director is another person who can have a marked influence on the progress of a company and it was this latter post that George Denley filled so adequately after his experience as a successful competition rider. George has already been mentioned in connection with the Velocette 'Do', the programmes for which bear testament to his keen sense of humour. The publicity aspect of the Sales Director's job is often taken for granted, but George will surely be remembered for his 'Dough for Bikes' campaign during the Depression and his strikingly effective design for the

The cover of a typical programme for the Velocette 'do'. The parody of the advertisements of the period is ingenious.

front of the 1938 and 1939 catalogues is illustrated at the bottom of page 81. He married Ethel Goodman and it is difficult to imagine a more harmonious couple.

That most vital department, the Accounts Office, was under the management of a Mr Harding until the late 1920s, a man who, like most persons accustomed to dealing with sordid pounds, shillings, and pence, gave the impression of very carefully counting every halfpenny that had to be expended. At one time, so we have been led to believe, he kept in his care certain commodities that he had to issue to the Works. Among these were candles that had occasionally to be used to light the interiors of bores in items being machined in the workshops which, in the Company's earlier days, were not lighted to the standards that are acceptable today.

A workman would therefore apply to Mr Harding for a candle with which to augment the normal lighting in order to complete the bore in the job upon which he was engaged. The story was told that Harding cut the candle into two parts and solemnly issued only half!

Philip Irving worked for Veloce for a period during the 1930s, leaving them to take up an appointment with the Vincent Company, then producing the Vincent HRD motor cycle. An Australian by birth, Phil is the son of a medical practitioner whose practice in that country of wide open spaces covered some hundreds of square miles. Like most of his fellow countrymen he is an outspoken type blessed with a keen sense of humour. As fellow members of the Veloce staff during his sojourn at Hall Green will vouch, he is a man who never tries to 'high hat' others, and if asked what were to him elementary questions was never too 'learned' to explain matters thoroughly and clearly. A logical debater, Phil always kept strictly to the point of any argument; resolutely refusing to be diverted down irrelevant side-tracks.

He left the Vincent Company before the war to rejoin Veloce and while with them designed and patented, in conjunction with them, the clever adjustment for the rear suspension. Later on, he 'infringed' this idea himself, when he designed the Vincent Girdraulic' front fork. He was also responsible for the Velocette Model O twin, and at the instigation of Eugene Goodman produced a design for an 'Everyman's' model that was never taken further than the drawing-board stage and was superseded by Charles Udall's design that came to fruition in the form of the LE.

Irving left Veloce to join Associated Motor Cycles Limited, just before the end of the war, having spent the war years in work designing jigs and equipment to produce Air Ministry sub-contract assemblies. He was also intimately concerned in the design and production of the Veloce military MAC and MAF models.

Charles Udall joined the Company in the capacity of a mechanic in the Repair Shop. He ultimately became involved with Harold Willis on development work and from there came into his own sphere in the Drawing Office. It was in the capacity of draughtsman that he worked on the M range of push-rod models and as related earlier, he evolved the basic layout for the LE model.

Harold Willis, Alec Bennett, and Freddie Hicks at the conclusion of the 1928 Junior TT (Second, First, and Fifth respectively).

No biography of Veloce Limited would be complete without a mention, and much more than a passing one, of Harold Willis. He became a Director of the Company and for over a decade, and until his sudden death in June 1939, he held the position that nowadays is usually known as Development Engineer.

He was the son of a prominent Birmingham cattle merchant but was apparently not interested in following his father's career and had spent some time in the employment of Messrs Belliss and Morcom, the engineering firm in that city. During the First World War he served as a midshipman in the Royal Navy, having spent some time at Dartmouth Naval College. He saw active service during the Battle of Jutland, during which action he had the gruelling experience of spending many hours in the water when his vessel was sunk. He never forgave the Germans and was heard to suggest that it would be a good plan to 'bore a hole in the middle of Germany to let in the sea and drown the lot of them!' When, in later years, the entry of Velocette machines in continental races took him into Germany he made no secret of his detestation of the inhabitants.

Willis was an active motor-cyclist and he competed in numerous trials and races. In the Isle of Man he had ridden Montgomery machines in the Junior TT races of 1924 and 1925. He finished fifth in the 1924 event, but he had to retire from the 1925 race. He vindicated himself by finishing in ninth place in the Senior event of that year, also on a Montgomery.

After the success of the 350 cc overhead camshaft model K that Percy Goodman had designed, when Alec Bennett won the Junior TT of 1926

Harold Willis being congratulated by Ethel Denley after winning the 'Hutchinson Hundred' event at Brooklands in 1927. His average speed was 86.39 mph.

by some ten minutes, the Company solicited the subscription of more working capital by a £10,000 Share issue. Many of the Company's employees became shareholders and because of his son's interest in motor cycles, Mr Willis Senior obtained a place in Veloce Limited for him. On taking up this post, Harold Willis assumed much of the responsibility for the racing programme.

Veloce Limited had been compelled to take bigger premises in order to cope with the increase in orders that followed the 1926 TT win and were by the end of the year installed in the factory at York Road, Hall Green, that is still their home today. The factory had previously been occupied by Messrs Humphries and Dawes who produced the OK marque of motor cycles there. It is interesting to recall that the late Walter Handley was Head Road Tester of the OK models and that a very firm friendship developed between him and Harold Willis. Mr Dawes remained for a while, using a portion of the factory to assemble bicycles.

The late Graham Walker used to recount his first meeting with Willis when the latter entered a 10 hp Reading Standard twin for the 1920 Colmore Cup Trial. It is difficult to imagine a more unsuitable mount for this type of event and on being questioned, Willis gave as his reason the need to find out what was wrong with motor cycles! This was typical of his approach to life.

When RWB joined Veloce in 1930, Willis was already there and was on the Board. He came into contact with HJW quite frequently and soon began to appreciate the latter's sense of humour and his priceless gift for coining apt and expressive terms and phrases quite on the spur of the moment. Some of them have become perpetuated in the motor-cyclist's terminology but unfortunately it would be quite impossible to remember them all.

His name 'double-knocker' for double overhead camshaft has come into almost universal usage. But other expressions such as 'nails' for valves and 'penny in the slot' with which he used to describe the falling of a broken-off valve-head into the combustion chamber are not so well known. He used a lot of foreign words instead of the English ones such as 'Boîte de vitesse' for gearbox and the positive-stop gearchange which he originated was often known as the 'Changement de pied'. A race-meeting was called 'Manifestation sportif'.

Talking about the behaviour of a certain make of machine during practice runs with the particular brand of girder fork that the makers of the machine had designed themselves, Willis described how, on the fast run down to Craig-ny-Baa, the riders were wondering whether to 'abandon ship' or hang on until 'cast off'! Of another rider who had changed makes and was asked what he thought of his new mount Willis reported, 'He speaks highly of the machinery but dislikes the navigation!' Surely a brief but accurate way of saying that there was plenty of power but poor steering qualities. Power was usually referred to as 'urge' by Willis and on one occasion, followed by some good brake horsepower readings on the test-bench during the autumn he remarked sadly 'Christmas urge! It will all have run out of the drain plug hole by June!'

The engine-testing equipment was manufactured by Messrs Heenan and Froude of Worcester and no reflection is meant or intended in mentioning that Willis mostly referred to them as Heenan, Froude and Ananias Limited, because he had often been disappointed by the performance of machines on the road with engines that had shown most promising brake horsepower figures on the bench.

Willis competed in the TT on several occasions while employed by Veloce Limited and he piloted his Junior Velocette into second place in the 1927 and 1928 events. He also won the 1927 Hutchinson 100 at Brooklands at an average speed of over 86 mph. As a racing man himself, Willis could see things from the rider's angle and it was this that prompted him to devise the positive-stop foot gear control when he realized how much time was lost per lap when using the conventional hand-operated control. Another of his much-copied ideas was the dual-seat, the prototype of which was at once called the 'Loch Ness Monster'. The original design was huge and ugly, hence the very descriptive name.

Mention has been made elsewhere of his name for various machines, such as 'Spring-Heel Jack', 'Whiffling Clara', and 'Roaring Anna'. Even his beloved aeroplane, which formed his sole hobby, was known affectionately as 'Clattering Kate'.

As Service Manager, RWB made a point of advising design staff of any failures that had occurred in service, particularly if the part failed on a new model. By constantly passing on the customers' grouses to them and taking to the Drawing Office any examples of broken parts sent in, the powers that be were nudged into taking action to eliminate the causes of the trouble.

Calling in one day, he found Willis seated alongside Charles Udall at one of the drawing-boards. As he opened the door, Willis looked up and remarked to Udall 'Here comes the bird of ill omen!' then turning to RWB he said 'What's broken now?' After that he always referred to Bob by this descriptive term.

It has been mentioned earlier that the petrol-tank transfers had been modified after the TT wins of 1926, 1928, and 1929 to include mention of this fact, even on the two-stroke GTP! Willis maintained that as long as the past successes were emblazoned on the tanks Veloce would never win another TT and he always had the '1066 and all that' bit cut off the transfers used on the machines that he prepared. Perhaps he was correct, for when the Company eventually reverted to the original transfer design in 1938 Stanley Woods won the Junior TT after breaking the lap record and easing up for the later laps!

This success, after so many years of hard work, together with the really excellent performance of the Senior racers in running the 'opposition' so close in the TT races of 1937 and 1938 was unfortunately spoiled for Willis because of his physical condition. For some time he had been in pain with sinus trouble possibly as a result of prolonged immersion in the seas during the war, and he finally decided to undergo an operation to get some relief. This decision was apparently taken against medical advice, but he had become so impatient of his state, which often prevented him from working, that he went into hospital. Tragically he contracted meningitis and he died on the eve of Stanley Woods's 1939 TT win.

The newspapers that carried the news of the Velocette success also included the obituary notice of one of the most colourful and likeable personalities that the motor-cycling industry has known. His passing cast a gloom over everything at Hall Green.

This chapter about the Company and those who contributed in their various ways to its growth, reputation, and prosperity is headed 'The Happy Family' for that is what the Goodman family succeeded in forming round them.

Obviously, it has been impossible to mention all those who have been, or are, concerned with the making of the section of motor-cycle history covered by this volume; even as it is the inclusion of just small details about some of those individuals whose names do appear has meant writing what some may think an over-long chapter upon a theme that may not be of general interest. However, in this age of huge commercial groups to which customers are probably known only as numbers there may be some who will care to read of an organization that did not subscribe to the statement that 'There is no sentiment in business.'

13
A Picture Gallery

Introduction

Since this book was reprinted during July 1974, quite a number of photographs of both an historic and an interesting nature have passed into the hands of the surviving author. By far the majority were donated by Mrs. E. Denley, the daughter of the founder of Veloce Limited, who herself was very actively involved with the business from 1916, when she joined her father's cycle business as a general clerk and typist, right through to her retirement in May 1955. When the factory moved to its final location in Hall Green, during 1926, she became responsible for the buying operation, as well as making sure the spare parts lists were accurate and helping her father with the accounts. When he died during August 1929, she continued with her buying activities and also assumed responsibility for the administration of the offices and the mechanisation of the accounts department. She also reorganised the service department and established a follow-on system. As a result, it became possible to dispatch parts on the day on which the order was received, a scheme that was continued very successfully by my late colleague, Bob Burgess.

Today, Ethel and George Denley live in quiet retirement, aged 91 and 88 respectively, not far from the site of the Hall Green Works in York Road. It pleases me greatly to be able to add these brief notes about Ethel Denley, for when the book was published originally, it had been her wish to avoid mention "because, it is a family story and the work people should take the limelight, not the bosses." Indeed, I was even dissuaded from mentioning that she is the girl with the rickshaw shown on page 14, such was her concern about appearing too prominently. Now at last I can restore the balance just a little, with her permission. Knowing Ethel and George as I do today, I can appreciate why the atmosphere throughout the Veloce workforce was like no other, for the friendship that has grown between us I value immensely.

Jeff Clew
February 1980

Even if a lightweight sidecar had been attached, this 1914 two-stroke outfit seems quite heavily laden. The photograph may have been taken during a publicity demonstration, in view of the gradient.

An early press photograph of the 1914 Ladies model, used by *Motor Cycle*. This machine has a Senspray carburettor, one of the options available at that time.

George Denley pauses during a South Birmingham Club trial during 1919. The white line across the road suggests some form of a test, which has drawn the attention of the bicycle-mounted onlooker.

A 1920 Model D two-stroke, with two-speed gear operated by means of a rack and pinion arrangement, controlled by the 'bath tap' at the side of the petrol tank.

Ethel Goodman astride a Model D, in the days when a manufacturer and members of his family rode the machines they made on every possible occasion.

A Works paper chase, one of many such events held during the 'twenties. There are three lady riders in the foreground, one with a sidecar outfit.

George Denley rode as a member of the Veloce Limited team, all two-stroke mounted, to gain a Gold Medal in the 1920 A-C.U. Six Days Trial.

Riding this machine, P. Muller, a Belgian rider, won a Gold Medal and a Cup in an unknown Continental speed event. It earned him factory help via the local agent.

A rare, but unfortunately not very sharp, photograph of the only Veloce car made. It looks as though John Goodman is occupying the rear seat.

A delightfully informal photograph of Honora Gale, riding her 1920 D2 model. She accompanied Ethel Goodman during motorcycle road events and is related to the Goodman family.

One of the more terrifying test hills of the 'twenties was Park Rash, not far from Kettlewell, in Yorkshire. George Denley carefully picks his way up the loose, stoney surface during the 1920 A-C.U. Six Days Trial.

George Denley shows his versatility by riding this two-stroke in the 1921 French Grand Prix, held at Le Mans. The cover over the flywheel is worthy of close inspection.

Riding what seems to be the same machine, George Denley brought his 250cc two-stroke to a creditable 7th place in the 1921 Junior TT.

Ethel Goodman shows her skill whilst riding a Model D two-stroke in the 'Coupe des Dames' event, held in the Parc de Prince, Paris circa 1921. She finished 2nd.

A study in concentration as the skittles are skilfully negotiated during the 'Coupe des Dames' event.

"Eric Peacock, the one-armed demon motorist who is now touring the halls", (1921). He featured in some of the early testimonials listed in the Velocette catalogues of the 'twenties. Note the foothold formed by an extension of the front wheel spindle.

·It would be interesting to know the story behind this photograph, in view of the venue, the traditional end of a very long ride.

George Denley poses by the roadside, presumably whilst on a touring holiday with this very nice 1926 ohc sidecar outfit.

The 1926 Junior TT Team Prize in its original presentation box, awarded to Veloce Limited folowing the achievement of their three ohc models in the Isle of Man. *(Les Brazier)*

The 1926 Junior TT riders, who formed the team entered by Veloce Ltd. This brought them their first TT win, a turning point in the fortunes of the company. Left to right: Gus Kuhn (5th), Alec Bennett (1st) and Fred Povey (9th).

A rare photograph of the Velocette workshop in the Isle of Man during the TT period, most probably in June 1928.

The Veloce General Office in 1928. The office boy looks especially young, whilst the poster on the far wall confirms the Velocette 1-2-5 victory in the 1928 Junior TT.

A photograph of the 'view' or inspection 'room' of the factory. Two-stroke flywheels, clutch chainwheels and pistons can be seen awaiting inspection, amongst other items.

This corner of the Tool Room shows quite clearly the machinery driven by belt from the overhead shafting.

Another view of the Tool Room. A box of cambox covers can be seen in the left foreground.

The Grinding Section, seen here, is overshadowed by a complexity of belt drives to the machines. Although described as either 'rooms' or 'sections', the various work areas were not physically subdivided.

In the Milling Section, Model U cylinders received attention, as did the gearbox shells and many other items, some of which can be seen in the photograph.

Machine Shop Bay No 1 seems to be handling the frame lugs from which the gearbox is suspended, as well as gearbox castings and two-stroke cylinders.

Machine Shop Bay No 3, shown here, is handling cambox bushes and also rear brake drums with their integral sprocket.

The Gearbox Fitting Section requires no special explanation, although the two-stroke model is still using the original design of three-speed gearbox with the face cam operated clutch.

The ohc models had their own, separate assembly line. The machines being assembled in the foreground have the Lucas Magdyno specification, necessitating the long, curved induction pipe for the carburettor to provide clearance.

Old clothes were needed here, in the Hardening Shop. A good place to be in the winter! Note the gas lamp illumination.

More dirty work in this area, where brazing, polishing and sandblasting take place. Note the frame headstocks piled to the left of the photograph.

The Enamelling Shop is by no means confined to male operatives, as can be seen in this photograph. Model U two-stroke frames have just been removed from the ovens; behind them, ohc petrol tanks have been lined and had their transfers affixed.

Noise was the main problem here, where engines were bench tested. An ohc engine is mounted on the brake in the foreground, and another on the brake at the rear.

1928 Model U two-strokes await dispatch. Some are fitted with the optional electric lighting, necessitating the use of the infamous Maglita of that period, there being no room to fit a Magdyno.

234

Veloce Ltd enjoyed good overseas sales. Here a batch of Model U two-strokes are being broken down into major units, prior to being crated for dispatch. The ohc models await their turn.

Note: The foregoing 16 photographs, together with several other photographs of the Works shown elsewhere in this book, form a special presentation album that was available in very limited numbers during 1928.

The 'Velocette Do' held in January 1929. Pride of place goes to Alec Bennett's 1928 Junior TT trophy. Percy Goodman is seated immediately behind the trophy and on his right, Ethel Goodman, with Alec Bennett next to her.

The TT Replica awarded to Freddie Hicks for winning the 1929 Junior TT at an average speed of 69.71mph. The inscription is worthy of note since it mentions the Tourist Trophy Trial. *(Les Brazier)*

The rarest Velocette of all – the 1929 dirt track model. The rider is Bert Clayton, associated with Claytons of Huddersfield, who were Velocette agents in that town. This machine was sold in July 1929; its engine (KDT149) still survives.

A later factory photograph, showing the assembly of four-speed foot gearchange gearboxes.

Stanley Woods toured Australia during 1936, taking with him his 'works' bikes to compete in Australian road races. Here he poses with his wife, seated on one of the 500cc singles. *(Dennis Quinlan)*

It is probable that this photograph is one of a series, taken for publicity purposes. It was taken at the time when the Ted Mellors/Franz Binder 1938/9 catalogue illustrations were devised. The man in the white coat is Harold Willis.

The memorial seat subscribed to by the management and members of Veloce Limited, in memory of Harold Willis. It was rescued just before the works were demolished and it is now, very fittingly, at Ballaugh, in the Isle of Man.

A studio portrait of Harold Willis, who died on the eve of the Velocette Junior TT win in 1939. He was sadly missed but has left behind a charisma all his own.

The last of a noble line, the now somewhat rare KSS model of 1948. Dowty front forks were fitted for the first and only time this season, as the Webb girder fork was no longer made.

Ethel Denley (neé Goodman) rides one of the first six of the new LE models at Bude, Cornwall, in July 1949. It had gone into production during October the year preceding.

Freddie Frith, Nigel Spring and Ken Bills pose at the end of the 1948 Junior TT, which Freddie won on his Mark VIII KTT. The man in the white overalls is Bill Mewis, who prepared the race-winning machine.

George Denley, now fulfilling the role of Sales Director, demonstrates the ease with which a 149cc LE Velocette can be threaded through the traffic in the centre of Birmingham during rush hour.

The last of the 'works' racers, fitted with telescopic front forks of Veloce design and manufacture.

A photograph of Percy Goodman, taken shortly before his untimely death in 1953. It seems ironic that the architect of so many highly successful models, including the ohc range, does not have his portrait hung in the National Motor Museum Hall of Fame.

These intrepid travellers, Fred and Doris Pickett, reached the Arctic Circle on their LE Velocette during 1954.

JRC's own 1954 MSS model, acquired from another Velocette enthusiast during 1978. It is in completely original condition, the dualseat having now been re-covered to the original specification. *(Les Brazier)*

JRC's USS two-stroke poses in rural surroundings that seem to fit the occasion. It is believed to be the only such model running in the UK. *(Les Brazier)*

A spread of colourful Velocette catalogues published during the thirties. *(Les Brazier)*

The classic '24 hour record breaking' poster, now a collectors' item. *(Les Brazier)*

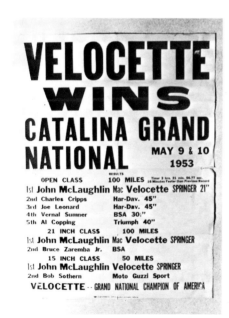

Velocettes had their successes in the USA too, including the Catalina Grand National of 1953. They repeated their success the second year, too. *(Les Brazier)*

Appendices

SOME NOTES ON VELOCETTE PART NUMBERS

Until the introduction of the LE model, a unique system of numbering component parts was in operation at the Hall Green Works. A brief description of this may be of interest to Velocette-owners or those for whom the marque has a special attraction.

Unlike some manufacturers, who 'invent' numbers to print in numerical order in their Spares Lists that have no real connection with the actual Part Numbers, Veloce Limited list the actual Works Part Numbers by which the particular part is known throughout the factory. Among most employees in factories conversations about their work includes many such numbers, used as a form of argot which is much quicker than giving a description of the items mentioned. Furthermore, there is less chance of misunderstanding. For example, one requires to refer to a valve so one refers to M2/2; there is no need for the person addressed to ask 'For what model?' The part number has told him all he needs to know and he can get out the detail drawing of the part concerned, should he so desire.

The example quoted is the number of an M-type valve, suitable for exhaust and inlet on both the first types of the MOV and MAC engines. MSS and other M-type engines have valves with part numbers starting M2 and all overhead camshaft valves have numbers starting K2.

When a modification is made to the part or a new M- or K-type engine is designed, the M2 or K2 acquires a suffix number, indicating a new part, not necessarily interchangeable with the original parts, e.g. M2/3, M2/4, K2/3, K2/4, etc. Throughout the M and K ranges all the valves follow this rule. Pistons on the M, K, and GTP models have the same basic number 27 prefixed respectively M, K, and RT. Very soon anyone having to deal with parts in Service, Stores, or Production acquires a working knowledge of many of the 'basic' numbers and can quote numbers from descriptions or vice versa.

A great advantage of not obscuring records with a series of catalogue numbers is that the original working drawing can be inspected at the Drawing Office by authorized persons, after locating the drawing in the filing-cabinet by using the part number. This is the system used at Hall Green. Engine parts use the prefix of the Works type letter; e.g. K (overhead camshaft models) and M (the MOV, MAC, MAF, MSS, Scrambler, Viper, and Venom, etc. series of push-rod models). The prefix also denotes the model upon which the part originated as it will be seen from the Veloce Parts Lists that there are parts with K prefixes used on M models, such as coil-type valve-springs K6/7; K7/6 on MOV, MAC, and MAF models in addition to the model upon which they were used first, the Mark II KSS and KTS models.

The locations upon the motor cycle can be ascertained approximately from the prefix letters used with some of the part numbers. Clutch parts have the prefix 'C' or 'CK', frame parts 'F' or 'FK', and gearbox parts by 'B' or 'BK'. In all these examples the 'K' denotes the parts were originally designed for the K models and were used first upon the overhead camshaft machines.

All rules have exceptions, or so it is said, and the system of using the initial letter of an assembly such as a frame by prefixing its parts with the prefix 'F' does not hold good throughout the range of spares. There are wheel bearings numbered with prefixes 'S' and 'KS' and sundry other items in wheel-hub and brake make-up where the prefixes 'W', 'A', and 'KA' appear in the lists.

For convenience there is what is called the Standard List, upon which appear all standard nuts, bolts, and washers. Additionally, the final-drive sprockets are included together with all standard studs, those straight lengths of steel threaded at both ends that are screwed into a casting and remain in place to carry the nuts that hold covers, etc. to the main part. All items on this list are prefixed 'SL' and all details of every bolt and stud, such as length, diameter, pitch of thread, length of plain portion, and other important details are readily available for reference. Gearbox sprocket width and pitch are indicated by different figures following the prefix, e.g. SL91: $\frac{1}{2}$ in. pitch $\times$ 0·305 in.; SL92: $\frac{1}{2}$ in. pitch $\times$ 0·205 in; and SL93: 0·625 in. $\times$ 0·75 in. The number of teeth is denoted by the figure following the oblique stroke.

The system of changing the figure in numerical sequence was not always in operation and prior to its adoption, the last two figures of the year during which a new part was introduced were used. This explains why part numbers such as B39/26 and C29/26 do not indicate a twenty-seventh change in specification as may be expected. Both were designed for and first used upon the gearboxes and clutches of the early K models, when the original cork-lined clutch was replaced by the seven-plate Ferodo-lined version in 1926, and the clutch operation was changed over from the 'frying-pan' operation to the current arrangement.

The futility of printing in Spare Parts Lists catalogue numbers from which the actual part numbers must first be ascertained before fulfilling an order is shown up very clearly when it comes to prices, because the same part is not always given the same catalogue number. A certain dealer who was 'in the know' was able to buy parts cheaper for a well-known make of machine by using a Spare Parts List applying to a different model from that for which he was ordering. He had found that identical parts carried different catalogue numbers in different lists and that the prices were not in line. He always ordered by quoting the catalogue number that was cheaper! You cannot do this with Velocette parts.

This extract from the original Mark II KSS Instruction Book, if used in conjunction with Veloce publication F 50/10R, will serve as a complete guide to the repair and maintenance of the overhead camshaft models.

ABRIDGED SPECIFICATION MODELS KSS and KTS

ENGINES. Type .. .. Single Cylinder, 4 stroke. Two overhead Valves operated by overhead Camshaft.

Bore and Stroke .. 74 mm. 81 mm.

Cubic Capacity (Swept Volume) .. .. 348 c.c.

Rated Horse-Power (A.C.U. Rating) .. 3.48 H.P. (One Horse Power per 100 c.c.).

Tappet Clearances (for Running) .. .. Inlet .006-in. Exhaust .010-in.

Tappet Clearances (for Timing) .. .. ,, .025-in. ,, .025-in.

Clearances set and checked when Engine is cold.

Position of Engine Serial Number .. Stamped (following the Serial letters "KSS") on near side of Crankcase below Cylinder Base Flange. Letters must be quoted with Serial number when referring to machine.

GEARBOXES. .. Type, 4 speed. Constant mesh. Foot controlled.

Ratios: Sprocket 15 tooth Top 6.42 3rd 7.75 2nd 10.2 1st 14.7
16 ,, ,, 6.02 ,, 7.26 ,, 9.55 ,, 13.8
17 ,, ,, 5.66 ,, 6.84 ,, 9.0 ,, 13.0

For Sidecar work use 15 tooth (smallest available) Sprocket. Gearbox Serial Number stamped on rear of Housing.

TRANSMISSION.

Primary Drive Driving Sprocket 21 teeth. Rear Driving Sprocket Variable (see above).

,, ,, Driven Sprocket 44 teeth. Rear Driven Sprocket 46 teeth.

Chains.. Primary: Pitch and Width .. .5-in. .305-in.
Roller Diameter .. .. .335-in.
Number of Pitches: 67.
Rear: Pitch and Width .. .625-in. .380-in.
Roller Diameter .. .. .4-in.
Number of Pitches. 99.

Wheels.. KTS Front WM3 × 19. KSS Front WM1 × 21.
,, Rear WM3 × 19. ,, Rear WM2 × 20.

Tyres .. ,, Front 19 × 3.25-in. ,, Front 21 × 3-in.
,, Rear 19 × 3.5-in. ,, Rear 20 × 3.25-in.

Frame .. Serial Number stamped on right-hand side of upper front Engine Lug.

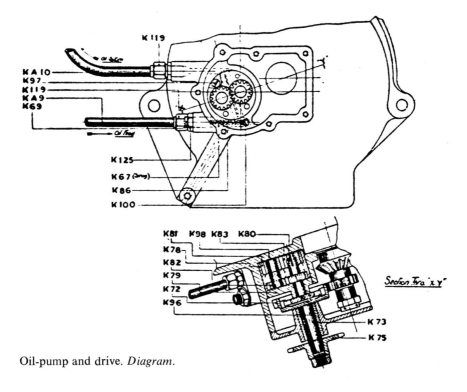

Oil-pump and drive. *Diagram.*

THE ENGINE LUBRICATION SYSTEM.

Oil is delivered by gravity to the feed side of a double, gear type oil pump fitted inside the timing case (behind the magneto chain case). This pump is driven by a coupling engaging with the inside of the magneto driving spindle. When the engine starts the feed side of the pump forces oil through a recess in the oil pump cover into the timing case, vertical shaft cover, and top bevel housing in which pressure is built up.

This pressure forces oil through a ball valve situated in the timing side mainshaft to the big end and through a groove in the camshaft main bearing into the cam chamber. (On engines prior to KSS 8101 oil is led by a pipe from the top bevel housing to a jet above the cams.) A flat is ground on the camshaft so as to overlap the groove in the bearing and form a passage for the oil at every turn of the shaft.

The oil which enters the mainshaft through the ball valve is taken through a passage drilled in the flywheel into a drilling in the crankpin of the big end. The big end is thus fed under pressure and oil is thrown out by the revolving bearing to lubricate the piston, cylinder walls and main bearings, afterwards draining down to the sump whence it is drawn by the return side of the oil pump to the oil tank. On all engines after KSS 8373 a filter is fitted between the sump and return pump. The filter plug is quite accessible and is just above the frame tube and below the magneto chain cover on the right-hand side of the machine.

In the upper part of the engine the oil fed into the cam chamber is distributed by the revolving cams to lubricate the rocker ends, rocker spindles and valves.

250

To prevent leakage of oil down the guides these are now fitted with leather oil retaining washers held in place by steel caps over the ends of the guides. All excess oil drains down the large pipe on the left-hand side of the engine and runs back into the sump.

Excess pressure in the system is relieved by the pressure release valve through which oil is by-passed to the feed side of the oil pump. This release valve is controlled by an adjustable screw adjacent to the oil feed union on the crankcase at the rear. It is correctly set before delivery of the machine and should not need re-adjustment in the ordinary course of service.

If for any reason it is necessary to re-adjust the pressure release, the adjusting screw should be turned clockwise to increase pressure or anti-clockwise to decrease it. Before the screw can be moved the lock nut must be slackened back anti-clockwise. Any adjustment needed should be made when the oil is thoroughly warm throughout (as after a run) and the

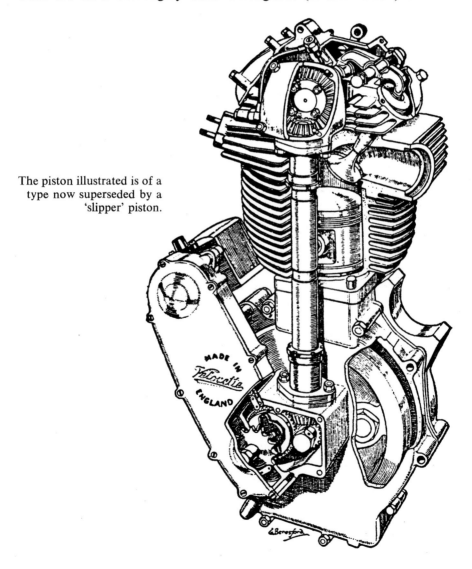

The piston illustrated is of a type now superseded by a 'slipper' piston.

screw should not be turned more than half a turn either way at any one time before checking the result of the adjustment—a small movement of the screw often has a big effect on the pressure.

An oil gauge is practically essential for checking purposes if any re-adjustment is made.

IMPORTANT. Before checking the pressure and the return of oil to the tank loosen and remove the lower section of the drain pipe from the Y pipe on the rocker box and arrange to collect any oil from the rocker box in a clean tin. This will ensure that the oil returned to the tank consists only of oil which has passed through the big end and provides a reliable check.

The oil pressure is checked by screwing an oil gauge into the hole provided in the bevel box cover (normally filled by a small hexagon headed plug). On early engines the gauge may be screwed into the hollow bolt which connects the oil pipe to the side of the bevel housing. These hollow bolts are drilled and fitted with a plug.

Normally and with engine oil well warmed up the pressure shown should be about 8 to 10 lbs. per square inch and the return of oil to the tank practically continuous, but in some cases it is possible to work with a slightly lower pressure provided that the return of oil to the tank does not become exceedingly intermittent or very small.

When the system is working correctly there will be both a pressure in the top bevel housing and a good return of oil to the tank—the one is not sufficient without the other.

Oil gauges should be used for checking purposes only and are not intended to be attached permanently to the machine.

The fact that the return is irregular sometimes give rise to enquiry, but it is quite in order. On starting the engine the return may be almost constant for a few moments due to the amount of oil which has drained to the bottom of the crankcase whilst the engine was stationary, and until this surplus is cleared the return flow will exceed normal. During normal running, however, the return is somewhat intermittent, and mixed with bubbles of air due, partly to the fact that the return side of the pump has practically double the capacity of the feed side, and partly to variations in the amount of oil suspended in the crankcase due to engine speed. For example, upon sudden acceleration the return flow may cease for a time, but will of course resume at a greater rate upon the engine being slowed down.

THE SUCTION FILTER

On all engines after KSS 8373 a suction filter is fitted to the crankcase and periodically this should be removed for cleaning. The filter plug is situated at the rear of the timing side crankcase (just above the frame tube and almost below the magneto chain cover).

Clean the crankcase around the filter plug before removal to avoid any dirt getting in when the plug is taken out. Unscrew the plug (anti-clockwise) and gently prise out the filter, using a small screw-driver at either side

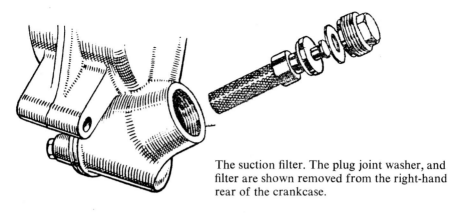

The suction filter. The plug joint washer, and filter are shown removed from the right-hand rear of the crankcase.

of the threaded hole. Do not lose the small lead seating washer which is fitted between the plug and the top of the filter.

Wash the filter in petrol or benzol. *Do not use paraffin* for cleaning filters. When re-fitting the filter plug do not force it down, as the lead washer is soft enough to give an air and oil tight joint without undue pressure.

Should the suction filter become choked the crankcase will be flooded with oil and excessive smoking at the exhaust will be noticeable.

THE CRANKSHAFT BALL VALVE

In the left hand thread nut on the timing side mainshaft a $\frac{1}{4}$-in. dia. steel bearing ball is held into contact by a light spring with a seating cut inside the nut. The purpose of the ball valve is to prevent oil draining by gravity from tank to crankcase sump when the engine is stationary.

Should it be found that the exhaust smokes excessively on starting or should the engine be difficult to start due to an accumulation of oil in the sump the cause is possibly this valve failing to close properly. Sludge or dirt in the oil through keeping oil too long in circulation may be responsible.

Remove the left hand thread nut from the mainshaft. Take care not to drop and lose the ball while taking off the nut. The spring will probably remain protruding from the shaft and may be pulled out carefully. Examine the spring and if damaged or distorted obtain a new spring, catalogue number K.115. Clean out the oil holes in the nut and clean the seating. The seating may be lapped, using a spare $\frac{1}{4}$-in. dia. bearing ball soldered to a short piece of brass bar, or the ball may be reseated by tapping it against the seating using a short punch whilst supporting the nut, open end upwards (with the ball on the seating) on a flat solid metal surface, such as the back of a bench vice. It is inadvisable to use much force as this tends to widen the seating and so reduce the unit pressure upon it making subsequent leakage more likely. If in any doubt as to the condition of the ball valve seating fit a new nut, catalogue number K.114/2.

CHECKING AND RESETTING THE VALVE CLEARANCES

The Fuel Tank must be removed in order to check or reset the clearances. Undo and remove the nuts securing the two rocker covers and take off the one at the front over the exhaust rocker. The Inlet cover can only be raised upon its studs and cannot be taken off unless the cylinder head is off the engine or the engine is out of the frame.

Set the crankshaft with the piston at top dead centre of the compression stroke. This position can most conveniently be found by pressing down the footstarter until the resistance of compression is felt (open throttle and air controls fully to provide "something to compress" in the cylinder). Having found the compression stroke take out the sparking plug and insert a spoke or straight piece of stiff wire through the plug hole to feel the piston. *Do not use a short length of wire—it may be dropped accidentally into the cylinder.* Holding the wire carefully move the crankshaft forward slowly until the piston is felt to reach its highest point in the cylinder, i.e., top dead centre. Check clearances with a "feeler" gauge. Inlet should be .006-in., Exhaust .010-in.

If re-adjustment is needed, loosen the rocker pin locknuts with the spanner provided, and then turn the rocker pins to increase or decrease the clearance, whichever is needed. To increase the clearance turn the exhaust rocker pin anti-clockwise and the inlet pin clockwise. To decrease the clearances turn the exhaust rocker pin clockwise and the inlet anti-clockwise. If reference is made to the illustration on page 223 it will be seen that the "V" marks are moved upwards to increase, or downwards to decrease clearances.

Always check and reset clearances when engine is cold. Finally refit rocker covers with a light smear of Jointing compound on the joint faces and fit and tighten the nuts evenly.

DECARBONISING THE ENGINE. (REMOVAL OF CYLINDER HEAD)

It is generally desirable to decarbonise the engine and to grind in the valves lightly on a new or recently overhauled engine after it has covered the first 2,000 miles. It is not, however, necessary or even advisable to repeat the process at anything like such frequent intervals, and often a very considerable mileage can be covered before it is necessary to decarbonise again.

The usual indications that the work is needed are a falling off in power and a tendency for the engine to pink excessively on accelerating and when pulling hard.

As the utmost care is needed to prevent the entry of dirt or foreign matter it is desirable to wash down the engine thoroughly with clean petrol or benzol before commencing any dismantling. Work should be carried out in surroundings as free as possible from dust and after removal of the head (as described below) the cover should be replaced on the bevel housing and clean rag or paper should be tied over the open ends of the bevel bush housing and vertical shaft cover.

Before the head can be removed the petrol tank has to be taken off. To do this turn off both petrol taps and remove the petrol pipe. Take out the bolt from the nose of the saddle and lift the front. Remove the three tank bolts. One through the frame at the back and the other two underneath

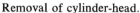

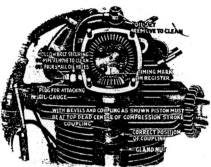

Removal of cylinder-head.

the tank at the front. See that the rubber buffers are not mixed so that they may be replaced in their correct places. Now lift off the tank.

Unscrew the ring holding the fixing chamber top to the mixing chamber of the carburetter and pull out the slides. Undo the exhaust pipe nut, disconnect the exhaust lifter cable from the lever on the head and remove the "Y" shaped oil drain pipe by loosening the union nuts which hold it to the head and the lower half of the pipe. Take out the sparking plug, and remove cylinder head steady strap.

THE IGNITION TIMING

Remove the Contact-breaker Cover from the Magneto and rotate the Crankshaft with the Footstarter until the Contact-points are fully open.

Check the gap with the gauge on the Magneto Spanner, and if not correct reset the adjustable point to give the right clearance.

Fix a Timing Disc and Pointer (as described in the last section) after removing the Dynamo Belt-cover.

Open the Throttle and Air Controls fully.

Engage the Footstarter and rotate the Crankshaft until compression is felt in the Cylinder.

Release the Footstarter, and then remove the Sparking-plug.

Set the Piston to Top dead-centre and adjust the Pointer to zero on the Timing-disc. Advance the ignition control fully.

Move the Crankshaft BACK about 60°, and with the fingers separate the Contact-points. Place between the Points a small strip of Cigarette-paper or paper of similar thickness (.001 to .0015-in.).

Release the Points on to the paper.

Checking. Rotate the Crankshaft forward very slowly whilst maintaining a light pull on the Cigarette-paper.

If the timing is correct, the grip of the Points on the paper will cease when the Crankshaft is 40° before top dead centre.

If not correct loosen the sprocket and re-set it.

Should no Timing-disc be available one can be made quite easily by marking out a card or metal disc in degrees by means of a Protractor.

Take off the Dynamo-belt cover, loosen the clamping bolt in the Dynamo-strap, turn the Dynamo in its mounting until the belt is loose, and remove the belt. Remove the cover from the front end of the rear chain—it is held at the front end by a nut to a stud on the Primary-chain cover. Lift the ear on the cover off the stud, at the same time pulling the cover forward out away from the rear part of the chain cover. Sometimes this is easier if the bolt holding the rear part of the cover to the mudguard valance is loosened first.

Remove the split cotters from the nut securing the rear driving Sprocket and from the nut on the Engine-shaft. Loosen the nut on the Gearshaft slightly. This nut is usually very tight, and the Spanner will need driving round with a hammer or mallet, and the rear Brake should be held on firmly while doing so to prevent the Sprocket turning.

Next engage top gear and remove the nut from the Engine-Shaft. This nut will also require to be driven round to start it and the Engine shaft prevented from turning by holding the rear Brake on. Both nuts unscrew anti-clockwise. Special spanners are provided in the tool kit for both these nuts, the pegged spanner (closed end) and the "Ring" spanner respectively.

Unscrew the nut right off the Engine-shaft with the Belt Pulley flange and Spring. Do not lose the plain washer which is used between the nut and the shoulder of the Shaft. Now unscrew and remove the nut from the Gearshaft, take off the plain washer behind it. Pull the Sprocket off the shaft, and unhook it out of the chain.

Take out all screws from around the edge of the Chain cover. Remove the single bolt securing the cover to the crankcase and take off the left-hand footrest and footrest square bar. Pull the outer half of the cover away from the inner part, being careful when separating them not to damage the Joint-packing. A distance tube will be found between the two halves. This fits over the edges of the covers around the holes, through which the fixing bolt passes. The purpose of the distance tube is to prevent oil leaking out, and to prevent the cover being crushed in when the bolt is tightened.

The sliding member or shock-absorber clutch may now be pulled out off the Engine shaft, but the sprocket and chain cannot be removed on account of the chain being of the "Endless" type, this making it necessary to take off at the same time the chain wheel from the Gearbox.

Remove the small grub screw and the locking plate† from the Flange of the Sleeve-gear nut on the clutch. It will be seen that the nut has four holes drilled in the Flange and the Peg-spanner is used to turn the nut. Again it will almost certainly be necessary to start the nut (anti-clockwise) by driving round the spanner. Remove the nut and pull off the Engine-sprocket and whole of the clutch with the chain. To start the clutch out of position it may be necessary to lever the back plate away from the face

† *Not fitted to pre-war models*

of the Gearbox. Be careful when the Clutch is removed not to lose the three small Thrust pins from the back-plate.

After re-assembling note that the Clutch will need re-adjustment.

THE ENGINE—REMOVAL FROM FRAME

Take off the Fuel Tank, Engine shaft shock absorber, Primary chain, and clutch as described in the sections dealing with these points.

Disconnect the cable from the positive terminal at the rear of the battery and pull out the plug from the commutator end of the dynamo. Take out the screws securing the Voltage-regulator to the dynamo strap and remove the Dynamo, Regulator and inner half of the Dynamo Belt Cover. Remove Exhaust pipe and Cylinder head steady. Remove Carburetter and disconnect Exhaust lifter and Magneto control cables.

Slightly loosen the bolts holding the rear engine plates to the crankcase and remove all the other bolts securing the front and rear engine plates to the frame and the bolts securing the front engine plates to the crankcase.

Lift the entire engine and gearbox units out of the frame. Finally, separate the engine from the gearbox by removing the bolts holding the rear engine plates to the crankcase.

DISMANTLING CYLINDER AND PISTON

Support the engine in a convenient position by gripping in a vice the front flange of the crankcase, supporting the rear of the engine from the bench by means of a steel bar bent to fit into one of the bolt holes and set to rest firmly on the bench. This takes a lot of the weight and prevents the Engine sliding down in the vice.

Take off the Cylinder Head as described on pages 222 and 223. With the flat of the hands against the front and rear of the Cylinder, push it sharply backwards and forwards alternately, exerting an upward pressure at the same time, to loosen the cylinder in the Crankcase. When free, pull it up carefully off the Piston. It is advisable to have an assistant to support the Piston as it is freed from the Cylinder in order to avoid damage, as Standard Two compression plates are fitted under the Cylinder.

Make a note before removing the piston which side of the engine the slot for the removal of the circlip is situated, or mark the piston so that it is put back into the same position. The flat machined face on the piston crown below the exhaust valve is marked "EX."

Remove one of the circlips from the piston and drive out the gudgeon pin from the opposite side. A soft metal punch must be used against the end of the pin to prevent damage. An assistant is essential when driving out the pin, so that the piston is supported on the opposite side to avoid damaging the connecting rod by setting it out of line.

The pin is a light driving fit with the piston cold.

REMOVAL OF PISTON RINGS

To remove the piston rings, gently expand the ends of the top piston ring away from the piston and insert three or four thin metal strips between the ring and the piston, sliding these round behind the ring until it is possible to slide the ring upwards over the piston crown. Take care not to spring the rings any more than is necessary to put the strips into place and to raise them out of the grooves as piston rings are rather brittle. This applies particularly to the slotted oil control ring. Some early engines have "stepped" section scraper rings in the third groove from the top and in a groove at the bottom of the skirt.

The current type of piston is of the "Slipper" pattern and carries two compression rings and a slotted oil control ring.

RECUTTING VALVE SEATS

The seatings in the Head can then be cleaned up by using a 45 deg. cutter with a pilot $\frac{5}{16}$-in. diameter, 4-in. long, for the inlet valve guide and a $\frac{3}{8}$-in. pilot will be needed for the exhaust guide.

After prolonged service, and repeated cutting, the Seatings may become sunk well below the surrounding surface of the combustion chamber, and this condition lowers the efficiency of the engine. In such circumstances it may be necessary for new valve seats to be inserted—a factory job.

The Valve guides are detachable, and may be removed and new ones fitted with a double diameter soft punch or drift. The small end should be $\frac{5}{16}$-in. diameter for about 2-in., and the remainder $\frac{1}{2}$-in. diameter approximately 4-in. long. Drive out the guides from inside the ports, but do not remove them unless they are worn or damaged so as to need replacement.

INSPECTION OF CYLINDER AND PISTON RINGS

The cylinder should now be inspected for condition of bore and piston rings. If the bore is worn badly or is scored, it will require re-boring and an oversize piston with rings. The original diameter of the bore is 2.913-in.

Re-boring is generally considered necessary when wear in excess of .008-in. has taken place, or the bore had become damaged or scored.

The rings when new, and when fitted to a new or re-bored cylinder, have gap clearances as follows:—

Compression rings .. .. .. .010-in.
Scraper ring .. .. .012-in.

Oversize pistons and rings are made in only two oversizes:—

plus .020-in. ($\frac{1}{2}$ mm) and plus .040-in. (1 mm).

No intermediate sizes are used. It is not practicable to fit oversize rings to a worn cylinder, unless the cylinder is re-bored and the appropriate larger piston fitted.

NOTE. If the cylinder is rebored and oversize piston is fitted, the mouth of the combustion chamber will have to be enlarged to clear the top land of the oversize piston.

REMOVAL OF MAGNETO AND TIMING COVER

Take out the screws securing the magneto chain cover and remove the cover. Undo all the screws securing the timing cover to the crankcase. Three of these are inside the chain case and one of them cannot be screwed right out as it will be found to foul the chain. Loosen and take off the large nut from the magneto chain case support stud which supports the back of the case to the crankcase. Pull the timing cover forward off the large stud and away from the crankcase bringing with it the magneto, the magneto chain and the sprockets, and when it is sufficiently far away take out the screw which could not previously be taken away. Do not lose the small coupling which drives the oil pump.

REMOVING TIMING PINION AND BOTTOM BEVELS

Take off the two nuts securing the bottom vertical bevel bush housing to the crank case. Tap the housing slightly from side to side to free it and draw it right up off the studs. Note the number of paper joint washers fitted between face joints so as to know how many to fit when re-assembling. Loosen and remove the ball valve nut from the end of the mainshaft: this nut is a left-hand thread. As it is removed it will expose the $\frac{1}{4}$-in. ball and the ball valve spring. Be careful not to lose the ball or damage the spring, which should be carefully pulled out from the end of the mainshaft. Take off the small tongued washer which is fitted over the mainshaft behind the ball valve nut. A small claw extractor will now be necessary to draw the magneto and pump driving pinion off the shaft. This pinion is not keyed. Finally, carefully prise off the bottom bevel pinion from the mainshaft—this can usually be done without difficulty by two small levers or screwdrivers. This pinion is a parallel fit on the shaft and is keyed in place. Note that there may be thin packing shims used behind this pinion for meshing purposes, and these should be retained for use when re-assembling.

SEPARATING THE CRANKCASE—REMOVAL OF MAIN-BEARINGS

The separation of the two halves of the crankcase is quite straight-forward and will be accomplished easily after taking out all securing studs and bolts.

The Mainbearings—a roller race on the near side and a ball race on the offside should be replaced if there is any trace of roughness or if any up and down play can be detected. The ball race and the outer rings of the roller race are readily removed without special tools if the Crankcase is heated first, and smartly brought down on to a solid wood surface to jarr them out of place; the centre ring of the roller race can be prised off the shaft.

Whilst the Crankcase is separated remove the oil-filter-plug from the offside rear. Clean out all oil passages.

THE OIL PUMP

It is best to avoid disturbing the oil pump, and unless it has to be removed for the renewal of worn or damaged parts it should be left in place. Should it require attention, however, or if it is necessary to clean out the oil passages in the crankcase it may be removed as follows:—

Remove the four fixing screws. *Do not attempt to remove the pump without heating the crankcase.* Heat the crankcase carefully over a gas ring to about 100 degrees Centigrade to expand the housing from the pump body, then holding the crankcase between several thicknesses of rag to protect the hands, raise it and bring it down smartly (timing case downwards) on to the flat top of the bench or other wood surface to jarr the pump cover and body out of place.

Having removed the pump, note that a brass shim K110 is fitted in the pump housing behind the pump body. Examine this, and should it show signs of wear obtain a new one. The pump spindle gears may now be taken out for inspection. The gears must be a close fit in the pump body, and must turn quite freely without end float.

Should new gears be fitted it may be found necessary carefully to lap these in, for which the following easily made equipment will be needed.

To maintain the pump cover truly concentric with the body, a split bush accurately turned to fit closely over the pump and cover and capable of being contacted on to them is required. Also a steel plate about $\frac{1}{4}$-in. thick and surface ground flat one side should be drilled, using the pump body as a guide, and tapped to take the four pump screws. The pump is then assembled and clamped in the split bush and secured to the steel plate with the four fixing screws. The ground flat face must be towards the pump body.

The lapping is done by rotating the pump spindle and running through the pump a mixture of Turkey stone powder and oil. **In no circumstances must emery powder or valve grinding compound be used.**

After lapping remove the pump from the plate and take it apart to clean away all abrasive matter. Refit the gears with clean oil and the pump is ready for re-fitting to the crankcase.

It should be noted that should the pump gears have locked due to foreign matter getting into the return side after being drawn up from the sump, a condition which may arise only in an early type engine without a suction filter, very great care is necessary to see that absolutely every trace of foreign matter is removed before re-assembly of the pump. Therefore in any instance when the pump spindle has sheared always make sure beyond possibility of doubt that the oil pipe which is cast into the timing half of the case and leads from the rear corner to the pump housing, is absolutely free from further pieces which might be drawn through to the pump and cause a repetition of the former trouble. In such cases, it is also essential to clean all external oil pipes and hoses and wash out the oil tank, subsequently re-filling with clean fresh oil.

In the event of it ever being necessary to extract the oil pump without the engine being dismantled, the following method may be adopted:—

Obtain a piece of flat mild steel approximately $4\frac{1}{2}$-in. long by $\frac{1}{2}$-in. wide by $\frac{1}{4}$-in. thick. Mark off the approximate centre and equi-distant from the centre drill two $\frac{1}{4}$-in. clearance holes $1\frac{3}{8}$-in. between centres. Also obtain two $\frac{1}{4}$-in. diameter studs approximately $1\frac{1}{2}$-in. long, threaded at both ends with $\frac{1}{4}$-in. $\times 26$ threads. From one end the thread should run down about 1-in., and from the other end about $\frac{1}{4}$-in. Two $\frac{1}{4}$-in. $\times 26$ thread nuts will also be required. Carefully remove the oil pump cover after taking out the four fixing screws, and then tap out for about three threads two opposite holes in the pump body to receive the $\frac{1}{4}$-in. studs. Fix the studs in position. If the drilled steel strip is then placed across the face of the bevel box and over the studs and the nuts are then run down on the studs, it will be possible to withdraw the pump when the crankcase has been sufficiently heated by tightening down each nut a little at a time so as to draw the pump out of the housing.

RE-FITTING THE OIL PUMP

To re-fit the pump heat up the crankcase, set the shim in place, and slide the pump into position, locating the pump carefully so that the four screws will fit into these holes in the crankcase, and so that the slot in the oil pump cover through which oil is delivered, is at the top.

It is of assistance in locating the shim and pump when fitting if two studs about $2\frac{1}{2}$-ins. long $\times \frac{3}{16}$ in. diameter, and threaded for about $\frac{1}{4}$-in. at one end and screwed into two opposite holes in the pump housing in the crankcase, so that the shim and the pump can be slid over them and into place. When the pump and cover are fully home, fit the four fixing screws and tighten them.

THE BIG-END BEARING

The Connecting rod should have no detectable vertical play, with oil in the bearing.

To dismantle the Flywheel assembly a heavy Box-Spanner will be needed. The crankpin nuts are invariably tight, and good leverage is required to shift them. The nuts are not locked.

A $\frac{3}{4}$-in. Whit. spanner (1.3-in. across the flats) and not exceeding $1\frac{3}{4}$-in. diameter around the hexagon will be needed.

The ends of the Crankpin are slightly tapered and the pin will have to be driven out of the Flywheels. For inspection it is of course only necessary to take off one Flywheel, which will permit the Connecting rod and the roller cage to be slid off the Crankpin, making all parts accessible for close inspection.

The Roller cage is supported on the Crankpin and occasionally wears the outer edges. This is not important provided that the Roller track in the centre is in good condition. Any pitting of the Roller-track calls for renewal of the affected part, and the Crankpin will have to be taken out of the other Flywheel.

Actually, the Crankpin is made up of two parts*—a hardened steel Sleeve being pressed on to a "soft" pin. Thus in the event of wear, the Sleeve only may be renewed.

The Standard diameter is 1.374-in.

REFITTING THE CRANKPIN

This construction makes it necessary to tighten both Crankpin-nuts evenly when fitting, otherwise the Sleeve might be moved on the pin.

* *Except before 1939 when the pins were made in one piece.*

When re-assembling the pin or fitting a new one, tap the pin carefully into the Flywheel and tighten down the nut only far enough to pull the edge of the Sleeve into light contact with the face of the Flywheel. Always make certain that the two faces are quite clean before fitting. It is immaterial which way round the pin is fitted, and as the Sleeve is recessed at both sides there is no need to register any oil hole in the Crankpin with the oil-hole in the Flywheel. Before fitting, however, make sure that the oil passage through the timing-side Mainshaft to the inner face of the Flywheel is quite clear, and also see that there is no restriction in the oil hole in the Crank pin sleeve.

SPECIAL NOTE

When the Crankpin is fitted it must be located so that the oil hole in the crankpin sleeve which runs through into the roller track is set to face to the rear at 90 degrees from the vertical with the fly wheels set at top dead centre.

Oversize rollers are also usually obtainable. The standard diameter is .1875-in., and there are two oversizes, .0002-in. and .0004-in. oversize respectively. In addition, should the hardened ring in the Connecting rod be worn or pitted, this also may be renewed.

With the Connecting rod mounted with rollers and cage in position on the Crankpin the slightest perceptible vertical play should be allowed with a dry bearing. Should there be slight stiffness this can usually be eliminated by carefully lapping out the ring in the rod or slightly polishing down the Crank-pin sleeve.

LINING UP THE FLYWHEELS

For lining up the Flywheels perfectly straightforward equipment is all that is required. The Flywheels should first be roughly lined up in the vice and then trued by placing the two Main-Bearings on their shafts, resting these on V blocks 5-in. from the shaft centres to the base and 2⅜-in. apart, and then checking with a Dial-gauge on the Mainshafts. The Shafts are allowed a maximum out of truth figure of .001-in.

REFITTING THE MAIN BEARINGS

NOTE SPECIALLY that the inner rings of the main bearings taper .001-in. per inch and must therefore be fitted the correct way round to their respective shafts. The "large" ends of the inner rings are always fitted adjacent to the Flywheel bosses, i.e., they are placed on the shafts "large end first."

The "large" ends will be found on inspection to have a pronounced radius, but as an extra check, "Hoffman" bearings have the maker's name and identification serial numbers stamped on the opposite side of the races so that when correctly fitted these marks should be outside and remote from the flywheels.

Should an attempt be made to fit the bearings the wrong way round it will be found that they will hardly go on to the mainshafts at all when pressed lightly into position with the fingers.

Heat the Crankcase halves before fitting the timing side ballrace or the outer ring of the roller race by immersing each half in boiling water until it is hot enough to allow the bearing and the outer ring to be dropped into the housings.

Before fitting the ballrace fit the oil retaining shim (K150) and any shims for taking up end float, but always fit the oil retainer next to the ballrace. No other shims must be fitted between the bearing and the oil retaining shim.

See that the outer ring of the roller race is fitted with lip at the bottom of the housing, otherwise it will be impossible to slide the Crankcase into place owing to the rollers being unable to enter the outer ring.

REFITTING FLYWHEELS TO CRANKCASE

As to the re-assembly of the Crankcase, no particular difficulty is likely to occur, but care is necessary to see that the Flywheel Assembly is set so that with perfect freedom when cold, there is no detectable sideplay.

The best method of doing this part of the work is first to fit the main bearings into the Crankcase, bolt the two halves of the Crankcase together (there is no joint packing used between them) and measure carefully the distance between the faces of the two inner rings of the Bearings. Use an internal micrometer for this. Next measure the width across between the main Bearing-bosses on the Flywheels. Any difference between the two dimensions may be made up by placing shims behind the outer rings of the bearings. As far as possible pack each side equally to keep the Flywheel Assembly central in the Crankcase. The shims are stocked in three thicknesses, .0003-in., .0005-in., and .012-in.

THE VERTICAL BEVELS AND BEVEL BUSH HOUSINGS

These seldom need attention, but if it is required to remove the bevels the housing must be rested, with the gear teeth downwards, and the flange face across the protected jaws of a vice or over a large tube or bush of suitable diameter. The bevel gear is removed by forcing it out of its retaining collar by tapping the slotted end downwards, using a brass or aluminium punch to avoid damaging the bevel.

To remove the bush, this has to be pressed out of the housing in the same direction. If a re-placement bush is fitted, it is essential that after fitting, the thrust face of the bush must be exactly the same distance from the joint face as the original, and it is therefore necessary to check this distance carefully before pressing out the old bush. If the distance is not correct trouble will be encountered in re-assembling the bevels, as if the thrust face stands out too far the meshing will be too tight, and if not enough there will be too much back lash between the teeth.

When re-fitting the bevel smear the bearing surface with clean oil, clean out the bush and push the bevel into place. Place the locating collar over the end of the bevel with the flat face downwards, and press it down into place. When finally fitted, the collar must allow the bevel to rotate freely without end float.

Having re-assembled the flywheels in the crankcase and bolted the two halves of the case together, it is necessary to fit the crankshaft bevel gear into place, making certain that the keyway slot in the gear is engaged with the key in the mainshaft, and that any spacing shims originally fitted are put back or replaced with new shims of similar thickness. Tap the gear firmly home and then fit the bottom bevel bush housing and vertical bevel into position with the same number of joint washers between the face joints as were used originally. Fit the washers and nuts on to the studs and tighten down carefully.

The aim is to get the bevels meshing for the full width of the teeth without backlash but with perfect freedom from tightness in all positions. If the pinions when checked are too slack remove them and take out a joint washer from the bush housing or fit an additional shim behind the crankshaft pinion. Re-assemble and check them again. Tight meshing can be rectified by fitting additional paper packings under the face of the vertical bevel bush housing or removing shims from behind the crankcase pinion.

The whole procedure is difficult to describe adequately, and some skill is needed to make a good job, but by careful selection of the correct thicknesses of shims and joint washers final correct setting can be achieved.

When meshed correctly remove the bevel bush housing, coat the face joints with good jointing compound and re-assemble, tightening the two nuts down carefully.

Fit the magneto driving gear in place on the shaft and tap it up into position. Follow it up with the small tongue washer and fit the ball valve spring into the end of the mainshaft. Stick the $\frac{1}{4}$-in. bearing ball into the left-hand thread nut with a light smear of soft clean grease and screw up the nut tight.

Finally fit the magneto chain case and timing cover with the magneto, magneto chain, sprockets, and bottom spindle and gear in place. See that the coupling is fitted on to the projection of the oil pump spindle.

It may be a little difficult to get the "Half time" gears meshed and coupling engaged with the recesses in the gear, but after one or two attempts success should be achieved.

Loosen the bottom and top gland nuts and push them respectively up and down the vertical shaft cover well clear of the threads. Prise out the spring circlip ring from the groove in the vertical shaft cover just above the bottom bevel bush housing, and slide it up the outside of the cover. This will allow the vertical shaft cover to slide down into the bottom bevel bush housing and the top coupling will be exposed. Remove the four nuts which hold the cover to the top bevel housing and pull off the cover. It is now that care is needed to set the engine to the correct position for the removal of the head. Rotate the crankshaft by means of the foot starter until the marks on the top bevels are in register. This will be made clear by reference to the illustration on page 223. It may be necessary to turn the engine anything up to twenty-one turns before the correct registering of the marks will be obtained according to the position in which the engine came to rest.

The slot in the top of the vertical shaft will be in line with the crankshaft and the piston, will be at the top of compression stroke when the marks register.

The cylinder head bolts may now be unscrewed by using the box spanner provided and the head lifted off the barrel. Take care not to damage the copper cylinder head gasket. It is best to take it off and hang it up until needed during reassembly. *Do not turn the crankshaft while the head is off or the timing will be upset.*

It is unnecessary to remove the cylinder barrel, and we do not advise disturbing it at all unless it has to be taken off for attention to the piston or piston rings. This is not likely to be needed except after a considerable mileage has been run. The cylinder piston and rings should be disturbed as little as possible. Frequent removal and reassembly sometimes cause prematurely heavy oil consumption.

REMOVAL OF VALVES

Loosen the lock nuts of both rocker pins with the spanner provided and take off the valve covers. Compress the springs of one of the valves and take out the cotter. We supply a valve spring compresser which is the best tool for this work. When ordering quote Part No. KA163/2. The compresser is designed so that one end bears on the valve spring top washer whilst the end of the compressing screw locates in the centre of the valve head. Now unscrew and take away the valve spring compresser and pull out the valve.

It is necessary to remove the rocker if the springs, with top and bottom washers, are to be taken out. This is done by using the spring compresser again, but as the valve is no longer in place a washer (SL6/35) must be placed over the plain tip of the screw to provide a bearing for the screw and to prevent damage to the end of the valve guide in which the tip should be located. After compressing the springs enough to clear the rocker, the rocker pin can be unscrewed and taken out allowing removal of rocker and thrust washer. This latter is fitted on the rocker pin between the rocker and the threaded end of the pin. After releasing the springs they can be lifted out together with the top and bottom washers. Also remove the oil retaining washers and caps from the valve guides.

It is best to provide two small boxes marked respectively "inlet" and "exhaust", so that the rockers, valve cotters, springs, etc., shall not be mixed. Actually the springs, top and bottom washers, and rockers are interchangeable between exhaust and inlet, but it is best to keep them separate after they have been in service.

The removal of the other valve, springs, and rocker is carried out in just the same way.

To clean the carbon from the piston crown and the head a soft metal scraper should be used to avoid scratching the surfaces. A strip of brass filed to an edge at one end is suitable. Do not in any circumstances clean or polish the piston top with emery cloth as abrasive may get between piston and cylinder and cause scoring and premature wear.

Before scraping away the carbon from the head the cavities through which the rockers project should be stuffed with clean rag to stop any carbon or dirt entering the cam chamber and getting into the camshaft bearings.

REFACING AND GRINDING IN VALVES, ETC.

Reface the seatings on a valve grinding machine equipped with a collett if such a machine is available. The seat angle is 45°.

An alternative method is to hold the stem carefully and as close to the head as possible in the chuck of a lathe or drilling machine, being careful not to mark the stem or otherwise damage it.

The valve head may then be cleaned and polished up with ordinary emery cloth, a fine grade being used for finishing purposes. It is desirable to true up the valve seats before grinding in the valves because although a valve is a comparatively cheap replacement it is necessary to avoid wearing the seats in the cylinder head by prolonged grinding as they are expensive to replace.

It is unlikely that the seatings in the cylinder head will require truing up with a cutter unless the machine has covered a considerable distance.

If recutting is needed see page 226.

If the seats appear to be in reasonably good order, the valves should be lightly ground in. To grind in the valves, use a very fine emery powder mixed with oil or paraffin, or one of the numerous brands of valve grinding compounds. These compounds are sometimes put up in double-ended tins, the coarse compound in one end and fine compound in the other. It is very seldom necessary to use the coarse variety on the valves. Use as little compound as possible smeared over the seating on the valve. Avoid getting any compound on to the stem or into the valve guide.

Slip the valve into position and hold the end of the stem near the cotter groove with a suitable holder which should be tightened on to the valve carefully to avoid damaging the stem or the edges of the cotter groove.

Rotate the valve backwards and forwards, maintaining the Valve head in contact with the seating by pulling lightly on the stem. Lift the valve frequently from the seating to prevent the formation of concentric rings and bring it down into another position, recommencing the back and forward movement for a further period.

After a few minutes light grinding the holder should be removed and the valve taken out. The compound should be wiped off the valve and off the seating in the head. The seatings should be a light grey in appearance, free from marks or black pits. As soon as a light grey seating is obtained all round the seat of the valve, and all round the seat in the head the grinding-in operation is complete, and the other valve should then be tackled.

Should the rockers and valve springs, etc., not have been removed, proceed to refit the valves as described later, but if the rockers and springs have been taken out the oil seal washers from the tops of the Inlet and Exhaust guides should be inspected. If the exhaust has been excessively smoky, or if the oil seal washers are worn or hard they should be replaced with new ones (Catalogue Nos. K252 and K253).

To refit first put in the valve spring bottom washer, the oil retaining washer and cap, the springs and the top washer, and compress the springs using the small washer SL6/35 as previously described. Put back the rocker, making sure that the rocker bush is quite clean. Clean the rocker spindle, oil the bearing surface, and screw it back into place, not forgetting the rocker thrust washer which is fitted between the left-hand side of the rocker and the threaded end of pin. Screw in the rocker spindle as far as it will go, but do not use force. Now unscrew the spindle until the "V" or arrow marked on the end of the spindle inside the hollow end of the hexagon is, in the case of the exhaust valve (the front one), facing the rear, or in the case of the inlet valve, facing the front. An illustration appears on another page showing the exact location of the pins. Having refitted the rocker, release the valve springs again, see that the valve guide is clean, wipe the valve stem with clean oil or grease and put the valve into position. It may be necessary to manoeuvre the valve spring about a little to let the valve stem pass through the oil seal and its cap. Having made sure that the valve is on the seating, refit the valve spring remover and compress the springs until it is possible to get the cotter into place. See that the cotter is properly engaged with the groove on the stem, and when this has been done release the screw so that springs will return to their correct position. Having refitted both valves and rockers, the valve clearances can be reset before the head is put back on to the engine, but it is desirable before setting the clearances to make sure that the camshaft has not been moved and that the marks on the bevels are in register. Here again reference to the illustration should make matters quite clear. The clearances are set by turning the rocker spindles to move the "V" marks or arrows downwards to decrease the clearance or upwards to increase them. Set the inlet clearance to .006-in. and the exhaust to .010-in. for running. These clearances are correct for a cold engine.

VALVE CLEARANCES FOR CHECKING TIMING

When the clearances have been set correctly tighten the rocker pin locknuts really tight. If it is desired to check the valve timing after the head has been re-fitted the clearances should both be set to .025-in., but if this is done do not forget to reset the clearances to the correct running clearances after the timing has been checked and reset.

THE CYLINDER HEAD JOINT

Unless this shows signs of leakage it will not need attention and the old gasket may be replaced. If there has been any leakage fit a new gasket.

See that both the joint faces are clean. No jointing compound should be used.

RE-FITTING THE CYLINDER HEAD

Re-fit the valve spring covers, using new paper packings, and make sure that the joint surfaces are quite clean. Use "Gasket Goo" or Seccotine on the metal surfaces. It is very important to replace the inlet cover as this cannot be re-fitted after the head is in place on the engine.

Fit the sparking plug before fitting the head on to the engine.

Make sure that the bevels are in the correct position (see illustration) and if the crankshaft has not been moved re-fit the head. Should the crankshaft have been moved and the timing deranged see below "Checking the Valve Timing".

Tighten the four bolts evenly with the box spanner provided. They should be tightened down a little at a time so as to pull down the head evenly. Do not tighten the bolts excessively as this will only cause distortion. Now re-fit the bevel housing cover (using a new paper packing), the exhaust lifter cable, exhaust nut, head steady strap, etc. Slide the vertical shaft cover up into the top bevel bush housing and slip the spring ring back into its groove. Screw up both gland nuts. If these have previously shown signs of leakage wrap a strand or two of asbestos string round the vertical shaft cover inside each nut before screwing them on to the bevel bush housings.

CHECKING THE VALVE TIMING

If the original setting has been lost through the camshaft or crankshaft having been accidentally turned when the cylinder head was off the engine it is first necessary to re-set the piston to top dead centre of compression stroke and at the same time make sure that the coupling slot in the bottom vertical bevel pinion is exactly in line with the two studs securing the bottom bevel bush housing to the crankcase, or in other words exactly parallel to the fore and aft centre line of the machine. As the bottom bevel pinion is cut with 23 teeth and is driven by a 22T. pinion on the crankshaft the flywheels may have to be turned anything up to 21 revolutions to get the exact position.

To make certain that the piston is on the correct stroke remove the contact breaker cover from the magneto and check the position of the contact breaker cam which (if the control is fully advanced) will have mounted the cam ring and the contact points will be separated.

To set the camshaft, rotate the top bevel pinion until the coupling slot is exactly in line with the bevel bush housing studs and the mark on the bevel in line with the mark on the crown wheel on the camshaft. Again, owing to the "hunting tooth timing" obtained by meshing a 23 T pinion with a 44 tooth crown wheel many turns may be needed before the timing marks will register.

Having set the crankshaft and camshaft with the vertical bevels correctly placed it will be seen that the vertical shaft, cover and couplings may be fitted and the head replaced without altering the position of the camshaft and crankshaft relative to one another and the timing will be correct.

To check, fit a timing disc to the crankshaft after removing the dynamo belt cover, see that the piston is exactly at the dead centre and attach a pointer to some fixed part of the engine and set the pointer to the zero on the disc.

It is necessary in order to check the timing accurately for the Exhaust Rocker to be removed when checking the Inlet valve timing and *vice versa*.

The timing for the cam now standardised (marked K17/10) is:—

Inlet opens 34 deg. before top dead centre.
Inlet closes 47 deg. after bottom dead centre.
Exhaust opens 64 deg. before bottom dead centre.
Exhaust closes 29 deg. after top dead centre.
When checked with .025 clearances on both valves.

Engines manufactured before 1939 may still have their original cams (K17/7) fitted, and in such cases the timing is:—

Inlet opens 35 deg. before top dead centre.
Inlet closes 65 deg. after bottom dead centre.
Exhaust opens 70 deg. before bottom dead centre.
Exhaust closes 30 deg. after top dead centre.
When checked with .025-in. clearance on both valves.

After checking and re-setting the timing do not omit to re-set the rocker pins to give the correct running valve clearances, *i.e.*, .006-in. inlet, .010-in. exhaust. Set cold.

The Inlet and Exhaust Cams are machined in one piece, so that should there be a marked variation in the reading from one Cam but the setting of the other be found correct the Cams and Rockers should be inspected for wear.

With new Cams and Rockers or those which are known to be in good condition it is sufficient to check only the Inlet opening and closing position if these are right the remainder of the setting follows automatically.

A new joint washer (K68/3) should be provided and the face joints cleaned carefully and lightly smeared with jointing compound. Tighten the screws carefully and evenly. It is specially advised that the engine should not be started until the magneto chain cover is fitted and all screws tightened, otherwise the oil pressure in the bottom bevel housing may burst the timing cover joint.

ADJUSTMENT OF MAGNETO CHAIN

The crankcase expands as it gets hot, and thus tends to tighten the chain. When cold the chain should have not less than ¾-in. side movement between the sprockets on one run of the chain. Hold the sprockets so that one run is tight when checking the slack.

To make the adjustment, loosen the three nuts holding the magneto to the chain case and prise up the magneto slightly until excess slack is taken up. Tighten the nuts and check chain again before re-fitting the chain cover. See that joint faces are clean and flat and smear with jointing compound. Re-fit cover, using a new joint washer (K240), and tighten the screws evenly and carefully.

ALTERATIONS TO COMPRESSION RATIO

As supplied the engine is fitted with two compression plates below the cylinder, and the vertical shaft is assembled with a thicker coupling at the top than at the bottom. The thickness (or depth) of the centre circular section of the top coupling is .187-in. between the tongues as against .125-in. in the case of the bottom one.

Should one or both of the compression plates be removed and the cylinder assembled without them, it is necessary to allow for the necessary vertical freedom of the shaft by substituting for the top coupling a coupling of similar thickness to the bottom one. It is of the utmost importance for this change to be made, otherwise the two vertical bevels would be forced apart and consequently damaged on tightening down the cylinder head bolts. If the compression ratio is raised therefore, **do not in any circumstances omit to change the coupling**.

Compression ratios obtainable are:—

Two compression plates fitted 7.6 to 1 approx.
One   ,,   ,,   ,, 7.95 to 1   ,,
No   ,,   ,,   ,, 8.4 to 1   ,,

RE-ASSEMBLING THE PISTON AND CYLINDER

Before refitting the Cylinder barrel, check the connecting rod for alignment if there is any indication from inspection of the Piston that it is not quite true or there is any reason to suspect that it may have been distorted. To check the Connecting Rod for accuracy, obtain a mandrel of the same diameter as the Gudgeon pin and not less than 5-in. long. Pass this through the smallend bush, set the Flywheels with the big-end at T.D.C. and verify by means of a surface gauge that the mandrel is parallel with the top machined face of the Crankcase and in line with the Crankshaft centre line. Examine the piston bosses to make sure that the smallend eye of the rod has had sufficient side clearance from the Piston, and has not been thrusting up against one of the bosses.

Tap the gudgeon pin into one of the piston bosses, so that it protrudes very slightly beyond the inside face of the boss. Slip the piston over the top of the connecting rod engaging the protruding end of the gudgeon pin in the small end bush which, should previously have been smeared with clean oil, and drive the gudgeon pin back into place, obtaining assistance when doing so to support the piston on the opposite side, as described in a previous section for the removal of the piston.

Note that the piston is marked "EX" on one of the flat machined surfaces on the crown. This side is fitted to the front, i.e., below the exhaust valve.

Take care not to drive the gudgeon pin too far, and thus damage the piston boss on the other side by forcing it too hard against the circlip which is fitted. When the gudgeon pin is in position fit the other circlip into its groove, making sure that it is correctly seated.

Wipe the piston clean, fit the rings into position, space them so that the slots are approximately equidistant from one another around the circumference of the piston, and smear the skirt of the piston with clean oil.

If the packing washer on top of the crankcase has been taken off or broken, fit a new one into position over the spigot at the bottom of the cylinder.

Wipe the inside of the cylinder bore with clean rag, lightly smear it with clean engine oil and proceed to slide it over the piston, compressing the piston rings in turn with the fingers so as to enter them in the cylinder, which should then slide down easily into place.

It is an advantage if help is available, as an extra pair of hands are very useful during this part of the work. See that the cylinder is fitted the correct way round, the cutaway portion of the fins being of course behind the vertical drive. As the utmost cleanliness must be observed during the foregoing operations, it is advised that the hands should be thoroughly wiped before carrying out this part of the work, as no dirt or foreign matter must be allowed to get on to the piston or cylinder bore, as this would be likely to cause damage.

DISMANTLING CAMSHAFT, TOP BEVELS, ETC.

NOTE.—In normal service there should be no need to remove the camshaft, but in course of time the replacement of the cams may become necessary. The following directions explain how to remove the camshaft and the vertical bevel bush housing and bevel, but if it is required only to substitute a new cam for one which has become worn, it is better to leave the bevel bush housing in place and to take away the bevel housing, camshaft, cams and bevel bush housing together, thus avoiding the necessity for re-meshing the bevel gears and re-making the joint between the bevel bush housing and the aluminium bevel housing. The procedure to be followed is therefore the same as detailed below except that the bevel bush housing remains undisturbed, and after removal of the small square cover from the left-hand side of the head, and the removal of the three nuts securing the bevel housing to the head the camshaft is tapped through the ballrace. Be careful, however, to replace any shims fitted between the small cover and the head or else the meshing of the bevels will be upset.

Proceed with the first part of the work as described on page 233 to remove valves, springs and rockers, etc. Next loosen and take off the two nuts securing the top vertical bevel pinion bush housing to the bevel housing and pull out the housing. It will save time when re-assembling if the number of joint washers between the face joint is noted, so that the same number of new ones may be used when re-fitting. Having removed the bush housing take out four screws, and remove the square cover at the sparking plug side of the head—and, note carefully the number (if any) of metal packing shims used between the cover and head, as these determine the lateral location of the camshaft. Now undo the three nuts holding the bevel housing, one at the bottom below the square camshaft ball race cover and the other two at the two top corners of the flange behind the large part of the housing on the offside of the head. Pull the bevel housing away with the shaft and cams.

To withdraw the cam a special puller is needed, and in no circumstances must the shaft be pressed through the cam to remove it as this would damage the bevel housing. Unless special facilities are at hand this is a works job.

The parallel part of the camshaft upon which the cam is fitted is slightly larger in diameter than the part which bears in the camshaft bush in the bevel housing, so that if a new bush is needed the cam has first to be drawn off and the key removed, and then the housing and bush must be heated to approximately 100 degrees Centigrade to expand the bush and permit the camshaft to be pushed out through the bearing.

The bush is of aluminium alloy pressed into place, and if a new bush is fitted it must be located as shown in the appended sketch. The bush must also be oil grooved so that the groove overlaps the ground flat in the shaft—for which grooving the old bush may be used as a pattern or guide.

When fitting the cam note that the inlet cam goes on first and is nearer the right hand or bevel gear end of the shaft. To distinguish the inlet from the exhaust cam note the position of the keyway in relation to the cams. The "peak" of the inlet cam is almost exactly above the keyway. Press the cam into position, setting it finally exactly .4375-in. from the end of the camshaft. See adjacent sketch.

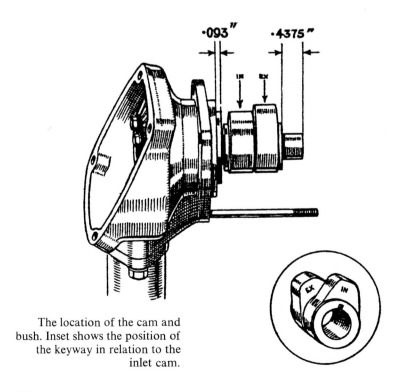

The location of the cam and bush. Inset shows the position of the keyway in relation to the inlet cam.

Refit the camshaft and top bevel housing to the head, using a smear of jointing compound on the triangular face joint. See that both faces are clean and flat, but do not use any joint washer between the metal faces. Tighten the three nuts carefully. Refit the square cover with any packing shims used originally and tighten the four screws. Finally clean face joints of bevel bush housing and bevel housing and obtain new joint washers (K120), slipping these in place over the two studs. Note that the same number as were originally fitted must be used. It is also most important only to use genuine packings as supplied by us as these are of the correct thickness. Use jointing compound on the metal faces.

Having tightened up the nuts evenly, check the fit of the bevel gears. These must mesh the full width of the teeth and must turn perfectly freely with no trace of backlash. Backlash, if any, may be taken out by reduction in the number of joint packings fitted between the bush housing and the bevel housing. It should also be noted that the fitting of additional shims behind the square cover on the left of the head allows the camshaft to move further over to the left and would increase the backlash between the bevels. It is not usually necessary to vary the number of shims or to fit one if none were used during initial assembly at works.

The final assembly of valves and springs, etc., and the re-setting of the tappet clearances is dealt with in the sections covering these respective jobs.

THE VERTICAL SHAFT AND COVER

From prolonged experience in the manufacture of engines of the overhead camshaft type, we are able to state that the life of the vertical shaft bushes which support the shaft in the cover is almost indefinite and their replacement is never in our experience necessary.

The "Oldham" couplings are, however, subject to some wear, and may after prolonged use require to be replaced to eliminate mechanical clatter. These couplings must be a light push fit in the slots in the vertical shaft, and even the slightest trace of play will give rise to noise of a much greater extent than might be anticipated from such a small degree of slackness.

Should new couplings fail to give that degree of fit required, due to slight wear in the slots, couplings oversize in width on the tongues may be obtained. These will almost certainly need the tongues "stoning" down to fit the slots.

Note that as assembled at works the engine has couplings of different centre thickness (or depth), and if one or both of the compression plates used below the cylinder are discarded in order to raise the compression ratio, the top coupling must be replaced by one similar to that used at the bottom.

For Mark I KSS/KTS and early MOV, MAC, and MSS models.

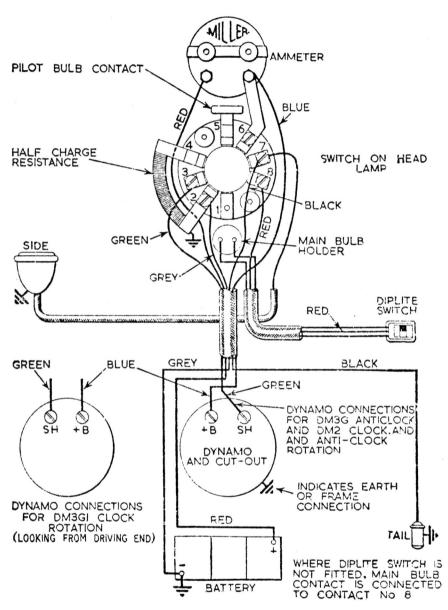

Wiring diagram for Miller SUS set incorporating 84 ES and 74 ES headlamps with dipping-switch and DM 3G dynamo.

WIRING DIAGRAMS: 2

For Mark II KSS/KTS and late MOV, MAC, and MSS models.

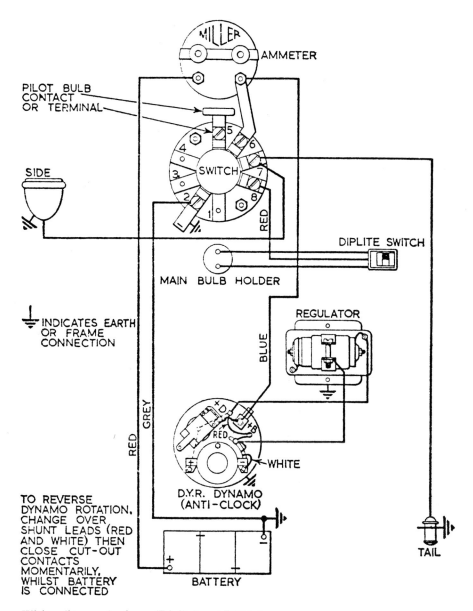

Wiring diagram for lamp (Diplite) and DVR dynamo.

For GTP and KTP models.

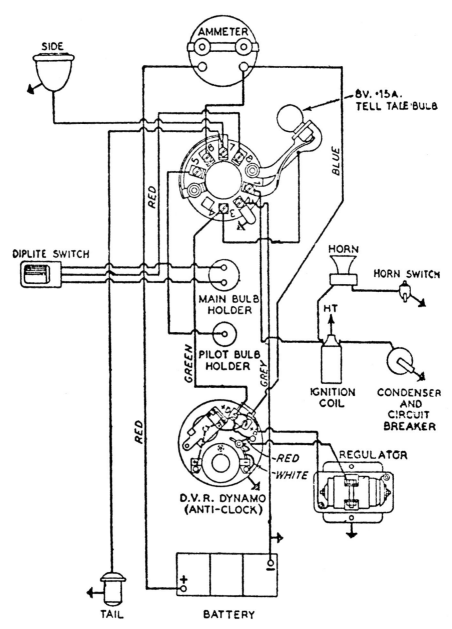

Wiring diagram for headlamp with Diplite coil ignition and DVR dynamo. GTP model.

For early GTP models and the 1930–1 KTP, the DM3G dynamo was fitted. This is a three-brush instrument that does not require a separate regulator in the circuit. Refer to Diagram 1 for the general layout.

276

ABRIDGED SPECIFICATION OF THE 1939 MODELS

	GTP	MOV	MAC	MSS	KSS	KTS
Engine						
No. of cylinders	1	1	1	1	1	1
Type	2-stroke	4-stroke	4-stroke	4-stroke	4-stroke	4-stroke
Valve operation	—	OHV	OHV	OHV	OHC	OHC
Cubic capacity	249 cc	248 cc	349 cc	495 cc	348 cc	348 cc
Tappet clearances (running)						
Inlet (in.)	—	0·003	0·003	0·005	0·006	0·006
Exhaust (in.)	—	0·006	0·006	0·010	0·010	0·010
Tappet clearances (timing)						
Inlet (in.)	—	0·010	0·010	0·025	0·025	0·025
Exhaust (in.)	—	0·015	0·015	0·025	0·025	0·025
Position of serial number	Offside of crankcase	On nearside of crankcase, below cylinder-base				
Gearbox						
Type	4-speed	4-speed	4-speed	4-speed	4-speed	4-speed
Final-drive sprocket (solo)	19	19	19	18	16	16
Gear ratios:						
First	14·2:1	16·1:1	14·0:1	11·25:1	13·8:1	13·8:1
Second	9·8:1	11·1:1	9·6:1	7·76:1	9·55:1	9·55:1
Third	7·45:1	8·45:1	7·3:1	5·91:1	7·26:1	7·26:1
Fourth	5·6:1	6·35:1	5·5:1	4·9:1	6·02:1	6·02:1
Position of serial number	Stamped on rear of housing					
Transmission						
Sprockets:						
Engine	27	19	22	23	21	21
Clutch	55	44	44	44	44	44
				Solo S/C		
Final drive	19	19	19	18 16	16*	16*
Rear wheel	52	52	52	46	46	46
Chains:						
Primary (pitches)	98	74	75	68	67	67
Size (in.)	0·375×0·225	0·5×0·305	0·5×0·305	0·5×0·305	0·5×0·305	0·5×0·305
Secondary (pitches)	114	108	108	99	99	99
Size (in.)	0·5×0·305	0·5×0·305	0·5×0·305	0·625×0·380	0·625×0·380	0·625×0·380
Wheels (rims)						
Front	WM1×19	WM2×19	WM2×19	WM3×19	WM1×21	WM3×19
Rear	WM1×19	WM2×19	WM2×19	WM2×19	WM2×20	WM3×19
Tyre sizes						
Front (in.)	19×3·0	19×3·25	19×3·25	19×3·5	21×3·0	19×3·25
Rear (in.)	19×3·0	19×3·25	19×3·25	19×4·0	20×3·25	19×3·5
Frame						
Position of serial number	R.-H. side below saddle	Stamped on right-hand side of upper front engine lug				

*Fifteenth-tooth sidecar

LIST OF VELOCE PATENTS

British Patent No.	Patentee(s)	Title	Date Granted	Brief Description
*15,377	P. J. Taylor	Roller-skates	Abandoned	New Veloce motors project
24,499	P. J. Taylor	Internal Combustion engines	21.10.1910	Unit-construction engine/gearbox
124,339	P. J. Goodman and Veloce Ltd	Engine-turning gear; clutches	15.6.1918	Kickstarter assembly
133,558	P. J. Goodman and Veloce Ltd	Internal combustion engines	7.1.1919	Two-stroke cylinder manufacture
135,694	P. J. Goodman and Veloce Ltd	Reciprocating pumps	23.1.1919	Oil pump
137,186	P. J. Goodman and Veloce Ltd	Motor cycles; gearing	20.3.1919	Rod-operated two-speed gear
137,688	P. J. Goodman and Veloce Ltd	Motor cycles	27.3.1919	Ball steering head
169,067	P. J. Goodman	Brakes	24.7.1920	Hub brake made by H. C. Webb, under licence
252,822	P. J. Goodman and Veloce Ltd	Internal combustion engines	13.3.1925	'K' engine design
312,788	P. J. Goodman, H. J. Willis and Veloce Ltd	Controlling variable speed gearing	6.6.1929	Positive stop foot gear change
338,704	E. F. Goodman and Veloce Ltd	Motor cycles	27.11.1930	Tank top panel, built-in conduit and coil compartment
426,983	H. J. Willis and Veloce Ltd	Improvements relating to motor cycle saddles	12.4.1935	'Loch Ness Monster' dual seat
511,875	P. E. Irving and Veloce Ltd	Improvements relating to spring mountings for the rear road wheels of motor cycles	25.8.1939	Adjustable rear suspension (coil springs) in arcuate slots
521,106	P. E. Irving and Veloce Ltd	Improvements relating to motor-cycle frames	13.5.1940	Adjustable rear suspension
521,107	P. E. Irving and Veloce Ltd	Improvements relating to driving chain adjustments for motor or other cycles	13.5.1940	Eccentric rear-fork chain adjustment
576,454	C. W. Udall and Veloce Ltd	Improvements relating to variable speed power transmission mechanisms	4.4.1946	Model LE gear-control mounting
582,601	C. W. Udall and Veloce Ltd	Improvements relating to motor-cycle supports	21.11.1946	Retractable centre stand linked with starting lever (Model LE)

*Note: Between 1909 and 1914 P. J. Taylor applied for the following patents, all of which were subsequently abandoned: 11,542 – 1909; 22,462 – 1911; 2,047 – 1912; 20,066 – 1913; 1,339 – 1914.

No further information is available other than the fact that they all related to engines or the lubrication thereof.

The Velocette Owners' Club

The formation of a Velocette Owners' Club was initiated by Mr. P. E. (Pete) Hatchett on the Veloce Stand during the 1956 Motor Cycle Show at Earls Court. An inaugural meeting was held on 5 March 1957, which was attended by 140 persons who are listed in the first issue of the Club's magazine *Fishtail* as being founder-members.

At the inaugural meeting the name of the Club was agreed and it was decided that the objects shall be the promotion of activities of a touring, social, and sporting nature, together with the exchange of technical and servicing information. Rules and regulations, the amount of the annual subscription, and the formation of an Executive Committee were also agreed as was the proposal to publish a Club magazine.

Membership is open to all owners of Velocette machines or those 'specials' in which are fitted an engine or engine and gearbox manufactured by Veloce Limited. Social membership is open to persons nominated by full members. The present membership is almost 600, including nearly 100 overseas members.

District Centres of the Club have been formed in many areas and they cover virtually the whole of the UK. Social activities in most Centres include such items as darts matches, film and slide shows, photographic competitions and, once a year a Christmas party and/or dinner dance. Another highlight of the year is a Club week-end, the venue depending on the organizing Centre.

Some of the Centres are affiliated to the Auto-Cycle Union in order to facilitate entry in sporting events under the Club name. The present Secretary is Mr. Alan Wright, 25 Crawley Close, Slip End, Luton, Beds., from whom further information about the Club is available.

The LE Velo Club

The LE Velo Club was formed in 1950 following a Rally held at Newlands Corner, Surrey, on 14 May. The Rally was initiated by Mr R. L. (Bob) Reid and was attended by more than fifty owners of the LE Velocette. It was proposed and agreed that a Club be formed and a pro-tem. Committee was elected with the express purpose of drafting the objects, rules, and regulations.

The first Committee Meeting was held on 17 May 1950 at which it was proposed that the Club be named the LE Velo Club. An annual subscription of 10s. was proposed and it was suggested that a regular Newsletter or Magazine be produced. Draft rules were prepared based on the qualification that the Club be open to owners of the model LE Velocette.

On 28 October 1950 the first General Meeting was held at which the Club Officers were elected. Forty-six members were present and the draft rules were accepted with an amendment to permit members to continue their membership even though they may no longer own an LE. The annual subscription was agreed at 15s.

Membership reached a peak or more than 700 during 1956 and now stands at just under 300. The objectives of the Club include the encouragement of social and touring activities and the dissemination of technical information. Runs are held regularly as instanced by the London Branch who hold a run every fortnight, summer and winter. Film shows are a feature of the social activities and also slide shows.

Tools required to carry out major overhauls are owned by the Club and are available to members on loan. The Club is associated with the Royal Automobile Club.

The present Membership Secretary is Mr. Malcolm Lewis, 5 Roseville Gardens, Codsall, Wolverhampton WV8 1A2. Telephone Codsall (09074) 3356. Branches of the Club have been formed in a number of areas, details of which are available from the Secretary.

Epilogue

While we were still writing this book the thought occurred to us that we must decide at which point to end the history, otherwise we would be forced to employ the expedient of one of the television companies and entitle it the 'continuing history'.

However, the decision has been made for us since we learn the manufacture of Velocette motor cycles is to cease, at least in the Hall Green Works.

And so yet another famous make fades from the scene and joins the ranks of those that are no longer in production, a matter of extreme regret to all those interested in British motor cycles and the cause of much sadness to those intimately connected with this family concern. We little thought that while we were writing the history of Veloce Limited we were also writing the obituary as far as the manufacture of motor cycles is concerned.

Note: Addresses correct at time of publication

Index

Whitworth, David 141, 142
Wilden, Doreen 207
Wilkes, George 204
Williams, Arthur 15
Williams, Edward 15
Williams, Fred 202
Williams, Harry 204
Williams, Jack 190
Willis, Harold 54, 60, 65, 66, 85, 121, 139, 177, 186, 188, 194, 195, 197, 211–214
Wilton Cycle and Motor Co. 21

Wolseley 16
Woodhead Monroe suspension units 86, 87
Woods, Stanley 131, 132, 133, 135, 139
Wyche Cutting 182
Wye Valley Trial 192

Xl-All saddle 19

York Road 212

Zenith-J.A.P. 168